D1191174

Marx's Economics

Marx's Economics

Origin and Development

Alexander Balinky

Rutgers, The State University

Heath Lexington Books
D. C. Heath and Company
Lexington, Massachusetts

Printed in the United States of America

Library of Congress Number: 70- 111481

TO

DONALD PIATT

JOSEPH SCHUMPETER

MAX GIDEONSE

Each, in His Own Way,
One of the Three Great Teachers in My Life

Contents

PART II

A Foreword

SCHUMPETER AND MARX

History is not so much a well-made play in set acts as a continuous performance of successive *ad lib* players. The year that Galileo died, Newton was born. In the year that Karl Marx died, 1883, Joseph Schumpeter was born. Precocious, he grew up in a Viennese environment where Marxians barked outside the academic gates.

And so we meet in Schumpeter that rarest of birds: a neoclassical economist who both *knew* the works of Marx and *admired* him. (By knowing Marx I do not mean that he had cut most of the pages of *Das Kapital*'s volume 1 and could quote the purple passages from the *Communist Manifesto*. And by admiration, I mean no less than that Schumpeter regarded Marx as one of the greatest social scientists who ever lived.)

To illustrate how rare it is for an economist to admire Marx in spite of *dis*liking his political goals, consider another scholar also born in 1883—Maynard Keynes. There is precious little evidence that Keynes interrupted many games of bridge to master the "turbid rubbish" of the German autodidact. Yet Keynes also disdained the bourgeois world of Queen Victoria. And only down the block, so to speak, from his Bloomsbury arrondissement lived the Fabian socialists. But perhaps the dullness of Sidney and Beatrice Webb, and the soufflé texture of Bernard Shaw's economics, turned his stomach and mind against the paradigms of socialism.

But *why* did Schumpeter have so high an opinion of Marx? This puzzle takes on a renewed interest now that there is a thirst for Marxism among the new generation; and, also, now that Schumpeter's stock is experiencing a flurry of revival on the bourse of intellectual history.

Let me state that, although I often heard Schumpeter praise Marx, I was never able to perceive from his remarks either an explication of the merits which made Marx deserving of the accolades, or—what is not quite the same thing—even the reasons why Schumpeter came to admire him. To use a characteristic Schumpeter evasion, his case for Marx was stronger than the sum of its parts.

We do not need an economist to praise Marx's sociology, history, and philosophy. (Nor, to digress, a non-economist to praise his economics!)

But Schumpeter *qua* economist actually rejected Marx's theory of surplus value as providing either (1) a valid (or logical) theory of "exploitation," or (2) insightful clues into the "laws of motion and transformation of capitalism." What is left then of Marx the economist? Fragmentary, and somewhat contradictory, reflections on overproduction, underconsumption, and periodic business cycles. Suggestive insights concerning technological innovation and the displacement of workers by machines. Certain pre-Leontief models of reproduction and balanced growth. To use another Schumpeter phrase, this is "respectable" work. But just that.

What I finally decided to be Marx's excellence in Schumpeter's eyes was not his "schema" but his grand "vision" of social change. Where a Macaulay conceived of whig society as the culmination of all evolution, and a Hayek looks back upon the epoch of Calvin Coolidge as a reattainable golden age, Marx peered at the social order from out the window of the British Museum to chant: This too will pass away. And it did. And it will.

Paul A. Samuelson
M. I. T.

Preface

Yet another book on Marx necessitates an immediate statement of purpose.

In an *Essay on Marxian Economics,* Joan Robinson makes the following point: "I have confined my argument to Marx's economic analysis in the narrow sense, and made no attempt to deal with the broad treatment of *history and sociology which form the most important part of Marx's doctrine.* This specialised approach is perhaps an *unnatural* one, and it is true that *no particular aspect of Marx's argument can be properly understood without a grasp of the whole."* [Italics mine.]

The primary purpose of this volume is to bridge this unnatural division of Marxian doctrine and thereby contribute toward a better understanding and appreciation of Marxian economics. But let me be more specific.

As a social philosopher, Marx was mainly concerned with unearthing the universal law of historical change. Dialectical materialism is more a method of analysis, an analytic device, than a theory purporting to provide specific answers to particular questions. It is one thing to say, as Marx did, that every society save the final one harbors within it the seeds of its own destruction. It is quite another to expose the laws of contradiction unique to a particular social order. The specific forces that once put an end to Slavery or Feudalism are not, according to Marx, the same as those which operate with equal dialectic inevitability to assure the demise of Capitalism. As a neo-Hegelian, Marx began with the philosophical proposition that, like all earlier systems, Capitalism must contradict itself out of existence. As an economist, on the other hand, he set himself the task of investigating the particular economic logic by which this would occur. Again, to paraphrase Professor Robinson's point, no part of Marx's economic analysis can be properly understood or appreciated except in the context of the system as a whole. The approach taken in this volume, therefore, is to focus on Marx's analysis of the laws of Capitalist development but to do so as a special case of the general theory. The result should be the emergence of a general yet comprehensive view of the Capitalist process as Marx, correctly or incorrectly, conceived of it.

There is no dearth of excellent, and not so excellent, books and articles on every aspect of Marxism as well as on the system as a whole. Nevertheless a problem exists for many who teach a course in Marxian economics at the

university level. Existing works which encompass the entire Marxian system
do provide the desired overview mentioned above. In the main, however,
such books have been written by noneconomists with fairly obvious consequences. The treatment of Marx's laws of Capitalist development tends to
be too superficial or brief for those seriously interested in Marxian economics. The fashion of economists, on the other hand, has been to concentrate
almost exclusively on Marxian economics at the expense of the philosophical,
historical, sociological, etc., framework of Marxism. It does not matter
here whether this is for reason of taste, talent, or methodological conviction.
A second purpose of this volume, therefore, is to make available a basic text
for use in university-level courses on Marxian economics. My endeavor to
attain the desired balance and perspective avowedly involves an element of
the pedagogical. Two final comments of an explanatory nature seem necessary.

At one time I had the privilege of studying Marxian economics with
Joseph Schumpeter, as well as assisting him in the teaching of a course on
the economics of Socialism at Harvard University. The reader will easily
detect the consequence of this experience, the strong influence of Professor
Schumpeter, on both my approach to and interpretation of Marxism. The
shortcomings of this book are, of course, entirely mine.

The reader will also observe that this book appears to come to an abrupt
end. This is entirely purposeful. If there is a single point in regard to Marx's
analysis of the laws of Capitalist development that I have tried to communicate above all others it is this: That while Capitalism is doomed, not all the
misery of the mass, nor suffering, nor tears, nor even revolutionary zeal can
bring the system to an end. Salvation must await the emergence of the objective circumstances for the Communist Revolution. The assurance of
Capitalism's demise is to be found in the contradictions inherent in the
Capitalist productive force. It is when the productive force breaks down of
its own accord that the objective circumstance for revolution appears. As
for the nature of these contradictions inherent in the Capitalist productive
force: that, of course, is what Marx's economic analysis and this survey of
it is all about. Beyond this point is to return to Marxian philosophy, history,
politics, and sociology. Marx's contribution to the economics of Socialism
and Communism remains. But that is quite another matter, the subject of
yet another volume which some day I hope to write.

I would like to take this opportunity to acknowledge some specific debts
in connection with this volume. I have benefited greatly from the careful and
critical reading of my manuscript by Professors Max Gideonse, Robert
Alexander and Paul Davidson of the Rutgers economics department. Very
special thanks is due Mrs. Catherine Tranfo, secretary of the Russian
Area Program, who not only typed this manuscript but freed me of many
administrative chores normally associated with the directorship of an area
program.

New Brunswick, New Jersey

Part I

I ·

The Essence of Marxism

Eulogizing at Karl Marx's graveside, Friedrich Engels tried to capture the essence of the Marxian theory of history in a single phrase. Man must first eat, said Engels, before he can philosophize. Indeed, well over two thousand years ago, the time had approached when man's capacity for serious reflection led him to question not only his own shortcomings but those of the institutions surrounding him. Some social theorists placed the blame for institutional imperfection upon the innate and inescapable imperfectibility of man. Others, as during the eighteenth and early nineteenth centuries, viewed man as naturally rational and good but as having been corrupted by defective elements in his environment.

In either case, no sooner had mankind risen above the all-consuming necessity of physical survival than some men began to grow dissatisfied with the discordance of a society anchored in social inequality. Certainly, since the time of Plato mankind has been conscious and troubled about the persistent inconsistency between an ethic or religion which preaches equality or brotherly love and an institutional setting in which the relationship of man to man is that of master to slave, superior to inferior, strong to weak, and rich to poor. As a consequence, many have searched for an avenue of escape from such contradiction. Scheme upon scheme for reshaping the world into one or another image has been put forth; with, one might add, no visible end in sight.

Marxism, Scientific Socialism, Bolshevism, Communism—call it what you will for the moment—is only one such scheme. Yet this particular creation of the intellect is frequently credited, as by the British scholar, R. N. Carew Hunt, with having both "brought into being the largest mass movement . . . since the rise of Christianity" and with being "the greatest subversive force in the modern world." [1] In view of the place thus accorded Marxism in world history, one may well begin with the following question: In what fundamental respect does Marxian Socialism differ from most, if not all, past and present varieties of non-Marxian socialism and social reform? This question appears all the more relevant in the face of the continuing preoccupation with "creeping socialism" in the West and the emergence of ideological diversity within the Communist bloc.

A glance at the historic soil and climate from which Marxism sprang will help to isolate the factors that differentiate it from other forms of socialism and social reform. Through his schemes or Utopias, pre-Marxian man sought, in the main, to satisfy his craving for social harmony. Plato assigned his philosopher-kings the task of training their subjects in obedience. Saint-Simon, in his *New Christianity,* searched for a society in which men would be bound together by "cords of social consonance." Rousseau sought to attain social unity by urging the abolition of all that which set man in "contradiction to himself." Universally, social critics and reformers strove to replace an accidental and discordant society with a planned one based on one or another system of logic and order. The basis of such blueprints was and remains largely ethical, religious, or aesthetic.

Communism, as an ideal alternative to the existing and imperfect world, reaches back far beyond Marx's day. Its several variants, of course, differ in detail. But more important, for the point at hand, pre-Marxian communism, from Plato's Republic to the early Christian communes and the settlements of the New World, had certain characteristic features. It was more concerned with renunciation of worldly goods, as a matter of moral superiority, than with the abolition of private property as such. Its intent was an equality not for the many but for the chosen few capable of attaining the requisite moral or spiritual apex. Its main purpose was to find a natural and therefore acceptable niche for everyone within the social hierarchy; thereby replacing restlessness, envy, and competing claims with cooperation and harmony.

Early social reform and socialism, utopian or otherwise, shared several underlying features with pre-Marxian communism. Both represented a quest for harmony in the sense alluded to above. Each stressed institutional imperfection over the inborn weakness of man. Both rested on the premise that rational and well-intentioned men could volitionally recast the economic, political, and social universe in accordance with their mental image of a better world.

Historically, Marxism represents a reaction against such a social philosophy. Marx had been at least as unhappy with the society of his day as his utopian contemporaries, probably for much the same complex of reasons. But Marx was equally dissatisfied with the prevailing naïveté regarding how to change existing institutions and what to put in their place. He was highly critical of all imaginative models of an improved world, especially ones designed by those who lacked working-class roots. Marx was particularly contemptuous of the notion that such a world could emerge on its own merit by being peddled in the courts and salons of Europe. Having equally little faith in salvation by example, he was also critical of those who organized or financed experimental islands as a solution.

Instead, Marx offered an ailing world salvation guaranteed by inexorable social-historical law. Insisting that he employed only the method of positive science, Marx claimed to have laid bare the social forces which had brought about the existing social order and which would, human will and morality aside, ultimately bring on the final and therefore perfect society. Thus, in a special sense, Marx both remained within the classical tradition and differed with those who advocated social reform. Since this point casts additional light on the essence of Marxism it deserves elaboration.

Eighteenth-century liberalism held that there are natural, social, and economic as well as physical laws; further, that man has to know what these laws are and behave in consonance with them in order to attain the best of all possible worlds. A clear presumption here is that capitalism, as a theoretical ideal, simply reflects that order of things which results when man ceases to behave in ways that would appear to violate the natural order of the social universe. Marx agreed that, indeed, there are such natural laws. He declared the dominant view of them, however, to be in error. Classical thought attributed continuing imperfection to the persistence of a gap between ideal (based on natural law) and actual behavior. Marx, on the other hand, looked upon the troubles of his generation as historically necessary; that is, as an unavoidable price which humanity had to pay in order to attain ultimate deliverance. Capitalism was not, in the minds of its ideologists, merely one milestone on the spiraling historical path toward a terminal social system. For Marx it was just that. He rejected not only the classical proposition that capitalist institutions were reflective of human nature, but reversed the very order of that relationship. That which we regard as human nature, thought Marx, is really nothing but a mirror of the objective, material circumstances of our existence.

Marxism may be differentiated in yet another and even more general way. The strategic factor in this case is the time dimension. In its broadest and strictest sense, Marxism concerns itself with *nearly* the full span of history. Its method, that of dialectical materialism, has been used to interpret all past and present institutions and events. Thus, looking both backward and forward, historical time is divided into seven stages: (1) Presocial, (2) Primitive Communism, (3) Formal Slavery, (4) Feudalism, (5) Capitalism, (6) Socialism, and (7) Communism.[2] The Presocial is that indeterminate period prior to the emergence of the social group and to which the method of dialectical materialism is said not to apply. Very briefly, Marxist doctrine characterizes the six stages of *social* history in the following way.

Primitive Communism represents the earliest stage during which man lives in a community. The mode of production is dominantly one of individual or family self-sufficiency; that is, a way of economic life not yet marked by division of labor and specialization. This implies the absence of private property rights in the means of production. It is not entirely accurate to speak of this period as one of collective ownership of the productive means since, according to Marxist theory, the very notion of ownership depends on the emergence of the next productive force. It is a society, in any case, in which there is no exploitation of man by man and no state which coerces the many for the benefit of the few. It is, in a word, a classless society.

The above state of affairs is not, however, destined to last. Primitive man, it is said, found it impossible to eke out even subsistence with such a rudimentary productive mode. Self-sufficiency had to give way to division of labor and specialization in response to the overwhelming force of economic scarcity. It is at this point that Marxists note the secular "Fall of Man." The logic of the new productive force requires that a relative few rise to the top in order to take command over an economic process which now calls not only for production but distribution and exchange as well. Marxist doctrine is anything but clear or specific about the actual means by which the few come to attain such power. Somehow ("by hook or by crook") a minority manages to become dominant over the majority. The doctrine alludes to such factors as superior intelligence, adaptability, and physical prowess. The result is the emergence of private ownership of the means of production. This, in turn, causes society to split into two primary classes: one class whose members own and control the means of livelihood and another whose members have been forcibly excluded from such ownership.

The resulting society is what Marxists mean by Formal Slavery. Here the owning and therefore ruling class not only owns the land, as the principal instrument of production, but acquires identical property rights over the dispossessed. The slave owns nothing, not even his own labor power. Thus the irreconcilable conflict between the two major classes begins and is not destined to end until the emergence of Socialism. Marxist doctrine makes little of the distinction between Slave and Feudal society. In the latter case the slave-owning class is replaced by a somewhat more stratified feudal nobility. The slave is now a serf or near-serf, with a few limited and theoretical rights.[3] Land remains the chief instrument of production and the fundamental schism between the two classes continues.

The Capitalist stage of history is characterized as one during which the dominance of the ruling class stems, most particularly, from the ownership of capital employed in commercial, industrial, and financial activity. A second distinctive feature, *vis-à-vis* Slavery and Feudalism, is that while the capitalist continues to own the physical means of production, he no longer possesses human beings as slaves. Because of the logic inherent in the Capitalist productive force, the worker comes to own his own labor power. The institutional arrangement of Capitalist society is such, however, that the worker is forced to sell his labor to capitalist-employers on the most unfavorable terms. Thus, the fundamental class conflict remains; the capitalist and worker becoming the two principal protagonists during this segment of the historical drama.

→ Thus no real change in the basic class structure of society is said to occur during the long period from the beginning of Formal Slavery to the end of Capitalism. The first fundamental transformation since Primitive Communism is made to coincide with the emergence of Socialism. At this point private ownership of the means of production gives way to collective ownership. Given Marx's definition of class (those who own and those who are excluded from the ownership of the means of production) it follows that Socialism becomes a classless society in a definitional sense. No longer does a ruling minority exploit and oppress the overwhelming majority. Thus as Feudalism is held to represent an advance over Slavery, and Capitalism over Feudalism, Socialism is said to be superior to Capitalism but not yet perfect or final like Communism.

It is precisely here that one finds yet another basic difference between Marxian and non-Marxian Socialism. Marxist doctrine does not settle for Socialism as a terminal society. Nor does it view Socialism as the last foreseeable answer to an imperfect world. Collective ownership of the means of production is viewed as a necessary but not a sufficient condition for final salvation. Socialism, wrote Marx, invariably bears the birthmarks of Capitalism from whose womb it emerges. Thus, according to Marxist doctrine, most post-Capitalist deviations from the ideal stem from the fact that Socialism necessarily inherits both economic and behavioral vestiges from the Capitalist system. A great deal remains to be done and many sacrifices lie ahead during the Socialist stage of development before the emergence of Communism is possible. Important changes must occur in the institutional setting, as well in man himself, before the promised land is reached. It is in this Marxian sense, therefore, that Socialism may be characterized as something of a purgatory midway between Capitalist hell and Communist heaven.

Communism, on the other hand, is seen as something far different than simply the furthest stage of social development that the human mind can visualize at a given point in time. Marx declared it to be terminal in the Hegelian sense of perfect. Further, as Marx put it, the absolute superiority and desirability of Communism is attributable *not* to its intrinsic moral or aesthetic quality but *vice versa*. It is the most moral and aesthetic society because it is the highest or final stage of social development. Finally, as against his predecessors, Marx envisaged a universal Communism based on material plenty, not asceticism; one to be enjoyed by all, not only the select few.

By way of summary, the following are the core propositions which, taken together, help to differentiate Marxism from other systems of social criticism and reform. (1) There are, in fact, social-historical laws which govern the universe; (2) such laws operate, in the final analysis, independent of human will or desire; (3) on the contrary, man's value system and the behavior pattern based on them are set by these laws; (4) relying on the method of positive science, man can discover what these laws are and how they operate and thereby comprehend the process by which society evolves to where and what it is; (5) with the same key man can unlock the door of the future and see, if only in contour form, the direction in which society will evolve and to what final end; (6) Communism, not Socialism, will be the terminal social order; (7) social improvement (which, for Marx, is synonymous with change) is inevitable not because of the fact or extent of human suffering but as a function of the laws themselves.[4]

This, then, is the sense in which Marx spoke of salvation and its inevitability. It is also the basis on which he staked out Scientific Socialism's claim to supremacy. As a scientist Marx was, according to his own word, entirely disinterested in both the ugliness of the existing and imperfect world or the beauty of the Communist ideal. Nor did he credit himself with preaching any ideas or ideals of his own construction. With a humbleness that is in striking contrast to the personal arrogance noted by so many of his biographers, Marx insisted that he was merely exposing to view the logic and direction of the historical process.

In order to distinguish his system of thought, especially from that of the utopians, Marx labeled his schema Scientific Socialism. More often it is simply referred to as Marxism and, as subsequently interpreted and amended by V. I. Lenin, as Marxism-Leninism. Depending upon the particular moment, country, or purpose at hand, today a third name may be added: Stalin, Khrushchev, Mao, for instance. In any case, correctly used and understood, Scientific Socialism or Marxism is *primarily* a system of ideas, a method for comprehending the social universe, not a blueprint of either a Socialist or Communist society. When Marx came to select a name for the party, one which he believed would lead mankind to its historic destiny, he chose the word "Communist." His purpose here was to distinguish that party from Louis Blanc's Socialist party which was already in existence in France. Marx also titled the 1848 Manifesto "Communist" because, as Engels tells us, Marx wanted to disassociate himself and his movement from the "multifarious social quacks" who had already appropriated the term Socialist. Nevertheless, even during Marx's lifetime, most of his followers came to refer to themselves as Socialists or Social Democrats. The designation "Bolshevik" did not make its appearance until 1903 when V. I. Lenin, Georgi V. Plekhanov, and certain others succeeded in getting most Russian Marxists to attend the Second Congress of the Russian Social-Democratic Labor party. It was at this congress, held in Brussels and London, that the historic split occurred. Those supporting Lenin's maximal policies, and who were in the majority, called themselves Bolsheviks. The others, who stood for gradualism and were in the minority, came to be known as Mensheviks. "Communist" as a synonym for "Bolshevik" did not come into popular use until the period of War Communism.

THE UTILITY OF UNDERSTANDING MARXISM FOR NON-MARXISTS

For well over a century Marxism has evoked drastically varying reactions. It has been and remains the object of penetrating study, criticism, deification, and attack. It has been dissected, synthesized, and "stood on its head." Most recently, parts of it have even been squeezed into mathematical formulas in order to facilitate closer inspection of its economic logic. For some, at one extreme, Marxism has already been proven to be factually wrong, logically inconsistent, and worthless as a predictive instrument. It has thus been labeled religious dogma, dismissed as utopian, charged with being crassly materialistic, and condemned as indecent bordering on the uncivilized. In the process of vilification the founders of Scientific Socialism have even been referred to as "crack-brained social deviates." At the opposite extreme there are still those who, in the words of Schumpeter, devoutly "finger the Marxian rosary." They pore over its doctrines in much the same fashion of Talmudic scholars. For them Marxism represents both the key to an understanding of the universe and an assurance of salvation. In their minds mortals like Marx and Lenin rank with the figures of Christ, Moses, and Mohammed.

As a system of thought, even an ideology, Marxism deserves neither treatment. Marx was neither angel nor devil, saint nor sinner. His works are neither Bible nor anathema. Like other high-powered intellectuals, Marx endeavored to illuminate and interpret the social process. And like the intellectual creations of other important social philosophers, Marx's system is both afflicted with serious error and replete with insights and remarkable vision. It may well be that it is Marx the prophet who has given Marxist ideology its survival value. Yet our principal concern in this volume must remain with Marx the scholar, the social philosopher, and economist. Our interest centers on the light that the Marxian system of thought has thrown, or has failed to cast, on the social process. What either extreme cares to make of it is quite another matter.

The relevant question, preceding an excursion into the details of Marxism, is why it should be studied at all. This question is especially pertinent to the American reader in view of the fact that the United States has proven to be the least fertile soil for the spread and acceptance of Marxist ideology, in theory or in practice. The hackneyed adage that "one should know the enemy" tends typically to lead away from dispassionate inquiry. The general notion that the pursuit of all knowledge, including Marxism, is an end in itself and needs no justification is true enough. Neither of the above propositions, however, provides the specific reasons why a non-Marxist should be *au courant* with Marxism. Some of the concrete advantages to be derived from such knowledge follow.

Most systems of thought would have faded into oblivion in the face of the sustained intellectual and emotional attacks that have been unleashed against Marxism. But like the few truly great ideas, Marxism has suffered eclipses only to spring back with renewed vitality in one or another part of the world. At this particular moment in world history, in fact, Marxism appears to be experiencing something of a Renaissance; especially in regard to Marx's theory of history and in connection with the so-called "New Left." Be that as it may, the general impact of Marxism on Western thought is undeniable. Whether we judge it right or wrong, a force for good or evil, one fact remains. The survival of Marxism as a *Weltanschauung* has served to prove its strength and appeal. This alone justifies its study even in the West. There are other reasons.

Familiarity with Marxism is essential for a sharper insight into the changing character of Capitalism. The bulk of Marx's writings consists of material dealing with the laws of Capitalist development and not with the organization and operation of Socialist or Communist society. Marx's principal concern was the social system of his day. His primary interest was in the dynamics of social change. He aimed his analytical guns on that Capitalism which, having once burst asunder the old Feudal ties, was now racing in the same self-propelled fashion toward Socialism; or so Marx believed. And, as we shall see, Marx left us a legacy of some correct or interesting insights and prophesies about Capitalism. Marxism is, of course, only one of various approaches to an understanding and criticism of the Capitalist order of things. Its value lies more in the method employed than in the specific content of Marxian deductions and conclusions. Nevertheless, Marx's critique is helpful in reminding us that Capitalism is dynamic, not static; that it is but one phase of historical development and not the end of the road. By its emphasis on the changing character of Capitalism, moreover, Marxist theory has shed some light on certain areas left dark by orthodox economic theory. It has brought into sharper relief such phenomena as the functional relationship between competition and monopoly, the role of innovation, equilibrium at less than full employment, and the concentration of capital in progressively fewer hands. Marxism has also served as an antidote to certain weaknesses in the classical and neoclassical position. The stress placed by Marxist doctrine on the irreconcilable class struggle, for example, has acted as a counterforce to uncritical acceptance of the notion of a general harmony of interests.

Capitalism aside, a knowledge of Marxism[5] is essential to a better and fuller understanding of another part of the world and a competing way of life. Of course, Marxist doctrine has undergone reinterpretation since its inception. There is no question but that it has also been the object of dramatic revisionism since the death of Stalin. A diminution of the force or importance of Marxist ideology in the USSR and the East European nations (far less so in China) is also observable; though this issue is not quite as simple as it may appear on the surface.[6] Nevertheless, Marxism remains as a highly articulated body of philosophical, sociological, political, and economic doctrine which underlies both movements and societies claiming to reflect its principles.

The fact of reinterpretation or revisionism does not, in any case, deny the existence of a body of doctrine which is still Marxist in its most fundamental sense. A working knowledge of the general principles and language of Marxism remains essential to an understanding of Communist-oriented societies. Familiarity with Marxist doctrine is necessary even to the comprehension of what such societies may be moving away from and the direction toward which they appear to be going. A knowledge of Marxism is useful, finally, in making possible meaningful East-West communications and even co-existence. One of the specific benefits accruing from such familiarity with Marxist doctrine is a keener awareness of the extent to which Communists use identical words differently than we do or act upon a set of premises quite unlike ours; without, one might add, any necessary intent to deceive.

THE WRITINGS OF MARX: A PRELIMINARY VIEW

Students of Marx generally agree that, in some vital regards, his writings are both enigmatic and changing in character. As such they invite continuing study and interpretation. Scores of books have been done on the general theme of "What Marx meant," and still others on "What Marx really meant." It is not inconceivable that a volume may yet appear bearing some such title as "What Marx Actually Believed But Did Not Say." Incontrovertibly, his works are anything but a model of organized clarity. In style and flavor they run the gamut from the steel-cold logic of the detached scientist to the white-hot phrases of the impassioned propagandist.

Marx's writings, in particular, tend to fall into three general categories. The first consists of innumerable items of an essentially polemic nature; articles and letters that contribute little to the mainstream of Marxian doctrine. Many of these were, in fact, the consequence of Marx's exceptional sensitivity to criticism and were written in the heat of personal controversy. The second category consists of such items as *The Class Struggles in France,*

The Eighteenth Brumaire of Louis Bonaparte, and (with Engels) *The Civil War in the United States.* These offer an analysis of specific historical events and bear only indirectly on the main and lasting body of Marxian theory. The final category includes such work as the *Poverty of Philosophy, Das Kapital, Value, Price and Profit, Theories of Surplus Value,* etc. These works are more nearly representative of the mainstream of Marx's theoretical system of thought. The classifications as offered above are by no means beyond argument and are intended only as suggestive of a problem. All too often a quotation from Marx, taken from one of his letters or polemic pieces, is cited in support or refutation of one of Marx's major theoretical arguments.

The precise relationship between the *Communist Manifesto* and *Das Kapital* deserves special attention. Marx avowedly declared the Capitalism of his day at death's door. The *Manifesto* is an eloquent and dramatic statement of that conviction. *Das Kapital* is the "scientific proof" offered by Marx in support of the thesis as put forth in the 1848 document. Since Scientific Socialism is a world view encompassing the entire span of social history, *Das Kapital* is, in that context, no more than a special case of Marx's general theory of socio-historical change. Understandably, however, Marx's preoccupation was with the structure of Capitalist society and with the economic logic by which it would destroy itself. *Das Kapital* is, therefore, primarily an economic treatise on the laws of Capitalist development. Its direct concern is with Capitalism and not with Socialism or Communism. The point holds even if we regard Marx's major works as a whole. Marx left posterity only the barest and vaguest blueprint of the structure of post-Capitalist societies and even less by way of a practical guide for their operation.

With the question of the validity of Marxian economics left aside for the moment, *Das Kapital* (which is the cornerstone of Marxian economics) leaves a great deal to be desired. Marx crystallized his credo during the early 1840's. He set down its main features in 1848. It took nearly two decades before the "scientific proof," in the form of volume I of *Das Kapital,* made its appearance. The German edition appeared in 1867 and the first English edition became available in 1886. The fact is that Marx was most reluctant to publish the material in question and had constantly to be prodded about it by his tiny coterie of disciples. One reason, without doubt, is that Marx had little personal taste for the subject matter of economics. When, following many years of study at the British Museum, numerous false starts, and several broken contracts with publishers, Marx finally finished the manuscript, he referred to it in bitterness as that "economic filth" for which he had been forced to sacrifice his and his family's life and happiness.

Once published *Das Kapital* became not only a major concern of many intellectuals but a point of discussion and debate among some of the more literate of the world's masses. Yet—and despite its impact—only a handful have actually read *Das Kapital* and fewer still really comprehend its complexities. The reasons are not difficult to isolate. Marx employed the technical language of the economist; a lingo with which even the most intelligent laymen are not familiar. Moreover, much that is in *Das Kapital* is at a level of abstraction and theoretical nicety which is not characteristic of public thinking or discussion. Even the professionals find the study of it a difficult and confusing assignment. It is badly organized. In it Marx raises a number of integral points only to drop them without further elucidation or without weaving them into the mainstream of his theoretical model. The balance between inductive and deductive reasoning is so poor that one easily loses the forest for the trees. Throughout *Das Kapital* is fraught with vagaries and ambiguities.

One difficulty is worthy of special note. Only the first volume (1867) of *Das Kapital* appeared during Marx's lifetime. The second (1885) and third (1894) were published posthumously under the editorship of Engels. The intervention of time and a second hand served to accentuate many of the difficulties already cited. The organizational relationship among these three volumes compounds the problem still further. The main lines of Marx's economic model appear in volume I. Volumes II and III are, in the main, additions to or subtractions from, reconsiderations and attempts at reconciliation, centering on the principal thesis. Which of several formulations on key issues, as between volume I and III for instance, Marx really had in mind is likely to remain in doubt.

MARXISM AS AN IDENTIFIABLE SYSTEM

There is no single source in which Marx or Engels, alone or together, set down their entire system as an organized and logical unit.[7] For this as well as certain other reasons about to be offered, a controversy has persisted over whether an identifiable system of Marxist thought really exists. This vintage issue has pushed itself into the foreground once again since the flareup of overt ideological conflict within the Communist bloc. There is a formidable school of thought in the West that argues along the following lines: The founders of Marxism were often so vague or contradictory that no one really knows what they meant or where they stood on a number of vital propositions. From the very beginning their disciples have read so much into and out of the writ that little is left beyond a heterodoxy of doctrine about which there is no general agreement. In any event, Marxism has long since degenerated into an instrument of convenience in the hands of Communist rulers. Its main purpose has been to serve the dissimilar personal or national interests of past leaders like Lenin, Stalin, and Khrushchev and present ones like Brezhnev and Kosygin, Mao, Tito, Hoxa, etc.

This view is by no means baseless. Yet there is another side to this question.

It is true that during his day Marx was already forced to reject as wrong many of the interpretations of his contemporaries. Late in life and in a very special context (that is often forgotten) Marx even denied that he was a Marxist. But was it not also J. M. Keynes who once remarked that he was not a Keynesian? The point is that Marxism is hardly unique in this regard. Any important and lasting ideology (or, if one may be permitted to draw the analogy, theology) is bound to suffer a similar fate. Christianity is no less an identifiable religion and is no less believed because its theology is interpreted or understood differently by Protestants and Catholics. Few would argue that Catholicism, as a major variant of Christianity, will disappear as a result of the fundamental changes that its theology is currently undergoing. Religion has been no less a world force because wars have been fought on its account and in its name. Who is to say that a Baptist is less of a Christian than an Episcopalian; or, by the same token, that Khrushchev has been less of a Marxist than Mao? What doctrinal differences do indicate is that there really is no such thing as "true" or orthodox Marxism except as it appears in the eyes of the beholder.

It is the fashion today to concentrate on the differences that exist among those regarding themselves as Marxists. There is, of course, that critical portion where doctrinal innovation has occurred and about which disagreement is sharp. But it is also well to bear in mind that many of these differences concern details, timing, and matters of day-to-day policy rather than methodology or the broad conclusions of Marxist doctrine. The deepest schisms that exist today center around the means to the end rather than on the ends themselves. There is no disagreement, for example, between Russian and Chinese ideologists over the point that Communism and not Socialism is the terminal social order. The point of issue, in this connection, has to do with timing, the readiness of the USSR to enter Communism, and certain details of organization of Communist society. All this aside, Marxists freely admit that Marx could not possibly have known or foreseen everything. Thus there is no *prima facie* reason for rejecting their contention that Marxism is a living and therefore changing doctrine. There is, moreover, no logical reason why one cannot accept this view without commitment regarding the validity of the Marxian schema. Except for those blinded by sectarianism, therefore, the existing heterodoxy need not pose an insurmountable problem. Marxism is an identifiable system of thought if it is understood to be the consequences of the coordinating, organizing, and interpretive labors performed by students of Scientific Socialism on both sides of the ideological barricades.

IS MARXISM SCIENTIFIC?

Virtually all reference works accord Karl Marx the status of one of the great intellectuals and movers of the modern age. The *Encyclopedia of the Social Sciences* ranks Marx as one of the world's major social philosophers and revolutionary leaders. It identifies him further as the "founder of the chief current in modern socialism." Still there are those who insist that neither the man nor his system of ideas is worthy of attention or continued study because Marxism is unscientific. The general argument is that Marx began with a preconceived notion that the world must or should rid itself of Capitalism. From this it is made to follow that the Marxian system is little more than a high-powered, pseudoscientific rationalization for what its founder wanted to see happen. As such, some dismiss Marxism as a case of wishful thinking. Others relegate it to the status of a creed which requires no proof. And still others would have Marxism interred alongside other outmoded doctrines which are of interest only to those who are concerned with the history of antiquated ideas.

Some subscribers to this view stress the purely moral or even the aesthetic nature of Marx's pronouncements. Many focus on the psychological factors underlying Marx's presumed alienation. One such theory is that as an adult Marx remained in a state of post-adolescent revolt against his father. Another is that Marx's disillusionment, followed by bitterness, stemmed from the fact that he was denied appointment to a university post even though he possessed all the formal credentials for such a position. A particularly popular notion is that Marx's alienation was directly the consequence of his sensitivity to the strong climate of Prussian anti-Semitism. Offered only partly in jest, a physiological theory has even been ventured. Marx is known to have suffered from an especially painful case of carbuncles. It is also a matter of record that he once wrote to Engels that some day the capitalists would long have cause to remember his (Marx's) carbuncles.

At a far more serious and impressive level, Marxism has been charged with being unscientific for the following three reasons. (1) Marx and Engels published their conclusions in the *Communist Manifesto* (1848) some twenty years before Marx gave the world the "scientific" proof in the form of *Das Kapital*. (2) The founders of Marxism ignored or reduced to unwarranted insignificance any fact or relationship that did not fit neatly into the mold of their preconceptions. (3) Marx the "coffee-house conspirator" has sullied Marx the social theorist or scientist beyond the point of repair.

But one cannot, on serious reflection, dismiss Marx or Marxism as unscientific quite so easily. The proposition that Marxism rests on certain unproved or unprovable premises is, of course, correct. Only Marxists claim that even their basic premises are scientifically derived and therefore incontrovertible. The fact of the matter is that Marxism is hardly unique in this regard. The same is true for any system of thought if pushed far enough back toward its premises. What really matters is whether the conclusions follow logically and what the weight of the empirical evidence shows. In the case of Marxism this remains to be seen. The weaknesses implicit in a psychological invalidation of Marxism are even more obvious. In the world scheme of things, what actually counts is not why a particular person gives birth to an idea, a system of thought, or an ideology. The strategic considerations here are whether that system enhances our comprehension of the universe and why it becomes a great world force. It has often been said that the road to hell is paved with good intentions. The reverse may also be true. Great discoveries can occur no matter how base, selfish, or distorted the motives of the discoverer may be. In any event it is hardly likely that Marxism will ever be proven right or wrong, or even understood, through psychoanalysis.

Let us turn now to the more substantive charges. A time lag between the public unveiling of a theory or system of thought and the publication of supporting evidence is not necessarily to indict that theory or system as unscientific. The line of demarcation between a truly great idea and the fruits of more pedestrian research is the intangible factor of insight. Thinking does not occur in a vacuum. It results from pressures and problems which cry out for solution. Thinkers sense relationships and develop hunches about the physical and social world around them Many such thinkers document their insights first and proclaim them publicly afterward. Others are pushed by circumstances or temperament into announcing a vision in advance of its verification. The fact that Marx and Engels were driven to give the world their vision in the *Communist Manifesto* some twenty years before the publication of *Das Kapital* casts more light on the circumstances of their day and their temperament than on the issue of whether Marxism is scientific.

Finally, there is the point that Marx ignored or rendered insignificant anything that did not fit the mold of his preconceptions. Ideally, of course, any hypothesis should be tested in terms of all the relevant variables. In practice, especially in the social sciences, this is hardly possible. There is no yardstick which can tell us whether or not or to what degree a particular fact supports or contravenes a given theory. Nor is there some formula to tell us how much weight to attach to one fact over another. Scores of volumes and articles have been written, pro and con, on the question of whether certain historical facts and events are consistent or inconsistent with the Marxian conclusions. That is as it should be. All investigators are forced to make such choices and place that weight on the data which to them seems warranted. We may disagree with what Marx included or excluded from his system. We can take issue with the relative stress that he placed on one factor over another. We may reject his conclusions. But we cannot brush Marxism aside as a simple rationalization or declare unscientific a method which is universally employed. Viewed in this light, Marxism is neither less nor more scientific than other equally impressive creations of the intellect.

It would seem that the question of whether Marxism is scientific belongs at the end rather than at the outset of an exposition on the Marxian system. The order is reversed here precisely because, in this writer's view, there are other questions which are far more relevant. Is the Marxian system logically consistent? Do the Marxian conclusions stand up in the face of empirical testing? Is it, indeed, even possible to subject Marx's predictions to statistical testing? What, in other words, is the predictive value of the Marxian model? Has Marxism, at least, illuminated and thereby helped us to understand something about the true nature of the social universe? First, however, one must know the Marxian premises, follow the logic leading to Marx's conclusions and predictions. It is to this limited objective that we now turn.

II.

The Hegelian Base of Marxism

THE RELATIONSHIP OF HEGELIANISM TO MARXISM

Tradition has it that an examination of Marxism, especially Marx's theory of history, begins with an exposition of its Hegelian base. The reasons behind this tradition are clearly stated by Joseph Schumpeter: "German-trained and speculative-minded as he [Marx] was, he had a thorough grounding and a passionate interest in philosophy. Pure philosophy of the German kind was his starting point and the love of his youth. For a time he thought of it as his true vocation. He was a Neo-Hegelian. . . . This background shows in all his writings wherever the opportunity offers itself. It is no wonder that his German and Russian readers, by bent of mind and training similarly disposed, should seize primarily upon this element and make it the master key to the system." [1]

But, then, Schumpeter goes on to say: "I believe this to be a mistake and an injustice to Marx's scientific powers. He retained his early love during the whole of his lifetime. He enjoyed certain formal analogies which may be found between his and Hegel's argument. He liked to testify to his Hegelianism and to use Hegelian phraseology. But this is all. Nowhere did he betray positive science to metaphysics. He says himself as much in the preface to the second edition of his first volume of *Das Kapital,* and that what he says there is true and no self-delusion can be proved by analyzing his argument, which everywhere rests upon social fact, and the true sources of his propositions none of which lies in the domain of philosophy." [2]

The extreme to which Schumpeter went in his insistence that Marx relied only on the method of positive science, that he was not at all a philosophic system-builder, is a good antidote to the more commonly held view that Marxism is anything but scientific. There is nothing in this one of Schumpeter's unsupported observations to justify our total dismissal of the Hegelian base of Marxism. This much may be said on behalf of Schumpeter's argument. Hegelian philosophy is far more embracing, complex, and metaphysical than is directly relevant to Marxism or our study of it here. Marx accepted those aspects of Hegelian philosophy which interested him, those that he found analytically useful, and rejected others. He modified or "inverted" Hegelianism in a fundamental sense to be discussed. Under the banner of Hegelianism, he claimed the truth of particular propositions which do not appear warranted by that philosophy. Thus, without breaking the tradition of starting with its Hegelian base, our treatment of Marxism will bend that tradition somewhat. To be more specific: We will consider here only those aspects of Hegelian philosophy necessary to an understanding of the language and meaning of Marx's theory, with special stress on the various respects in which Marx differs or goes beyond the Hegelian framework.

THE HEGELIAN FRAMEWORK

Even the barest and most relevant essentials of Hegelianism require an initial statement regarding the dominant philosophical position to which the philosophy of Georg Wilhelm Friedrich Hegel represented a reaction. Seventeenth-century empiricism had culminated by the eighteenth century in a materialistic concept of the universe. Such philosophers regarded the world as a large and complex clock-like machine which, for all time, operated in accordance with certain immutable laws. And when religious orthodoxy insisted on a place for God, philosophers like Descartes satisfied that requirement. God, it was said, created the world and pushed the button to set the mechanism in motion; then, by His own choice, no longer interfered with the natural order of the universe. It was only a short step for an outright materialist like Diderot to rule God out as entirely unessential to the whole process.

The philosophers with whom Hegel took issue employed the method of formal logic. Because of its relevance to that which follows, a word about its meaning is called for. Formal logic, first systematized by Aristotle, defines things in terms of their essential properties. It is based on such propositions as $X = X$; which is a way of saying that an object is not different from itself. Thus something is either X or non-X and cannot be both at the same time. An object, say a pipe, is defined as such because it embodies those features to which a pipe must conform if it is to be a pipe. The statement that a pen is a pen and not a pencil and that both are writing instruments as against a spoon involves the use of formal logic. The syllogism is the mode of argument employed by formal logic. Thus the classic:

> All men are mortal
> Socrates is a man;
> Therefore Socrates is mortal.

The purpose of formal logic is to facilitate thinking. It is to enable us to distinguish one thing from another by a clear-cut definition of the subject.

The dominance of philosophical materialism during the eighteenth century did not, however, succeed in blotting out an opposing view of the universe. A reaction against materialism set in and a revival of philosophical idealism, spearheaded by Kant and Hegel, occurred toward the end of the eighteenth century. The principal charge levied against materialist philosophy was its failure to comprehend the true nature of change because its approach was metaphysical and its method that of formal or static logic. Hegelianism, the essential tenets of which follow, represents a criticism of and a departure from philosophical materialism.

The universe is composed of a system of dynamic and related categories such as quantity, existence, causality, substance, and quality. The sum of these dynamic categories comprises a totality called the *Idea*, the *Whole*, or the *Absolute*. The Absolute constitutes the only reality; it alone is completely real. The parts which make it up partake of reality, possess a greater or lesser degree of reality, only as they are related to and seen in terms of the Absolute. The Absolute also possesses such attributes as creative power, truth, and rationality. It is the source or originator of the universe and thus also the creator of the mind. The universe is run on a rational principle called the World Spirit. Thus rationality is truth and truth is reality (hence Hegel's "whatever is rational is real, and whatever is real is rational").

Our primary interest here, as was Marx's, is with the phenomenon and mechanism of movement or change. A connecting link exists between the categories that make up the Absolute. That link is dialectical[3] in the special sense that careful scrutiny of any concept will necessarily lead to the next and different one. This is so because nature—the parts observable at any given point short of the full unfolding of the Absolute—exists and is seen in "contradiction yet in unity." Every part of the Absolute, in other words, contains polar opposites which are related. Thus the idea of black requires the notion of white, hot requires cold, good requires bad. As for the concept of existing in unity, East and West are opposites yet one leads to the other. The Absolute is composed, however, not only of abstraction or thought but also the totality of experience. It encompasses the time element and everything that transpires over time. Events (history), along with our awareness of them, are therefore also subject to the same dialectical process. The dialectic rules over history as well as over thought, both being part of the Absolute. Thus historical change is really the process by which the Absolute unfolds, gradually revealing progressively more of its true self.

The actual mechanics of movement or historical change is explained with the aid of a triad called "thesis–antithesis–synthesis." The idea about an existing thing, institution, or event (at any given point in the unfolding of the Absolute) is known as the *thesis*. On contemplation, each existing thesis is found to possess a fundamental contradiction as a result of which it breaks down. This is the *antithesis*, which denies or negates the thesis. But the antithesis also suffers from the same ailment and breaks down in consequence of its own internal contradiction. The result is the emergence of a *synthesis*, which negates the antithesis, thereby becoming the "negation of the negation." It is characteristic of the synthesis, however, that it embodies the true or valid elements of the antithesis and also of the initial thesis. Thus this triad represents steps or stages in the movement toward the Absolute. But no sooner is the synthesis examined than it too is found to be defective or contradictory. A new thesis emerges and the spiraling movement of thesis–antithesis–synthesis begins all over again. When, if ever, will it cease? Recall the Hegelian view of history as the process of the Absolute (which is perfect in its ultimate sense) gradually unfolding. There comes a point, therefore, when a thesis evolves which—even if contemplated for eternity—fails to reveal any flaws or contradictions. It no longer gives rise to an antithesis and further change or movement halts. In that instance the Absolute has been reached and with it arrives the final truth, reality, rationality, and perfection.

MARX'S MODIFICATIONS OF HEGELIANISM:
DIALECTICAL MATERIALISM

We have already observed that Marx accepted certain fundamental Hegelian concepts, rejected others, and, some say, misused still others. Again, the crux of the matter is to be found in the controversy between philosophical idealism and materialism. Hegel's main concern, as we have seen, was not so much with what those like Diderot and Holbach had done with God as with the problem of change. His basic criticism of eighteenth-century materialism—based as it was on the idea of fixed laws, a machine-like universe, and a system of formal logic—was that it failed to cope with the process of change. Marx took a stand somewhere between these two views on this issue. On the one hand, he felt that the exponents of materialism had served a useful if limited purpose. He welcomed the attention that they focused on the presence of a natural order and universal law. He particularly liked the stress placed by that philosophy on the existence of an objective reality. Certainly Marx had no objection to having God declared obsolete. On the other hand, Marx too was deeply concerned with the process of change and agreed that a purely mechanistic philosophy offered no satisfactory explanation of change. This was why Hegelianism appealed to Marx quite as much as it did. But let us be more specific.

Which features of Hegelianism did Marx accept without modification and why? First, and probably most important, was the dialectic (the triad of thesis–antithesis–synthesis) itself. The Hegelian dialectic is both an optimistic and a fatalistic doctrine. It is optimistic because change always results from the reconciliation of conflict, with each stage in the spiral coming closer to the Absolute or perfection. It is fatalistic because Hegel maintained that the universe is sustained by reason and each development is part of reason's plan. Thus the dialectic provided Marx not only with a universal key to causation but assured him that struggle—for Marx it was class struggle—was the essence of both the universe and improvement. It was, in other words, this philosophical framework which enabled Marx to say that each social order is an improvement over the one before it and to guarantee the "suffering masses" salvation under Full Communism as the terminal society.

The "Law of the Transformation of Quantity into Quality" is a second feature of Hegelian philosophy which Marx found especially inviting. According to this "law," everything—be it substance, institutions, or ideas— is always in a state of flux. This constant change is not discernible, however, except at a critical point known as the "Node." It may be helpful to formulate the underlying principle here in two propositions. (1) Nothing undergoes quantitative variation without a resulting qualitative transformation. (2) Cognizance in regard to such transformation, i.e., the emergence of new qualities, occurs in "leaps" or "jumps" rather than gradually or continuously. Social progress, thought Marx, is subject to this same law. It appears to take place not by a gradual, perceptible process but by sudden spurts. Social revolutions then, to employ Hegelian phraseology, are nodal points in the continuous unfolding of the Absolute. Marx spoke of the Communist Revolution as a "dialectical leap" from Capitalism to Socialism.

A third feature of Hegelianism that attracted Marx was its system of dialectic as against formal logic. The Hegelian system of logic rests on the fundamental proposition that all phenomena are continually in a state of becoming something else. From this it is made to follow that X can never be equal to X since no two things can ever be identical. By employing dialectic logic it is thus possible to arrive at the following statement: To say that Capitalism is some one thing, i.e., that X is equal to X, means that a thing is equal to itself only *if* it remains the same. But this is to say that it does not exist since all existing things are in a constant state of change. There is no need here to consider the pros and cons of the two systems of logic, each of which has its own internal consistency. What is of special interest to us is why Marx (and most particularly his followers) was attracted to the system of dialectic logic. Marx was drawn to it, above all, precisely because it derives from the notion that everything is always in a state of becoming something else. It is thus also possible to levy the charge that static or formal logic can serve as an instrument of rationalization in the hands of a ruling class intent on blocking social change. Dialectic logic, on the other hand, as Marx saw it, exposed to view the inevitability of revolutionary change.

We turn now to Marx's differences with and the extent to which he went beyond the Hegelian framework. Marx rejected philosophical idealism. In his words: "My dialectic method is not only different from the Hegelian, but is its direct opposite. To Hegel, the life-process of the human brain, *i.e., the* process of thinking, which, under the name of "the idea," he even transforms into an independent subject, is the demiurge [creator] of the real world, and the real world is only the external, phenomenal form of the 'idea.' With me, on the contrary, the ideal is nothing else than the material world reflected by the human mind, and translated into terms of thought."[4] Marx, in other words, claimed that he had found Hegel standing on his head and that he, Marx, had "set him the right way up."

The question of whether Marx was correct in viewing Hegel as a subjective idealist in the pattern of Kant and Berkeley need not detain us here. The issue of whether Hegel really meant that the Idea is the only reality remains a point of controversy.[5] The neo-Hegelian influence of Ludwig Feuerbach on Marx in this connection is more significant for an understanding of Marx's theory of history. Feuerbach had maintained that ideas were merely reflections of material conditions, which, in turn, determined *individual* being. Marx was impressed with the notion of the dependence of ideas on the objective, material situation. In its purest form, however, such a materialist view could lead (as, indeed, it did in the case of Feuerbach) to the proposition that "Man is what he eats." Marx was unwilling to accept so narrow a view. He departed from Feuerbach by shifting the emphasis from material conditions determining *individual* consciousness to that of determining *social* being. Marx's focus was thus on the institutional arrangements of society. This difference with Feuerbach is but one of the reasons why the well-known Marxian proposition that "man must first eat before he can philosophize" ought not to be taken too literally or interpreted too narrowly.

Marx's so-called inversion of Hegelianism, his rejection of philosophical *idealism,* is the single most important distinction between Hegel's philosophy and dialectical materialism. There are numerous other respects in which Marx departed from Hegelian orthodoxy, two of which deserve special mention. In the case of his theory of history, Marx selected a single element—the productive force—within the social universe and made that and that alone the independent variable in history. Everything else is said to take its form and to change as the dialectic operates within this productive force.[6] There appears to be nothing in the Hegelian system, however, that imbues any single element with such special power or independence, thus turning all other elements into dependent variables. Secondly, Marx clearly had no Hegelian warrant for treating the dialectic as a predictive instrument. "Philosophy comes too late," according to Hegel, "to teach the world what it should be. . . . The owl of Minerva begins its flight when the shades of twilight have already fallen."

There are, finally, two related philosophical questions which were of particular importance to Marx and, therefore, to our understanding of Marxism. One has to do with Marx's premise about the nature of human nature. The other concerns Marx's epistemology, i.e., his "activist theory of knowledge" as it is sometimes called. The following two propositions, subscribed to by Marx, are basic here. (1) Reality is not mind but matter. Thus the material world, which precedes that of the mind, exists whether we are aware of it or not. (2) Human nature is not some one, particular, unchangeable, and definable thing. Thus, in his search for a scientific theory about society and social relations, Marx became deeply interested in the existing relationship among three variables: thinking, being, and social action. The question that Marx was asking, in other words, was this: How does man come to any real knowledge of the material world and what is the link between such knowledge and social action? The reason for Marx's special concern with this question—his interest in the interaction between man and his material environment—should already be fairly obvious from all that has been said thus far. It will become even more so when we examine his theory of history; a theory which poses no logical contradiction between the notion of the inevitability of social change in a predictable direction and the equal necessity for revolutionaries and revolutionary action.

Marx's activist theory of knowledge represents the resolution of what, to the Marxist mind, is only an apparent inconsistency between the notion of inevitability and the necessity for human action. Marx's initial premise is that people are, in the first instance, simply bundles of egoistic *and* social inclinations who crave nothing more specific than something stable and eternal. Such a view of the nature of man constitutes a clear rejection of two far more commonly held convictions. The first is that man is born with a specific set of "instincts" or "drives" which shape his social behavior. One hears frequently enough that man is *by nature* self-seeking, aggressive, accumulative, competitive, etc., etc.[6] The second conviction follows from the first. Particular features of society, the institution of private property, competition, the act of capital accumulation, for instance, are regarded as deeply rooted in human nature. The institutional arrangements of society and all the events that transpire are thus said to be simply a reflection of that which is "instinctive" or "natural" in man. To attribute the precise opposite to Marx, i.e., that man is born or is by nature cooperative, brotherly loving, and so on, would constitute a serious misreading of what Marx really meant. It would be more accurate—and for all practical purposes correct enough—to interpret Marx as having believed that social man is born *tabula rasa* and that his subsequent ideas, value, systems, and patterns of social behavior merely reflect the objective circumstances of his existence. Again, as we shall soon see, it comes down to the character of the productive force at a given stage of historical development.

How does man, as thus conceived, gain knowledge about the material world? What are the social consequence of such knowledge? Marx took issue with the once prevailing view that knowledge of the external world resulted from the impact of sensations on our minds. What disturbed him in particular was the implicit assumption here that sensations are passive; for, if that be the case, two conclusions can be made to follow. (1) Objective truth is unattainable; if all men were born wearing black-lensed glasses and never once removed them, snow would always be black and no one would ever know that it is anything else. (2) There is no necessary force in operation which would result in man's conscious effort to change his environment. But Marx would not accept these conclusions and offered the following explanation instead. Thought gives us access to the material world but is not a part of it. The external world provides certain sensations which have an impact on the mind. The impact of these sensations, however, does not result in *direct* knowledge of the material universe. The first stage results only in stimuli to knowledge. We can only know something by reacting to the stimuli. It comes to us, therefore, only through the resulting action which is set in motion by the effect of the stimuli of the material world on our minds. This knowledge, though it comes to us in stages, nevertheless represents segments of an undeniable and objective truth. Thus as our knowledge grows we come closer and closer to absolute truth itself.

What does all of this mean in a more concrete sense and what are its policy implications for an orthodox Marxist? It means, first, that theory and action are synonymous. Theory which does not end in action is sterile, and action, without the supporting theory, is without meaning or purpose. Second, it means that any statement, pronouncement, or promise by an individual or political party cannot be taken at face value. An idea or theory is proven to be correct or incorrect, true or false, by how it works out in practice and what changes have resulted. What someone thinks or believes and says, or the motivation behind it, at any given moment is quite another matter. Third, it means that the object of theory or philosophy (Hegel notwithstanding) is not merely to understand the world but to change it since understanding and change are organically linked. This then, is the philosophical framework within which Marxists not only assure us of the inevitability of social change and its direction, but reconcile such inevitability with the equal necessity for human action and direction. Man does what he must! Or, as Marxists put it, man is truly free only when he does that which is historically necessary.

MARX'S PHILOSOPHICAL OUTLOOK: A SUMMARY

According to Marx, idealism and materialism are the only two philosophical systems possible. The same may be said about the two systems of logic: formal and dialectical. As Marx interpreted it, and despite its various shades and distinctions, idealism fundamentally holds to the primacy of mind over matter. It asserts that objective truth is unattainable since knowledge is determined by sensations. Thus, and for the reasons already noted, Marx declared idealism to be a religious, an antiscientific or, at best, a non-scientific point of view. Marx set against this philosophy a system he called dialectical materialism which, to his mind, offered the only possible scientific account of the real world. It was scientific because of its materialist base, the only terms in which science can deal. Relying on a different, a dialectic, system of logic it was able to explain the process of change. It was not mechanistic, leaving room for man's role in the revolutionary process. Dialectical materialism is thus held out to be the key to understanding the true nature of the social universe. Correctly used, according to Marx, it enables one to comprehend the links among ideas, institutions, and events. It enables us to know how and why we came to the present and what, in general terms, lies ahead.

III·

Marx's Theory of History: Its Principal Tenets

Marx's general purpose was to discover the underlying force responsible for social change. His special intent was to gain an insight into the fate of Capitalism. He reasoned that a knowledge of the forces shaping past and present institutions and events would also provide a glimpse into those of the future. To that end he sought a universal explanation of the process by which movement occurs from point to point in historical time. The economic or, as it is sometimes called, the materialist interpretation of history is Marx's answer.

THE BASIC PROPOSITION

In his search for a single-factor, universal explanation of historical movement Marx began by asking: what is *the* principle that governs all human relations? He found that principle in the common activity which all men share: the necessity to create the means with which to support life. This is what Engels had in mind when he confirmed that ". . . mankind must first of all eat and drink, have shelter and clothing . . ."; live, in other words, before he can start to do or think of anything else. This, too, is the basis on which Marx and Engels declared that, in the final analysis, the cause of all historical change is to be found, not in man's mind, not in his growing insight into absolute truth and justice, but in the changes that occur within the mode of production. This, in essence, was the great discovery made by Marx which Engels equated in importance to Darwin's law of evolution in organic nature. This was "the simple fact, hitherto concealed by an overgrowth of ideology," that Marx had unearthed and which Schumpeter declared to be one of the greatest individual achievements to this day.[1]

The quintessence of Marx's theory of history may, without error, be set down as follows: The *ultimate* causes of *all* social changes are to be sought in the changes in the *mode of production*. But to stop here involves the same deceptive brevity and simplicity as would an investigation of the pricing process which begins and ends with the familiar proposition that supply and demand determine price with nothing else or more said. In both cases it is necessary to reach far behind the words themselves; unless, of course, one is satisfied with tautologies. The significance, the truth or falsity, of Marx's theory of history depends on numerous and sometimes complex considerations. A good deal hinges, for instance, on one's interpretation of what Marx actually subsumed under the category productive force, i.e., how narrowly or broadly this concept is defined. The word ultimately (elsewhere Marx and Engels prefer the phrase in the final analysis) carries with it a far more critical connotation than may appear on the surface. Did Marx really take the productive force to be the single independent variable determining every other element of a universe composed entirely of dependent variables? Let us look into these matters.

A SYSTEM OF CLASSIFICATION: DEFINITIONS AND RELATIONSHIPS

According to Marx, the social universe is conceptually divisible into two basic parts: (1) A bottom layer which is called the economic base or substructure, and (2) a top layer, encompassing all else, which is known as the superstructure. The economic base is, in turn, made up of two subelements: (a) The productive *force* and (b) production *relations*. Since the productive force is the critical variable in the Marxian historical system it is well to begin with it.

By productive force Marx meant the sum of the means with which to support life. It is especially important to guard against too narrow or too broad a view of what Marx had in mind in this case. To interpret the materialist theory of history, as some of Marx's popular critics have, as maintaining that the introduction of the steam engine set the entire course and content of Capitalist civilization is to reduce that theory to unjustified absurdity. To subsume nearly everything within the social universe under the productive force, as some of Marx's followers have done in an effort to save the theory, is to render it a truism. Marx meant something far more than that technology determines history and much less than that everything in the social universe determines everything. Objectively speaking, Marx considered labor and land (including natural resources of every description), along with tools and machinery, as components of the productive force. Moreover, such factors as the quality, availability, distribution, and organization of the three elements—as well as their relationship to each other[2]— are also included in Marx's definition of the productive force. Finally, Marx included exchange and distribution, their state of development or degree of sophistication, as part of the productive force of any society.

The productive force—which is represented as a relationship between men and things—gives rise to the second element within the substructure: production relations. This is represented as a relationship between men and men based on the relationship of men to things. The relationship here, in other words, is between a dependent and an independent variable. The initial (dialectic) change occurs within the productive force, i.e., in the relationship between men and things. This in turn, though with a time lag, necessitates a corresponding change in production relations, i.e., in the relationship between men and men. Thus the productive force plus the corresponding production relations makes up the economic base on which the superstructure is said to rest and depend.

The superstructure of a given epoch may be defined as the totality of an existing civilization minus the economic base on which it rests. It may be helpful to conceive of this upper layer in terms of the following related elements:

1. *Institutions:* Church, army, school, court, etc.
2. *Events:* Wars, discoveries, revolutions, colonization, etc.
3. *Ideas:* Ideas about institutions and events; value systems, attitudes, mores, philosophies, theologies, etc.

Thus, for example, the superstructure is said to encompass not only the church but religious wars fought over presumed differences in theology. Given this framework and language, we turn now to the question of what the economic interpretation of history maintains.

A PROBLEM OF INTERPRETATION: THE APPROACH TO BE FOLLOWED

Marx and Engels stated and restated the essence of the Marxian theory of history in many places and in a variety of ways. The following is typical: "In the social production of their means of existence men enter into definite, necessary relations which are independent of their will, productive relationships which correspond to a definite stage of development of their material productive forces. The aggregate of these productive relationships constitutes the economic structure of society, the real basis on which a juridical and political superstructure arises, and to which definite forms of social consciousness correspond. The mode of production of the material means of existence conditions the whole process of social, political, and intellectual life."

The problem with this statement, or any one of its many variants, is that it has been understood so differently by Marxists and non-Marxists alike. M. M. Bober interpreted the above proposition as meaning that the productive force is the "alpha and omega" of history, that the change occurring within the productive force is the "prime" or "sole" cause of history, with everything else being a "vexatious parenthetical digression." Lionel H. Robbins, in his criticism of the Marxian theory of history, arrived at a still narrower interpretation of what Marx had in mind. According to L. H. Robbins, Marx had not only made the productive force the ultimate determinant of history but conceived of it in purely technological terms (i.e., as an aggregate of techniques of production existing at a point in time). R. N. Carew Hunt summed it up this way: All that Marx really meant was that the manner in which men produce sets the entire "complex of ideas and institutions" which make up the society in question. Joseph Schumpeter distilled Marx's theory of history into the following two propositions: (1) The productive force is the basic determinant of social structures which, in turn, "breed" attitudes, forms of behavior and civilizations; (2) the productive force has a logic of its own and changes in accordance to necessities inherent in it in such a way as to generate its own successor. Harry Laidler, on the other hand, interpreted Marx as having said no more than that the productive force is the preponderating influence in the process of historical change and in shaping the political, social, intellectual, etc., elements of the superstructure. G. D. H. Cole similarly represented Marx as having meant little more than that the "economic" is the most important force operating within a totality of heterogeneous forces.[3]

Given such diversity of interpretation, our plan is to approach Marx's theory of history in two stages. This chapter will set forth, in some detail, the main tenets of the Marxian theory of history as understood or interpreted by this writer. The chapter that follows will be concerned with such questions and issues as these: (1) Why does such diversity of interpretation in regard to Marx's theory of history exist and persist? (2) Is it possible to arrive at some reasonable resolutions of these differences? (3) What are the crucial issues involved? In essence Chapter 4 represents a defense of the interpretation of Marx's theory of history as presented here.

THE THEORY AND ITS APPLICATION

As we have already observed, Marx accepted the general Hegelian proposition regarding the cause and manner of *all* change, physical as well as social, but limited his interest to the social process. Recall, as well, that Marx departed from orthodox Hegelianism in a number of important respects. The economic interpretation of history is thus within, yet goes outside or beyond, its Hegelian philosophical framework. According to Marx's theory, history does not change because someone conceives of some new or rational idea. The specific content of a civilization is not altered because man comes to see truth or justice in a different light. All historical change originates within the productive force; which, to stress the point again, is not some idea but a physical, objective reality existing quite apart from the mind of man. The productive force, which has a logic of its own, changes dialectically in the manner already described. Each such productive force, save the last, contains within it both the seeds of its own destruction and the logical necessity of producing its successor. There comes a point in the case of any one productive force, in other words, when it breaks down of its own accord, when it can no longer meet the economic needs of man. The productive force is thus the single independent variable in the Marxian historical system and the initial change is viewed as endogenous rather than exogenous in nature.

Marx's theory of history further maintains that each productive force generates a corresponding production relation. To put it another way: a given relationship of man to things necessitates a particular relationship of man to man. Primitive Communism and Slavery lend themselves nicely for purposes of illustration here. The productive force of Primitive Communism is characterized as one of self-sufficiency. It is as yet undifferentiated by division of labor and specialization and, therefore, by distribution and exchange. The corresponding production relation is that of cooperation and "collective" ownership resulting in a classless and, therefore, in a nonexploiting society. At a certain point, however, the productive force of Primitive Communism is bound to break down and a new one emerge. The inability of a productive force characterized by self-sufficiency to meet the economic requirements of society causes the emergence of the next productive force based on division of labor and specialization. This, in turn, changes the relationship of men to things from "collective" to private ownership of the means of production. A corruption, taking the form of the institution of private property, is introduced. All of this necessitates a corresponding change in the relationship of man to man, that is, in the production relations. Society splits into two fundamental classes antagonistic to each other: (1) the relative few who own and control the means of livelihood, and (2) the many who are forcibly excluded from such ownership. Man's relationship to man thus changes from that of cooperation and classlessness to that of class and struggle between master and slave, exploiter and exploited, oppressor and oppressed. Hence the difference in the relationship of man to man during the periods of Primitive Communism and Slavery. But the productive force dominant during the slave epoch is equally doomed. It, too, will eventually break down and give rise to the next and so on until Full Communism emerges. There follows, in each case, a corresponding change in production relations. Thus the particular configuration of an existing productive force determines not only the absence or presence of classes, exploitation, and struggle but the particular form that each of these takes at any given point in history. The *Communist Manifesto* makes the point: "The history of all hitherto existing society is the history of class struggles. Freeman and slave, patrician and plebeian, lord and serf, guildmaster and journeyman, in a word, oppressor and oppressed, stood in constant opposition to one another. . . . In the earlier epochs of history, we find almost everywhere a complicated arrangement of society into various orders, a manifold gradation of social rank. In ancient Rome we have patricians, knights, plebeians, slaves; in the Middle Ages, feudal lords, vassals, guildmasters, journeymen, apprentices, serfs; . . . The modern bourgeois society that has sprouted from the ruins of feudal society has not done away with class antagonisms. *It has but established new classes, new conditions of oppression, new forms of struggle in place of the old ones.*" [Italics mine.]

This, then, is the economic base on which the superstructure is said to rest and depend. The economic interpretation of history goes on to maintain that every element of the superstructure arises and takes its definite form from the substructure, changing with each change in the economic base. In Marx's words: "The mode of production of the material means of existence conditions the whole process of social, political, and intellectual life." Engels stated it thus: "the production of the immediate material means of subsistence and consequently the degree of economic development attained by a given people or during a given epoch form the foundations upon which State institutions, the legal conceptions, the arts and even the religious ideas of the people concerned have been evolved, and in the light of which these things must be explained."

But let us be somewhat more specific in regard to these statements and what they really imply. What Marx and Engels tell us is this. (1) The content of all institutions—political, social, religious, legal, military, educational, etc.—at a point in historical time is set or determined by the character of the productive force *dominant* at that same time. (2) The ideas—ethical, political, legal, religious, etc.—that prevail, as well as the behavior patterns based on existing value systems, also reflect that same productive force. (3) Historical events such as wars, crusades, revolutions, and so on, which surround the institutions and ideas in question, cannot be correctly understood or interpreted except in terms of the two propositions above. (4) At some critical point an existing productive force breaks down of its own accord. A new and different one emerges and then becomes dominant. (5) This endogeneous change results in a corresponding change not only in the production relations but in all the appropriate elements within the superstructure. A different set of institutions, ideas, values, etc., emerges; more congenial, more consistent with the logical requirements of the new productive force.

To push the point just one step further consider this illustration of what Marx and Engels had in mind. Assume the dominance of a Feudal productive force with these main features: (1) land as the principal agent of production; (2) agriculture as the primary economic activity; (3) a "closed" system of economic organization (that is, absence of markets) where that which is produced is, in the main, also consumed within the same economic unit called the manor. The corresponding production relation is basically that of lord and serf, however many subclasses or gradations in rank there are. Feudal society (the superstructure), its institutions, ideas, etc., reflects the character of this particular economic base. That is to say, government takes on the form of monarchy and political theory culminates in the doctrine of the divine right of kings. By the same token, religion is institutionalized in the medieval church with its specific theology and so on. Assume now the emergence of a new productive force with a different set of characteristics. Capital replaces land as the main agent of production. The focus of economic activity changes from agriculture to commerce, industry, and finance. The organizational center of that activity shifts from the manor to the city and the factory. The process of exchange, money, and credit assumes greater importance. The economic and political dominance of the landowning nobility gives way to domination by a new class composed of merchants and industrialists—the bourgeoisie. The serf is replaced by the industrial worker. The class struggle is now between the capitalist and the proletariat. The appearance of the Capitalist economic base causes corresponding changes in the superstructure: monarchy gives way to democracy (bourgeois), the Protestant Reformation takes place, etc.

Certain aspects of this theory are of particular interest and thus call for further comment or special emphasis. The first of these concerns the relationship of ideas to the economic base. As Engels put it, "moral theories are the product . . . of the economic stage which society had reached at that particular epoch." Philosophers "from Descartes to Hegel and from Hobbes to Feuerbach" did not arrive at their ideas by pure reason, as they had presumed. Rather, their "very ideas are but the outgrowth of the conditions of bourgeois production and bourgeois property." What else, asks the *Communist Manifesto,* "does the history of ideas prove than that intellectual production changes its character in proportion as material production is changed." The *Manifesto* goes even further and maintains that the ideas or morality dominant at any one time reflect the will or interest of the ruling class: "Your very ideas are but the outgrowth of the conditions of your bourgeois production and bourgeois property, just as your jurisprudence is but the will of your class made into law for all, a will whose essential character and direction are determined by the economical conditions of existence of your class." All of this is why Marxists do not credit pre-Marxian, as well as non-Marxian, historians with comprehending the true nature of a given civilization or with understanding the correct cause of historical change. According to the economic interpretation of history, men may indeed believe that their struggles and wars are fought over such lofty principles as political or religious freedom or some other equally superficial ideological consideration. In fact, they record these illusions in their history books. This then is the "overlayer of ideology" through which, according to Engels, Marx had broken in order to get to the truth.

The inevitability aspect of the economic interpretation of history is a second feature that deserves special attention. The laws of history, wrote Marx, work "with iron necessity toward inevitable results." All that a backward country need do to see its own future is to look at the state of development of an advanced nation. Failure to understand these laws of development makes it appear as if these forces work "blindly, violently, destructively." But once we discover what they are, Marx tells us, we also learn that no society can "overleap the natural phases of its evolution nor shuffle out of them by a stroke of the pen." All that is possible, concedes Marx, is to "shorten and lessen the birth pangs." In that sense, therefore, that which comes about is really neither good nor bad but a matter of historical necessity. Indeed, the term "historical necessity," in much of the Marxian literature, is barely distinguishable from the word "desirable." Marx thus sees the social universe as being in a constant state of flux but moving, with "iron necessity," toward a known end called Communism. The productive force, not human will or desire, is the prime mover. Men are said to believe as they do and to act accordingly because they must, as a reflection of the objective circumstances of their economic existence. The objective condition through most of history is characterized as one of society divided into haves and have-nots locked in struggle. Class struggle, with all it implies, is represented as the very essence of change, of progress, of life itself. Each man plays a necessary historical role depending on which side of the class barricades he is destined to be. Viewed dispassionately, therefore, no one is to be blamed for his actions since everyone only does that which is historically necessary. The economic logic of the pre-Socialist economic base forces the ruling minority to exploit the dispossessed majority. The individual capitalist, Marx reminds us, is not really such a bad fellow. The same applies to the pre-Socialist worker who cannot be blamed for his earlier ignorance or stopped from taking over when the proper time comes. Thus we could not, even if we wished, halt the march of history. What is possible, Marx assures us, is to understand the workings of the laws of history and thereby predict the future. It was just such knowledge, based on positive science rather than philosophy, that Marx claimed and on the basis of which he offered the "suffering masses" ultimate salvation. This is also the context within which Marx declared that "History does nothing . . . man makes his own history . . . [even though] he does not do so out of conditions chosen by himself."

The Marxian theory of history is, thirdly, an optimistic doctrine. This point is singled out here, most particularly, as support for the view that one cannot brush aside the Hegelian base of Marxism quite as easily as does Joseph Schumpeter. Marx's view of the dialectic is both optimistic and fatalistic. It is optimistic because historical change always results from the reconciliation of conflict; with each stage in the thesis–antithesis–synthesis spiral there is a step upward or closer to the perfect social order. (The reader will recall that the synthesis embodies not only the new but those aspects of the preceding thesis and antithesis which remain valid.) The dialectic is fatalistic because it leaves no room for the accidental or the irrational in history. The social universe is sustained by natural socio-historical law and each development is part of that law's plan. That this is Hegelian may easily be shown by substituting Absolute for Communism, reason's plan or "World Spirit" for socio-historical law, and so on. This is the philosophical framework within which Marx contended that: (1) Feudalism is better than Slavery, (2) Capitalism is an improvement over Feudalism, (3) Socialism is superior to Capitalism, and (4) Communism is the perfect and therefore terminal social order. It is also the basis on which Marx rejected that aspect of eighteenth-century philosophy which conceived of reason as man's ability to know absolute truth as well as to formulate an ethical system based on right and wrong. Thus it is that Marx looked upon the process of historical change with cold but approving objectivity.

The time-lag factor in the Marxian historical system is, at least in this writer's opinion, one of the most interesting and underexplored facets of the economic interpretation of history. According to this theory, the causal relationships involved are neither direct nor instantaneous and need not necessarily be understood by human intelligence at any given point in the process of social development. The very existence of prevailing institutions, ideas, codes, etc. of a set character introduces a time lag between a change in the economic base and corresponding changes in the superstructure. The theory maintains that a given change in the productive force is followed by a period (of undefined length) during which there occurs a gradual, imperceptible change in production relations and in the various elements of the superstructure. The new will eventually and inevitably win out over the old; but not, as we are about to see, immediately or even quickly, and not without a struggle. Schumpeter alludes to this time lag factor when he writes that "Social structures, types and attitudes are coins that do not readily melt. Once they are formed they persist . . . and . . . different structures and types display different degrees of this ability to survive."[4] That is to say, as it relates to ideas and patterns of behavior, a change from one economic base to the next is followed by a transitional period during which most people still retain the ideas, values, and behavior patterns which correspond to the earlier productive force. V. I. Lenin stressed the further point that certain attitudes such as "bourgeois nationalism" and religion tend to persevere longer than most. Marxians call this phenomenon "vestigialness."

The many theoretical and policy ramifications of this time-lag factor are well worth considering at some length but cannot be undertaken at this point. Several illustrations, based on the Marxian interpretation of history, must therefore suffice. Assume, again, that a given change initiates within the existing Feudal productive force. Say that emergence of the next or Capitalist productive force involves the appearance of steam power. Neither Marx nor Engels maintained, however, that the change from the Feudal to the Capitalist productive force would cause an immediate alteration in the existing production relations or in the many elements of the superstructure.

According to Marx's theory of history, the emergence of the Capitalist productive force was surrounded by struggle. It was resisted by the historically doomed landowning nobility whose class interest lay in trying to preserve the now economically outmoded Feudal productive force. For some time, in fact, the old ruling class may even succeed in retaining its political dominance even though it has lost its economic supremacy. Moreover, early in the period of Capitalist development, the fundamental class conflict between worker and capitalist was obscured by the fact that the bourgeoisie used the proletariat in its battle to destroy the old ruling class. Thus the new production relation, that of the capitalist-employer and wage worker; does not immediately become apparent. At the same time, modern factories do not suddenly appear and cities do not spring up over night. The factory may be preceded by home industry and the Feudal manor will only gradually disappear. Or take the change from a Capitalist to a Socialist economic base as a case in point. According to the Marxian interpretation of history, the emergence of a Socialist productive force as such does not cause an immediate and corresponding set of changes in mass ideas and behavior. The fact that the Socialist Revolution occurs and that the means of production are nationalized does not in and of itself enable the masses to manage the economic or even the political affairs of the new society! To a greater or lesser degree everyone, even a Communist party member, is held to be afflicted with the social ailment of vestigialness. A necessary conflict is said to arise between the logical requirements of the newly emerged Socialist productive force and the persistence of bourgeois institutions, ideas, values, and forms of behavior. This is so, according to Marx, because "What we have to deal with here is a communist society, not as if it had *developed on a basis of its own*, but on the contrary as *it emerges from capitalist society*, which is thus in every respect tainted economically, morally and intellectually with the hereditary diseases of the old society from whose womb it is emerging." [Italics mine.] There is a lag, in other words, between the moment that the Socialist productive force emerges and the time that most workers and peasants shed their vestiges. Just how long people must live and work in an environment dominated by a Socialist productive force before they cease to be religious, before they rise above all other forms of "superstition," and before there occurs a change in attitude toward private property rights, work, and each other is left unspecified. Thus and until the people are ready to govern themselves the Communist party must rule on the principle of the dictatorship of the proletariat.

What, finally, does the Marxian theory of history tell us about the *rate* of social change? Is all such change necessarily sudden, violent, bloody, revolutionary or could it, under certain circumstances, also be gradual, bloodless, evolutionary? Appropriate quotations from the works of Marx and Engels can, in fact, be found in support of either view. But our interest here is in Marx's *theory* of historical change and not in Leninist strategy and tactics. Thus viewed the whole issue of revolution *versus* evolution, violent or peaceful transition, turns out to be largely irrelevant. In this regard Marx was, indeed, a Hegelian. He saw the process of historical movement, first of all, as one of gradual, imperceptible, and continuous change. As dialectic logic has it, A is never equal to A since nothing ever remains the same. Cognizance, the awareness of major social change, on the other hand, occurs only at critical (nodal) points in the process. Social change is thus both evolutionary and revolutionary, gradual and sudden, peaceful and violent. Revolution, viewed in this context, is simply the stage at which society becomes aware that the existing productive force has reached its final breaking point. This is what Marx meant by "the objective circumstance for revolution" which, in the case of Capitalism, he characterized: "The monopoly of capital becomes a fetter upon the mode of production . . . the means of production . . . at last reach a point where they become incompatible with their capitalist integument. This integument is burst asunder. The knell of capitalist private property sounds. The expropriators are expropriated."

MARX'S THEORY OF SOCIAL CLASSES:

THE CLASS STRUGGLE

The concept of class and class struggle plays an undeniably pivotal role in the Marxian schema. The proposition that "The history of all hitherto existing society is the history of class struggle" is one of the broadest and most dramatic statements appearing in the *Communist Manifesto*. Still, for reasons to be noted, one may agree with Schumpeter when he accords Marx's theory of social classes no more status than that of "the crippled sister of the economic interpretation of history."

The Marxian theory of social classes, such as it is, contains two essential elements: classification and antagonism. Economists generally, those in the neoclassical tradition most particularly, tend to classify groups within society in terms of their functional relationship to the economic process. Thus we have the well-known category of the worker, the landlord, the capitalist, and the entrepreneur as agents of production. Each factor is regarded as essential to production and each is said to receive its share—in the form of wages, rent, interest, and profit—in the distributive process. The assumption here, sometimes left implicit but often explicitly stated, is that there exists an economic harmony of interests and/or a single distributive principle (i.e., marginal productivity theory). But such functional differences did not interest Marx or suit his purposes. Instead he selected the institution of private property and made that *the* stratifying principle on the basis of which all pre-Socialist societies are divided. Society is split, according to Marx, on the basis of private ownership of the means of production versus exclusion from such ownership. The dominant means of production—land, capital—differs as between (say) the Slave and the Capitalist epoch. But the principle of private ownership of the productive means versus exclusion from such ownership remains unchanged. A minority, whose composition changes over time, retains ownership and control over the means of production. The vast majority, denied ownership rights, is said to have no other choice but to submit to exploitation in order to survive.

At no time did Marx lose sight of the fact that the two classes were not homogeneous. He recognized the existence of gradations or subgroups within each class lasting through the final stage of Capitalist development. Marx even admitted that historically significant rifts could occur among groups within a class. Once again, however, he resorted to the phrase "in the final analysis" in order to insist that the real force behind history is to be found only in the class war between the haves and the have-nots. In reference to his own day, Marx regarded the independent farmer and artisan, the self-employed doctor or lawyer, as anomalies which—given the dynamics of the Capitalist process—would tend to rise upward or merge with the working class. What remains, becoming all the more clearly distinguishable as Capitalism matures, is the raw struggle between the two fundamental classes. What Marx saw, underneath it all, were exploiters and exploited pitted against each other by the logic of the productive force. Thus the force that moves the world is said to be not the will of man nor even the clash of nations, as many historians would have it, but the class struggle. What Marx had to say about the precise form that this class struggle takes during the Capitalist and post-Capitalist periods of history is yet another matter and considerably beyond the scope of this chapter.

The fact is that Marx had never developed a systematic theory of social classes despite the amount of time he devoted to it or the emphasis that he placed on the class struggle. Perhaps the entire concept of class and struggle was so central in his mind that he felt no need to define the obvious. It is more likely, however, that Marx experienced great difficulty in working out a meaningful theory of social classes which would serve the purpose and be logically consistent with his economic interpretation of history. The result, in any case, is that Marx's theory of social classes is one of the weakest and least realistic aspects of Marxist theory.

The point at issue, to approach the matter from a somewhat different side, is why so great an intellect as Marx settled for such an inferior theory of social class. But first, and in all fairness to Marx, it must be stated that little progress has been made in developing an adequate theory of social classes even to the present. A functional concept of class may suffice for the purposes of economic theory. Something more is required if one is to understand the dynamics of the full social process. There are, of course, other theories of social classes and conflict than the Marxian one. The current world situation calls to mind the theories that see society divided and in conflict along racial lines. Existing antagonisms between specific occupational groups leave something to be said for a division-of-labor theory of classes as well. These are but two of many such theories from which to select. The crucial issue is that there exists an inescapable relationship between the theory of social classes selected and one's view of history as well as the forces responsible for social change. Marx was keenly aware of this integral relationship; which is why his theory of social classes is not an independent doctrine but an extension of his theory of history.

Given the materialist theory of history, Marx appears to have had no other logical choice but to develop the theory of social classes that he did. The dialectic framework of that theory prescribed not only that there be two (and only two) basic classes but that they exist in sharp antagonism to one another. As we have seen, antagonism or struggle is, as viewed by Marx, the essence of all history and historical movement. The classes had, moreover, to be purely economic in nature since the character of the productive force is said to determine all aspects of the corresponding civilization. How else, except by defining classes in terms of ownership versus exclusion from ownership of the means of production, could Marx have arrived at the proposition that Socialism is a classless society? The precise manner in which Marx weaves this sociology of history and class with economic analysis will be seen in the chapters concerned with the Marxian laws of Capitalist development.[5]

IV·

Marx's Theory of History: An Overview

WHAT THE THEORY DOES NOT MAINTAIN

An overview of Marx's theory of history might well begin with some observations as to what this theory does not maintain and where it is not meant to apply. The economic interpretation of history does *not* maintain: (1) that men are moved, even in the main, by economic motives; (2) that the content of a civilization—the character of its institutions and ideas—can be understood in terms of such motives; or (3) that economic motivation is the force underlying historical change. The point is stressed here because even Engels came dangerously close to holding such a superficial view of the Marxian theory of history. What Marx, in fact, endeavored to do was to expose the material conditions (i.e., the productive force) which shape the content of existing institutions and ideas and to explain the process by which these elements of the superstructure change over time. What really interested Marx, in this connection, was the manner in which social groups accounted for their own being and their particular mode of behavior.

Secondly, Marx's theory of history does not simply maintain that the productive force is but one or even the most important determinant of history. Nor does it, for that matter, merely hold that no civilization could exist without the productive force. No one seriously questions the fact that all civilizations *depend* upon the existence of a productive force as earlier defined. Most would grant that the productive force has great historical significance. But Marx's theory of history would hardly be worth considering were it to say nothing more than that man must first eat (stay alive) before he can philosophize (do all else)? Who would deny that civilizations *depend* on rainfall and sunshine, water and air? It is quite another matter to say that every facet of the superstructure, all historical change, is determined by some special character of the water or air. Yet this is really what the economic interpretation of history tells us. It is, of course, for us to decide whether this theory confuses the condition for human existence with the causal forces behind the historical movement.[1]

THE CRUCIAL ISSUE: THE "KICKBACK EFFECT"

We come now to a question which is crucial in any assessment of the Marxian theory of history. How much this theory really explains is closely linked to an issue which, simply as a shorthand device, I will henceforth refer to as the "kickback effect." Precisely what did Marx maintain about the causal relationship between the economic base and the superstructure of society? Did he, in fact, regard the productive force as the single independent variable; thereby treating the superstructure as entirely passive or dependent? Or did he admit to an interaction between substructure and superstructure, with all that such an admission implies? To take the latter view is to concede that the productive force, however important, is but one of a multitude of complex and interacting factors responsible for shaping the course of history. It raises such further questions as these. How much weight is to be placed on the economic base and on the various elements within the superstructure? What are the implications for historical change, or our ability to understand it, of endless chains of such interactions?

Late in his life—following many years of controversy over the economic interpretation of history—Engels endeavored to settle this issue of the "kickback effect" once and for all. In a now famous letter to Joseph Block, written in 1890, Engels, speaking for himself as well as for Marx, said: "According to the materialist conception of history the determining element ... is *ultimately* the production and reproduction in real life. More than this neither Marx nor I have ever asserted. If, therefore, somebody twists this into the statement that the economic element is the *only* determining one, he transforms it into a meaningless, abstract and absurd phrase. . . . the various elements of the superstructure . . . also exercise their influence . . . and in many cases preponderate in determining their form. There is an interaction of all those elements in which, amid all the endless *hosts* of accidents . . . the economic movement finally asserts itself as necessary. . . . Marx and I ourselves are partly to blame for the fact that younger writers sometimes lay more stress on the economic factor than is due to it. We had to emphasize this main principle in opposition to our adversaries, who denied it, and we had not always the time, the place or opportunity to allow the other elements involved in the interaction to come into their rights."

Thus Engels, perhaps even more so than Marx, both insisted on the primacy of the productive force and admitted that the various elements of the superstructure do leave an imprint on the substructure, i.e., that the relationship is two-way and complex. The primacy of the economic is obscured, the argument goes on, by the time-lag factor as well by the fact that social change is perceived in "leaps." But while all of this may and indeed does satisfy the faithful, it strikes a non-Marxist as little more than a magnificent piece of equivocation. The heart of this matter lies, of course, in the meaning attached to such words as "ultimate," "necessary," "final," and "primary." Here, however, rereading the words of Marx or Engels is of little help. Admirers as well as critics of Marx's theory of history have made serious efforts to resolve the "kickback effect" problem. There are those, like G. D. H. Cole, who suggest that the productive force is only the initial stimulus which may or may not evoke a response because the universe is full of abortive stimuli. But this still leaves to the imagination the question of what within the universe acts as the selector and therefore the true determinant of history. Joseph Schumpeter, in an effort to square the same circle, maintained that while ideas and values were not for Marx the prime movers of history, they did play the role of transmission belts between the economic base and the superstructure. One wonders, though, whether this tells us anything more than what has already been said without resolving the real issue.

What, then, are we to make of the above equivocation? Marx and Engels permit an interaction between the substructure and superstructure and are thus able to end the *Communist Manifesto* with the exhortation: "Workers of the world, unite!" By insisting, at the same time, on the primacy of the productive force they fail to work out the nature of the interaction between the economic role and the related one of man's mind, intelligence, and all the rest. Since the productive force is said to ultimately assert itself, what remains for the elements within the superstructure to do? The central question remains unanswered. It is well enough to say that man has the ability to transform his environment and that only in that way can he gain knowledge about the world. The notion that man is the master of his own destiny makes realistic sense only if one grants that the idea (intelligence, etc.) is an independent variable capable of affecting the environment in a primary way. But the only point that Marx and Engels grant is that an interaction exists. Nothing is established regarding the primacy of the elements of the superstructure or the principle governing the interaction. It would seem that once an interaction is allowed the purity or primacy of the substructure is affected and the ultimacy of the economic base as the determinant of all history is meaningless.

There is no question but that Marx and Engels were aware and greatly troubled over this difficulty. The number of times that they and their disciples treated various elements of the superstructure as belonging to the economic base attests to this. It is, again, the old conflict between Marx the scientist and Marx the revolutionary. The founders of Scientific Socialism needed to have it both ways. They appealed to the inexorability of historical law as a guarantee that a terrestial paradise for all would ultimately emerge. At the same time they organized or wanted organized a revolutionary party which would direct the battle for the overthrow of Capitalism. The academician in Marx forced him to admit the "kickback effect" but the other side of him prevented his working out its real implications. For once the notion of a two-way causal relationship is taken seriously the possibilities and complexities become infinite and the question of what, except everything, determines history remains.

Undeniably, the economic interpretation of history can and has been read differently on this point. But these facts remain. Marx's prognostication of doom for the Capitalist system stems from his analysis of contradictions which he found to be inherent in the Capitalist *productive force*. Moreover (as any examination of Marxist literature will bear out), Marxists typically interpret history as if the productive force is, in fact, the single determining factor. Many problems and pitfalls connected with the application of Marx's theory to a particular historical situation can, indeed, be avoided by recognizing an interaction between the economic base and the superstructure. To do so, however, is necessarily at the expense of that glamor and significance which Marx's theory of history does possess. All of this is why the economic interpretation of history should be allowed to stand or fall on the one basis, the one-way relationship, on which it does say something significant. This also accounts for the bias in favor of the narrower interpretation of this theory as it appears in the preceding chapter. The conclusion one reaches about its validity is something else again.

SOME SPECIAL CONSIDERATIONS

In assessing the economic interpretation of history, the reader is asked to keep the following five summary considerations in mind. (1) According to this theory, all social change is endogenous and initiates within the productive force as the single independent variable in this system. (2) A given change in the productive force necessarily results in a corresponding change in the *entire* configuration of the superstructure. The emergence of the Capitalist productive force, for example, does not alter the religious side of the superstructure without, at the same time, causing a logically related change in the form of government, the educational system, the institution of marriage and the family, etc. What Marx tells us, in other words, is that there is a distinctly Slave, Feudal, Capitalist, Socialist, and Communist way of thinking and behaving, of governing, of family life, of worshiping or not worshiping, and so on. With the relationship of the economic base to the superstructure set aside for the moment, the possibility that the various elements of the superstructure may indeed be logically linked at any given point in history is one of the most interesting and underexplored facets of Marx's theory of history. (3) Marx's conscious and purposeful quest was for a universal principle of social change. Recall the question with which he began: "What is *the* principle that governs *all* human relations?" This desire on the part of Marx to formulate a theory that would correctly explain all past, present, and future phenomena and events is hardly unique and certainly understandable. (4) Marx's theory of history involves two basic elements each of which must be judged by its own set of standards. One is the primacy of economic causation and the other is the general Hegelian framework. The first proposition is, in fact, far more widely accepted than the second even by those who are not Marxists. Marxists, of course, draw no such dichotomy and accept both propositions with equal conviction. (5) It must also be noted that Marx was far from satisfied with his own theory of history. He had, at one time in his life, every intention of writing a book on dialectical materialism. Had he done so there is a good possibility that the true scholar in Marx would have forced him to face up to some of the weaknesses and to reconsider certain of the views associated with the economic interpretation of history. Instead, for nearly two decades, he trapped himself in a task which culminated as *Das Kapital*. Based on history's judgment, one cannot but wonder whether a book on dialectical materialism might not have been the greater contribution.

AN ASSESSMENT OF THE THEORY

We come now to some of the specific features of the Marxian theory of history, beginning with its Hegelian base. No attempt is made here to compare philosophies or reach any final philosophical conclusions. The continuing controversies over philosophical systems had best be left to the philosophers. The intent in that which follows is to do no more than raise some of the questions and to point out what certain critics of Marx's theory of history have had to say in regard to its Hegelian base.

Hegelianism has been attacked, first of all, for its unwarranted optimism. Hegel has been interpreted, at least by some, as having said that whatever happens is necessarily right and therefore good because it cannot be any other way. If the cosmos is directed by reason, with laws of its own, then indeed nothing irrational can occur. And every natural disaster, every barbaric act of man or of an entire nation, is only part of nature's reasoned plan. Recall Marx's point, speaking as a Hegelian, that each social order is necessarily better than the one preceding it. This type of dialectical reasoning can easily lead to the rather absurd conclusion that Nazism was preferable to that which came before it and that Nazi concentration camps were an unavoidable part of history's rational plan. Similar conclusions appear inescapable when one tends to equate historical necessity with desirability. Knowledge of the past provides us with sufficient evidence (in all, perhaps, but a metaphysical sense) that history does not quite move in this way. Enough retrogression, decay, and reappearance of the undesirable have occurred to leave some room for pessimism about the future. So much depends, in any case, on what one means by "good" and "progress."

The principle of the dialectic—the notion that all change results from a reconciliation of opposites—has also been seriously challenged. Critics view the dialectic as a gross oversimplification inasmuch as this principle forces everything within a very complex universe into the mold of either a protagonist or an antagonist. No one questions the existence—past, present, or future—of conflict within the social universe. Where great doubt exists is on the matter of whether, on the one hand, everything within the universe is in conflict and, on the other, whether that which does exist in contradiction is necessarily reconcilable. Might there not be, for example, qualitatively different forms of conflict some of which may and others may not be resolvable?

Marx, of course, has been additionally criticized for the specific use (or, as some prefer, abuse) to which he put the dialectic in his theory of history. The application of so highly abstract a concept as the Hegelian dialectic to the concreteness and reality of history has certainly been questioned. Critics find it especially difficult to conceive of the stream of history as starting at some one point and coming to a known end. How for that matter, the same critics ask, is it possible to break into this unending process and declare this or that to be the thesis, the antithesis, or synthesis? Marx and, most particularly, his followers have been even more sharply criticized for the extreme to which they have pushed dialectical materialism as the only truly scientific method. It is one thing to recognize and credit the concept of the dialectic as a useful tool in our comprehension of conflicting forces and purposes in historical change and social development. It is quite another to interpret everything through it, as have the Marxists, and thus to declare any other approach as unscientific. It is still another, as we have already observed, to go entirely beyond the Hegelian warrant and use the dialectic as an instrument for predicting the future. To attribute such exclusive scientific power to dialectical materialism is to imply (1) that formal logic is unnecessary or is a contradiction of the scientific method; (2) that there was no such thing as true science before Marx's lifetime; and (3) that the only scientific discoveries made today are those made by Marxists. In all fairness it must also be noted that such an extreme—this kind of barren scholasticism to which dialectical materialism had degenerated during the Stalinist period—is no longer characteristic at least of Soviet and East European Marxism. There remains the matter of Marx's theory of knowledge. Marx ended up by saying that man is master of his own destiny and that history is predetermined. Whether he succeeds in reconciling these two propositions through his activist theory of knowledge is something else to be left to the philosophers.

Thus Marx really offers no explanation of what, in the first and last instance, causes the productive force to change other than the principle of the Hegelian dialectic. To the extent, therefore, that the economic interpretation of history rests on this base it must share many of the same charges levied at Hegelianism. Edmund Wilson, in *To the Finland Station,* does not stand alone when he dismisses the dialectic as that "mythical and magical triangle" which since the time of the Greeks has stood as a symbol of certainty and power. Karl R. Popper, in his remarkable book *The Open Society and Its Enemies,* quotes Schopenhauer on Hegel as follows: "Should you ever intend to dull the wits of a young man and to incapacitate his brains for any kind of thought whatever, then you cannot do better than give him Hegel to read. For these monstrous accumulations of words that annul and contradict one another drive the mind into tormenting itself with vain attempts to think anything whatever in connection with them, until finally it collapses from sheer exhaustion. Thus any ability to think is so thoroughly destroyed that the young man will ultimately mistake empty and hollow verbiage for real thought."[2] But the fact that Hegelianism remains a powerful force despite, perhaps even because of, its weaknesses is attested to by the following two items which appear in the same source. Popper quotes Schopenhauer again as saying about Hegel: "He exerted, not on philosophy alone but on all forms of German literature, a devastating, or more strictly speaking, a stupefying, one could also say, a pestiferous, influence. To combat this influence forcefully and on every occasion is the duty of everybody who is able to judge independently. *For if we are silent, who will speak?*"[3] Finally, speaking his own mind, Popper says: "I mention this fact mainly because I wish to show how difficult and, at the same time, how urgent it is to continue Schopenhauer's fight against this shallow cant. . . . At least the new generation should be helped to free themselves from this intellectual fraud, the greatest, perhaps, in the history of our civilization. . . . The Hegelian farce has done enough harm. We must stop it. We must speak—even at the price of soiling ourselves by touching this scandalous thing which, unfortunately *without success,* was so clearly exposed a hundred years ago."[4] [Italics mine.]

We turn now to the question of the primacy of economic causation. As already observed, Marx did not rest content with the general Hegelian proposition that all change occurs dialectically. He found the productive force alone within the social universe to be the prime mover and determinant of history. But this view immediately raises two general lines of questions. (1) What proof is there that history changes and that the content of all civilizations is determined by a single factor or force within the social universe? (2) Granting such a possibility, what further evidence is there that the economic rather than some one other variable is thus determining? Marx's theory of history, which offers positive answers to both questions, is understandably appealing in certain respects. It satisfies man's desire for a neat and sure explanation of all social phenomena. It offers a convenience and a sense of security to those who like to squeeze all things into a precast mold. Most social theorists, nevertheless, find society far too complex to be understood or explained in terms of *a* principle which singles out one factor as determining.

To be more specific, Marx's theory of history leaves many vital questions without satisfactory answers. There is no room in this theory for the effect on history of simple chance. Sheer accident is a factor which no less distinguished a philosopher than Bertrand Russell deems to be an important though not the exclusive determinant of history. Suppose that the delicate negotiations resulting in Lenin's re-entry into Russia in 1917 had gone the other way. It is difficult to deny the difference that this would have made in the timing as well as in the direction of the Bolshevik Revolution. The Marxian theory also fails to offer a satisfying explanation of why differing ideologies, theologies, and mores have emerged out of what by every reasonable standard is the same economic base. It is difficult, indeed, to see what great difference there was between the French and German productive force which made one society the "cradle of democracy" and the other so receptive to the "Führer" principle. Thirdly, it is one thing to recognize that "great men" do not simply mold society to their image or make history by the sheer force of their will. It is quite another to insist that a given productive force will necessarily generate someone or some leader who will espouse a corresponding ideology. It is very much open to doubt whether there would, in fact, have been a philosophy known as Utilitarianism without the biological entity named Jeremy Bentham, Scientific Socialism without Karl Marx, or *the* Bolshevik Revolution without V. I. Lenin.

There are, of course, many other theories of history and alternative explanations of the historical process. There exists the very eligible possibility that it is really the mind or nature of man and his intelligence, as expressed through his will and his emotions, which brings about the initial change. Moreover, that it is the constant interaction of this factor with the environment which determines the ethos and substance of civilization and changes within it. One can argue, as has been done, along the following lines.[5]

It is the factor of intelligence (ideas) which separates man from beast. Without this distinguishing mutation man, or even his mode of production, would make about as much history as animals with their mode of production. Even initial ideas are not merely reflections of the material environment. Subsequent ideas evolve out of the aggregate of previously accumulated ones without, necessarily, the intervention of external facts. Man's ideas—what he thinks or believes—result from a complex of things. Man differs from the "lower forms" not only because he possesses the instrument of intelligence but because he is driven or motivated by certain desires and feels certain emotions. Love, pity, hate, envy, and sympathy as well as the desire for creature comforts, status, power, self or social improvement, and recognition all make up a portion of what we call human nature.

This is not to say that the physical environment does not bear upon man's ideas. A given set of geographical circumstances plays a significant part in giving direction to the mode of production. People living in a mountainous area may, generally, come to be hardy, independent, or freedom-loving but undeveloped in terms of their propensities for communication and commerce. Whereas those living along a navigable river, say, may become facile in trade and communication but more homogeneous and less independent than mountain people. But even within the same geographical area unaccountable differences among people arise. Not all feel the same emotions, are driven by identical desires, or react to the material stimuli in the same way. Differing degrees of sharpnesses of intelligence and varying scales of sensitivities and emotional capabilities result in differing reactions even to the same physical environment. Similar observations may be made about the impact of different degrees of economic scarcity upon the content of civilization and so on. None of this means, however, that geography, the productive force, or any other single physical factor is the sole determinant of the character of a civilization or the content of all ideas.

Certainly, science and inventions are responsive to economic needs and are limited by the availability of resources. Many areas of scientific endeavor are devoted to an improvement in the productive force as well as to the betterment of man's physical and social well-being. But can we say, as did Marx, that all invention and scientific discovery is but a reflection of the logic of the productive force? Again, factors such as psychological or even religious motivation, curiosity, and accident cannot be dismissed in connection with the origin of scientific ideas. In any case, and whatever its origin, once science exists it asks its own questions, supplies some of its own stimuli, and develops its own spheres of interest. Science is not a mere handmaiden to economic necessity.

The environment is full of provoking and challenging stimuli. Not everyone will be alive to it or see the hints implicit in it. Among the multitude who may be driven by the desire to improve things a few may, by viewing existing things differently, sense a need or devise a way of satisfying it. Innovation or scientific discovery is not just a matter of an automatic response to stimuli. The presence of a certain type of mind is required. History is not a result of a mechanical reaction of passive and ignorant human beings to an all-determining physical environment. Material circumstances change. Resources become depleted. Diminishing returns may plague mature economies. What is made of these changes in the material world depends on how the innovators perceive things and what they do to solve the problem. But the existence of such men at the precise moment of need is not automatically assured. Otherwise all problems would be solved, no civilization would collapse, and the future would be a certainty even if we did not know its exact form.

History is determined not by a single factor but by a whole complex of things entering into the determination of human nature as it exists in relation to the physical environment. Geography, certain human traits, religious and psychological forces, institutions, and values are all intimately allied and exist in mutual interaction. It is the sum of these parts and their interaction that shapes the character of civilizations and sets the direction of change. Nor does that change necessarily need to be in dramatic leaps or revolutions. It may take the form of slow and imperceptible departures from that which exists. History may result from a slow, often modest, process of contributions of the greater intelligences and stronger personalities reacting to and acting upon their environment.

What, then, can be said on the positive side? Marx's approach to a theory of history—whatever the final verdict—was both more novel and less simplistic than many of the theories which preceded it. On the one hand, it has served as a challenge to such other singular approaches as the idealist, providential, great man, accidental, and climatic theories of history. Yet if a monistic theory of history is possible, it may be that Marx has shown the way even if we should arrive at an entirely different destination. Marx's impact on our approach to the understanding of history is undeniable. His theory has made a significant contribution toward making history something more than a mere description of past events. It has focused attention on the continuity of the historical process and the dynamic nature of institutions and our ideas about them. It has called the attention of the economist to the importance of the historical framework within which economic analysis takes place. Its Hegelian base continues to remind us that the existence of eternal principles and absolute values is still an open question.

Above all, however, Marx's theory of history has caused us to recognize and credit the undeniably important role that economic factors and forces play in society and its history. Marx might have come a shade closer to the truth had he recognized the possibility of an inverse causal relationship between the productive force and the superstructure. To be specific: (1) the more primitive the productive force, the harder the struggle for economic survival, the stronger and the more direct is the impact of the economic base on the total culture of society; (2) the less primitive the productive force, the further man rises above the physical margin of subsistence, the more complex his desires and goals become, and the less their content reflects or is determined by the economic base. This may be why Marxists so often select an early period of history or primitive societies when they wish to illustrate the "truth" of the economic interpretation of history. Be that as it may. If this theory of history has only served to shake us loose from the earlier neglect of economic considerations, if it has enabled us to interpret that which once went unnoticed or was simply not understood, it has already served a most useful purpose and warrants our interest.

Part II

V ·

An Introduction to Marxian Economics

As we have seen, Marx the social philosopher was mainly concerned with unearthing the universal law of historical change. It has also been observed that dialectical materialism is more an analytical device or method than a theory purporting to provide specific answers to particular questions. It is one thing to say, for instance, that every society harbors the seeds of its own destruction. It is quite another to expose the laws of contradiction unique to a particular social order. According to Marxist doctrine, the specific forces that once put an end to Slavery or Feudalism are not the same as those which operate with equal dialectic inevitability to assure the demise of Capitalism. As a Hegelian, Marx began with the philosophical premise that, like all earlier social systems, Capitalism must contradict itself out of existence. As an economist Marx set himself the task of investigating the particular economic logic by which this would occur. This, then, is the subject matter of all that is to follow. The end product should, hopefully, be the emergence of a general yet comprehensive view of the Capitalist process as Marx, correctly or incorrectly, conceived of it.

The subject matter of Marxian economics naturally and logically divides itself into two basic parts: (1) the essential elements in the Marxian model and (2) the forces of contradiction. The first part includes such items as Marx's labor theory of value and price; his so-called subsistence theory of wages; the meaning and derivation of surplus value and profit; the division of surplus into industrial profit, interest, and rent; the structure of capital, capital circulation, and accumulation—as well as such related questions as commodity exchange, innovation, etc. The second part includes such matters as the increasing organic compositions of capital; the law of falling profits; economic imperialism; the various crises (i.e., disproportionality in production, underconsumption, credit, innovation, etc.); the reserve army; the increasing misery of the working class—all leading to the Revolution.

The basic distinction between Marxian and orthodox economics is so well and succinctly stated by Joan Robinson as to deserve full quotation. According to Mrs. Robinson, "The fundamental differences between Marxian and traditional orthodox economics are, first, that orthodox economists accept the capitalist system as part of the eternal order of Nature, while Marx regards it as a passing phase in the transition from the feudal economy of the past to the socialist economy of the future. And, second, that the orthodox economists argue in terms of a harmony of interests between the various sections of the community, while Marx conceives of economic life in terms of a conflict of interests between owners of property who do not work and workers who own no property."

Mrs. Robinson finds, moreover, that these two basic points of difference are linked: "These two points of difference are not unconnected—for if the system is taken for granted and the shares of the various classes in the social product are determined by inexorable natural law, all interests unite in requiring an increase in the total to be divided. But if the possibility of changing the system is once admitted, those who hope to gain and those who fear to lose by the change are immediately ranged in opposite camps."

And, finally, Mrs. Robinson distinguishes between the two economics in terms of the motivational factor: "The orthodox economists, on the whole, identified themselves with the system and assumed the role of its apologists, while Marx set himself to understand the working of capitalism in order to hasten its overthrow. Marx was conscious of his purpose. The economists were in general unconscious. They wrote as they did because it seemed to them the only possible way to write, and they believed themselves to be endowed with scientific impartiality. Their preconceptions emerge rather in the problems which they chose to study and the assumptions on which they worked than in overt political doctrine."[1]

Mrs. Robinson is somewhat less explicit on some related points of difference which focus on economic methodology. The manner in which Marx connected the economic interpretation of history with the operation of the Capitalist engine is noteworthy. Instead of assuming away (if only for purposes of analysis) the role and impact of government, Marx made his theory of the state an integral part of the economic process. Instead of regarding certain institutional arrangements as fixed, he treated them as variables operating in the economy. He assigned to the institution of private property and property relations a central role in the process of Capitalist destruction. Stressing conflict rather than harmony of economic interests, Marx made the class struggle a vital force *within* the economic process. In short, Marx viewed the Capitalist system in a temporal perspective and as existing in irreconcilable conflict.

But nothing said above contradicts the fact that Marx's economics is also heavily steeped in both the classical French and, most particularly, the English tradition. In regard to the French influence, François Quesnay and his *Tableau économique* must certainly be mentioned as instrumental in Marx's conception of the process of reproduction as a whole. The nature and extent to which Marx was influenced by the French socialists, on the other hand, is more nearly related to Marx the political activist than Marx the economic theorist. The depth to which Marx's economics bears the stamp of the English economists is far more significant to an understanding of Marxian economics.

The Marxian theory of value is a prime case in point. Marx not only followed the British classical economists by making a theory of value the starting point, if not the matrix, of his entire theory of Capitalist development but did so despite the fact that a cost of production theory of value caused him incalculable theoretical difficulties and problems from which Marxian economics is today not yet fully liberated. From a more practical standpoint, the Marxian "law of value" has plagued Soviet economists and planners for nearly the full span of Bolshevik history. It is only now or quite recently—and then, in the main, for purely operational reasons— that the Soviets are beginning to free themselves of this particular ideological fetter.

The point about the importance of the British and especially the Ricardian influence on Marx stands despite the controversy over whether the labor theory of value is really essential to the significance of the Marxian system of economics. I have in mind the view held by Joan Robinson, among others, "that no point of substance in Marx's argument depends upon the labour theory of value"; [2] that the theory is essentially irrelevant to the main issue, which is the analysis of the distribution of total income between the working class and the capitalists and the relationship of this distribution to crisis. This view may well be so or, at least, prove to be the way out. The fact remains that an understanding of Marxian economics requires some attention to the details of the labor theory of value and its place among or relationship to the other elements of Marx's economic model.

It is in this context that a comment about whether Marx and Ricardo held to the same or to different labor theories of value may prove to be illuminating for that which immediately follows. Marx's and Ricardo's theories of value may be viewed as one in the following sense. Both had worked out a theory of value within the context of a purely competitive economy in a state of perfect equilibrium. Neither concerned himself with the element of monopoly or imperfect competition. Each had worked out the refinements of "socially necessary" and "homogeneous" labor time. Both faced the methodological problems involved in an effort to rule the natural agents and capital out of the valuation process.

Yet behind mere words or method, beyond the "bare theorem," some real difference appears to exist. The crux of the matter lies in this: Ricardo's concept of value is that of exchange or relative value. The value of a commodity is simply its power to command other commodities in exchange for itself; a power which, in turn, is determined by the relative labor contents involved. Following Aristotle, Marx begins with the basic premise that the value of a commodity consists of some element intrinsic to it, something that exists independently of that commodity's power to command all other things in exchange for itself. The fact that Marx found that intrinsic element to be labor—and labor alone—may well be the bridge that enabled him to move into the area of social implication. This much is certain: Marx and Ricardo drew different social implications from a labor theory of value. Ricardo was influenced by John Locke, who espoused a similar theory. Locke defended the institution of private property with the argument that man was entitled to own anything into which he had put his own labor. Ricardo and other British economists added the further assumption that employers and workers bargained on equal terms in a free labor market. Marx drew a precisely opposite set of conclusions and thereby turned a labor theory of value to an end which was neither envisaged nor intended by the classical economists. If all value was due to its labor content then why, asked Marx, should any share of the resulting product accrue to those who did not work?

VI·

The Marxian Law of Value:
The Initial Version

The Marxian theory of value and price progresses from an initial version as found in volume I of *Das Kapital,* to second and third versions as developed in volume III. Our immediate concern will be with the first version to be followed by the second and third. But even in the first case our approach will be to state the theory of value in its simplest or crudest form and then to add the necessary refinements.

THE REQUIRED TERMINOLOGY AND DISTINCTIONS

Marx begins by drawing the familiar distinction between *use* and *exchange* value. An item is said to possess use value if it has the power to satisfy some human need or desire. But since an identical item may render different degrees of utility in the possession of various users it must be regarded as a subjective phenomenon and therefore incapable of precise measurement. Use value alone is to be found only in a society so primitive that it is not as yet differentiated by specialization and division of labor and therefore by the process of exchange. For a modern economy, characterized by what Marx calls commodity production, the significance of use value lies in the fact that it is a necessary but not a sufficient condition for the existence of exchange value. Exchange value, on the other hand, refers to how much of everything else any one item can command for itself in the market. It is this objective and quantitatively ascertainable measure that is of principal interest to economists, as it was to Marx.

In this connection, Marx makes the further distinction between two basic types of economies and their resulting output. There is, first, the primitive economy where production is undertaken by and for the direct consumption of the producer. Here the producer is interested in having produced only that which has some direct use value to him. Marx calls this a case of "production for consumption" and refers to the resulting output as a "product." There is, secondly, the modern economy where the producer's objective is to produce something having use value for others than himself. Here, given the institution of private property and the existence of markets, any one producer gains command over some of those items produced by others which do render him use value. Marx calls this second case "production for exchange" and the resulting output a "commodity." Thus it is the "commodity" and not the "product," "commodity production" and not "production for consumption" that is analytically central in the Marxian theory of value and price. This, as well, is the context within which Marx defines a commodity as anything which possesses *both* use and exchange value, and price as its monetary expression.

Two further observations in this same connection. In order to make his point about the character of the modern Capitalist economy, Marx symbolizes the circulation of commodities (the case of "simple exchange") from production to consumption as: $C-M-C$. Here C stands for the various commodities produced which embody equal quantities of labor. M represents money which serves as the medium of exchange. The path of commodity circulation may then be traced as follows: An initial producer (P_1) produces a given commodity (C_1), which has no use value for him, in order to receive an amount of (M) equal to the quantity of labor embodied in the production of (C_1). This sale of (C_1) by (P_1) for (M) constitutes stage I of the process. Stage II involves the purchase by (P_1) of some commodity of use value to him (C_2) which is equal to the amount of labor embodied in the production of (C_1) and for which the amount of (M) is just sufficient. The same sale-purchase transaction may, of course, be traced for (P_2), (P_3) . . . (Pn) and (C_3), (C_4) . . . (Cn). The principle involved here is simply the exchange of labor-content equivalences.

Marx attaches considerable analytic as well as social significance to the above; that is, to the fact that the modern Capitalist economy is characterized by commodity production. The institutional arrangement of $C-M-C$ constitutes a break in the direct production-consumption relation. In the main, man no longer produces that which is of use value to him. He produces instead for the impersonal market, i.e., for exchange. Marx is quite clear regarding the social implication in this case. The $C-M-C$ arrangement is a critical factor in altering the nature of the production relation—man's relationship to man. But this temporal divorce between production and satisfaction is not quite the same yet as the related Marxian notion about "production for profit" *versus* "production for use." Marx was equally clear about the fact that commodity production does not disappear with the end of Capitalism.

One final distinction before coming to a statement of the crude labor theory of value. Marx also followed in the path of predecessors by distinguishing between *normal* (long-run) and *market* (short-run) value and by being primarily concerned with the former. The normal value of a commodity is said to be that long-run, average magnitude around which all short-run or market values fluctuate and toward which they invariably tend.

To put it another way, a commodity is at its normal value when supply and demand are in equilibrium. Market value represents any temporary departure above or below a commodity's normal value. Thus at the theoretical point of perfect equilibrium market and normal value are one. In this first version, Marx did relatively little theorizing about the economic forces underlying the short-run fluctuations of market values around their respective long-run normal values. He noted the frequency with which such oscillations occur. Referring to such movements as "abnormalities," he cited "supply and demand," "monopolies," and "some other modifications I must now pass by" as causal factors. Marx concluded that since, in the long run, these deviations cancel each other out only the determinants of normal value deserve full investigation.

THE THEORY OF VALUE: ITS CRUDEST FORM

As noted earlier, Marx held to the basic premise that the value of a commodity consists of some element intrinsic to it; something that exists independently of that commodity's power to command all other things in exchange for itself. He was looking, in other words, for some one objective ingredient common to all commodities and in terms of which, therefore, commodities would exchange for each other. Marx found that common element to be the labor embodied in the creation of a commodity. In his words: "What is the common substance of all commodities? It is labor. To produce a commodity a certain amount of labor must be bestowed upon it, or worked up in it." A commodity has value, he explained further, because "it is only the material envelope of the human labor spent upon it." Marx meant by labor "the expenditure of human brain, nerves, muscles, etc." This, one must add, is the "recent scientific discovery" that Marx said "marks, indeed, an epoch in the development of the human race."

Marx stated the fundamental proposition in many different ways and in many different places. One of the briefest is this: "The value of a commodity, therefore, varies directly as the quantity, and inversely as the productiveness, of the labor incorporated in it." This statement may also be expressed in either of these two ways. (1) Commodities which possess the same amount of labor have the same value, or (2) the relative values of commodities are determined by the respective quantities of labor fixed in them. To offer the simplest possible illustration: Assume that it requires 100 units of labor to produce a pair of shoes and 500 labor units to produce a briefcase. In that event a briefcase will exchange for or command five pairs of shoes and a single pair of shoes will exchange for one-fifth of a briefcase. And so on for n commodities. But thus stated Marx's theory of price is, at best, a vulgarization which can only serve as a first approximation. Any reasonably objective assessment of it must take into account not only (1) the many theoretical refinements made by Marx but (2) the second and third versions of Marx's theory of price as found, most particularly, in the third volume of *Das Kapital*.

THE NECESSARY REFINEMENTS

The proposition that labor is a property common to or present in all commodities is, as Marx himself admitted, a purposeful truism. If this were the only point at issue one could just as easily, and with as little significance, select some one other single ingredient present in or common to all commodities. But Marx had, of course, quite another point in mind. His purpose was to relate the process of value creation, i.e., the act of production, with the distribution of the resulting output. If he could establish the fact that human labor—and labor alone—was value-creating, it could be made to follow that only those who worked were entitled to share in the resulting output. This, then, is the context within which Marx set out to show why or how such elements as land, raw materials, capital goods, etc., do not enter into the valuation process, i.e., do not, in and of themselves, create or add to normal exchange value.

The essence of Marx's approach to eliminating, first, the natural agents from the valuation process was to draw a line between such natural agents and commodities. Recall his definition of a commodity as something that has *both* use and exchange value. Marx argued that such items, for instance, as uncultivated or unimproved land, uncut trees, and unmined ore were free and uncommitted gifts of nature and not commodities. A commodity is said to come into existence—and with that exchange value emerges—only at the point where human labor is combined with one or more natural agents. This is what Marx meant by an "act of production." Until such a moment, in other words, as "social labor" is applied to them the natural agents are inert or of no *economic* value.[1]

Marx disposed of entrepreneurship as an element in the valuation process with fair ease. Given the economic interpretation of history in general and the Marxian theory of social classes in particular, Marx really had no other logical choice but to treat entrepreneurship as a form of labor. It was not that he lacked appreciation of that function, as we shall see. But since, in his general scheme, there could only be two basic economic classes and a single principle of division between them, Marx simply relegated entrepreneurship to the status of highly skilled mental labor and counted it as part of the total labor embodied in the production of a commodity.

A labor theory of value poses special difficulties in regard to the role of capital in the valuation process. Both Ricardo and Marx were aware of some—by no means all—of the theoretical complexities involved. (Marx was, perhaps, even more keenly aware of these problems if one may judge from the amount of space he devoted to them.) Ricardo recognized the fact that the price realized for the sale of a commodity includes a net return which accrues to the owners of capital goods used in the production of that commodity. He indicated that the return to capital is connected with the time element involved in the productive process and the fact that the period from initial investment to the sale of the finished product varies from industry to industry. Ricardo pointed to these factors as causing the actual price relationships to deviate from the ratios of labor content. But, at least according to some students of Ricardo, he was not aware of how the above views regarding capital contradicted the essential validity of his labor theory of value.

Marx grappled with this capital problem in its Ricardian setting and, in doing so, came somewhat closer to sensing the contradictions involved. As a result, Marx took a different analytic path. He began with the simple proposition that a commodity is produced by the utilization of some combination of labor and physical instruments, i.e., machinery, tools, equipment, etc. He referred to this combination as the "means of production" necessary to the creation of any commodity. (It is important here not to confuse the "means of production" with what Marx calls the "mode of production," which refers to the productive force plus production relations as discussed in the preceding chapter.) This being the case, Marx conceived of the capital fund as being composed of two organically related parts: (1) variable capital and (2) constant capital. It is a distinction, as we shall see, that is central to the whole of the Marxian économic schema. The difference may be expressed in real as well as in money capital terms. In real terms, variable capital represents the "human" or "living" labor that enters into the productive process. Constant capital is the means of production entering into that same process of production. In its second sense, variable capital is that portion of the total capital fund paid out in wages for the employment of workers used in production. Constant capital is that amount spent for the purchase of everything else necessary to production—raw materials, machinery, equipment, etc.

Given the above conceptual framework, the crux of Marx's argument here is that only variable capital—"living" labor—employed in production is actually value-*creating*. Constant capital—the means of production—though necessary to production, becomes relevant only when or as it is set in motion by or combined with "living" labor. Marx writes, "A machine, which does not serve the purposes of labor, is useless. . . . Living labor must seize upon these things and rouse them from their death-sleep, change them from mere possible use-values into real and effective ones. . . . contact with living labor, is the sole means by which they [the means of production] can be made to retain their character of use-values, and be utilized." Moreover, according to Marx, the utilization of constant capital in commodity production results only in the simple transference of the exchange value of the means of production in question. Thus Marx arrives at the proposition that the means of production is but "past," "frozen," or "stored up" labor. The exchange value of a commodity is a function, therefore, not only of the currently utilized or "live" labor but that quantity of "past" or "frozen" labor that entered into the process of conceiving and forging the instruments of production.

Thus it was that Marx ruled all but labor out of the valuation process in the first version of his theory of value. In doing so, however, he went to considerable length in order to stress that it is the *full* labor content which is determining. Marx meant by this the sum of all labor, mental as well as physical, past and present, with allowance for depreciation, expended at each stage of the productive process. But he did not endeavor, nor even claim that it was possible, to sum the full labor content embodied in the various commodities. According to Marx, the resulting exchange ratios somehow worked themselves out in the economy. His concern was with the theory of it—the process as it worked itself out in the market—and here Marx took two considerations into account: (1) that various levels of mental and physical skill entered into the creation of each commodity and (2) that it would be meaningless to sum such qualitatively different units. A valid analysis called for some "pure and simple" or "abstract" quantitative unit of measurement.

Marx made time—the hour, day, or week—the common denominator in terms of which the magnitude of labor content could be expressed. The various skills and levels of skill embodied in a given commodity had also to be reduced to a single or homogeneous quantity. The labor content of any commodity could then be expressed as so many hours of abstract or homogeneous labor. Commodities could, in turn, be compared in terms of their respective contents of such abstract units of labor. But this raises the question of how, by what mechanism, the many levels of labor skill are homogenized into the abstraction Marx calls "pure and simple" labor. It implies the existence of some schedule of weights by which, for example, one clock hour of work by a cabinet-maker is worth five times that of a clock hour of work by an ordinary carpenter and ten times that of a floor sweeper and so on.

The critical question, of course, is how such weights are set or determined in relation to the multitude of skills involved in the production process. Here Marx appears at his weakest and most evasive in providing an answer. He raises this question, specifically and with directness, in one of his works but only to say: "This is not the place to discover the laws regulating this reduction. It is clear, however, that such reduction does take place." Elsewhere he tells us that "it is competition that sets up the scale" and appeals to experience as showing that "this reduction is . . . established by a social process . . . and fixed by custom." What it comes to, in the final analysis, is that Marx asks his readers to take this as an article of faith, "for simplicity's sake" and in order to "save ourselves the trouble of making the reduction."[2]

Two further refinements regarding the character of the labor that enters into the valuation process deserve special mention. The first concerns Marx's distinction between mental or physical exertion as such and socially useful labor. If an item is to have exchange value (if it is properly a commodity) it must, as already observed, be both useful and have labor embodied in it. Some few things—the ordinary air we breathe or water flowing freely in a stream—have utility but no exchange value because no labor is expended in their creation. On the other hand, a great deal of mental or physical exertion can be expended on something without that item possessing exchange value; for example, where such effort is put into something that no one desires or is willing to buy. Thus, according to Marx, only that labor which is crystallized into something society wants counts in the determination of exchange value.

Marx found recognition of this point both analytically necessary and troublesome; troublesome because it inevitably gives rise to the following question. What forces determine whether and the extent to which a given outlay of labor is more or less socially useful? Here, again, Marx offers the social process as the answer. In the final analysis it is the market that decides. If, at any one moment in time, a given magnitude of labor is spent on something society wants less than some alternative item, then the value of labor expended in the first direction is diminished and the value of labor in the alternative direction is enhanced. This is reflected in the economy by a deviation of market from normal exchange value. Market value falls below normal value in the first and rises above normal value in the second case. In the short run, therefore, one line of production or industry will suffer a special type of loss and another will experience a special type of gain. (This windfall, plus or minus, is something quite apart from Marx's "surplus value," which is yet to be considered.) The presence of such windfalls will, according to Marx, finally cause labor to be reallocated in such a way that in the long run market and normal value will coincide.

The related and last refinement to be mentioned here concerns Marx's view that it is only "socially necessary" labor which is value-determining. By socially necessary, in this sense, Marx meant that labor "necessary for its production in a given state of society, under certain social average conditions of production, with a given social average intensity, and average skill of the laborer employed." Using Marx's well-known case of textile production, the precise meaning of this qualification may (inferentially at least) be illustrated at three levels: industry as a whole, a firm within an industry, and a single worker within the firm. Let us consider first the case of a textile industry capricious enough to use gold rather than steel spindles. In summing the labor content of the yarn produced (in this instance "frozen labor") only the labor required to produce steel spindles would count since this is all that is technically required for the making of such yarn in the society in question. Thus the normal value of the yarn produced by the industry would reflect only the labor cost of steel spindles even though gold ones were actually used. Now suppose that the industry as a whole does operate with steel spindles with the exception of one eccentric capitalist whose firm produces the same yarn using gold spindles. The normal value of that one firm's yarn would be set not by its own labor content but that of the industry as a whole. Finally, Marx recognized that even within the same skill or job classification workers could differ in regard to efficiency, intensity of work, or productivity. Whose labor is counted, that of the most or least efficient worker? Marx maintains that the normal value of a commodity reflects the labor of average skill and intensity. The force of competition in the labor market is presumed to result in the rewarding of the most efficient workers by lifting them to higher job categories. The least efficient would, by the same token, be driven out of the skill or job in question.

Marx goes further by injecting the elements of time and change into his concept of socially necessary labor. According to Marx, the quantity of "pure and simple" labor which is socially necessary at any one point in time is a function of the productivity of labor; which, in turn, is a function of the organic composition of capital. The principles involved here, both short and long run, may best be illustrated by starting with the short run and assuming an initial change in the organic composition of capital of the single firm within an industry. As we shall see in some detail later, Marx makes it a part of the logic of the Capitalist economy that some one firm within an industry will get command over a new technique or machine, one that is not at first available to the other firms within that industry. The innovating firm thus undergoes a change in its organic composition of capital, i.e., in [its $c/c + v$ or] the value relationship between the constant and total capital outlay. According to Marx, a rise in c relative to $[c + v]$ increases the productivity of labor; which means that the labor time required for the production of a given commodity falls. Thus, in the short run, the innovating firm can produce a given quantity of the commodity in question with a smaller *total* labor expenditure than any of its competitors. From the standpoint of the innovating firm, in other words, the quantity of total labor required to produce a given volume of output falls relative to its own past or the current cost of all other firms within that industry. Despite this reduction in the labor time required, however, the innovating firm is able— in the short run—to sell its output at a price set in the market which reflects the socially necessary labor content as an *average for the industry* as a whole. According to Marx, the innovating firm may, in fact, shade the price somewhat in order to gain a somewhat larger market. But, again, this represents a short-run phenomenon. Thus, but only for a time, the innovating firm is able to realize an extraordinary gain because it can sell its commodity at a price determined by the industry-wide socially necessary labor cost rather than its own which is below the average for that industry. Once more it is important to stress that this extraordinary gain is something other than surplus value, which is still to be discussed.

Just how long the innovating firm can continue to realize such extraordinary gains from any single complex of innovations is said to depend upon certain frictional and institutional factors or rigidities, i.e., flow and quality of entrepreneurial talent, patent laws, etc. In the long run, according to Marx, the forces of competition will cause progressively more firms to adopt the same or similar techniques or means of production. *Ceteris paribus* this will result in a fall in the *average* (industry-wide) amount of socially necessary labor required for a given volume of output. The long-run tendency, therefore, is not only the wiping out of extraordinary gain but a corresponding fall in the normal exchange value of the commodity in question. Thus Marx established a direct relationship between a change in the amount of socially necessary labor time required to produce a given commodity and a change in its normal exchange value.

THE ROLE OF MONEY IN THE VALUATION
PROCESS: FIRST VERSION

Marx contributed little to monetary theory as such. His views regarding the role of banking, credit, etc., in the capitalist process will be discussed later in connection with his theory of interest and certain other aspects of his economic model. In the present context, it is necessary only to point out that Marx accorded money a relatively simple and neutral role in the valuation process. He regarded metallic money as but one of a multitude of commodities. Its distinctive feature is that it serves as a common measure of values. According to Marx, the value of such money is determined by precisely the same factors which set the normal exchange value of all other commodities. He maintained, in other words, that the value of, say, an ounce of gold was determined by the amount of labor (as defined above) required to produce it. Price, in this sense, is then the monetary expression of exchange value. Thus, according to Marx, a commodity sells for that amount of money (expressed in marks, dollars, yen, etc.) behind which there is that quantity of precious metal which contains the same amount of labor as the commodity in question.

Here, as elsewhere, Marx injected a certain note of social criticism. The monetization of the economic process, according to Marx, not only masks the true social character of production (i.e., the bonds between producers in the market) but obscures the fact that labor alone creates economic value. The consequence is an impersonalization of the economic process which, if only by implication, Marx condemns.

SUMMARY

Having defined terms and noted the principal refinements and qualifications, we may state the first version of the Marxian labor theory of value as follows: The normal exchange value of a commodity is determined by the quantity of "pure and simple," socially necessary, labor which is embodied in that commodity at all stages of its production. Thus, in volume I of *Das Kapital*, Marx contends that commodities exchange for one another in terms of the labor content embodied within *each* commodity *individually*. To repeat, in modified form, an earlier illustration: if a pair of shoes represents 100 abstract, socially necessary units of labor and a briefcase 500 such units, a briefcase will sell for five times that of a pair of shoes at perfect equilibrium. The only deviation from the true labor content, in this first version, would be the short-run fluctuations of *market* value around long-run *normal* value.

Marx was well aware of the so-called Smithian value paradox, as it bears on a theory of value, but did not appear to be troubled by it. The point at issue here is why such essentials as ordinary air or water, which have infinite use value, have no exchange value; while diamonds, which are far less essential, possess so high an exchange value. Marx explains this phenomenon in terms of labor requirements. Ordinary air and water, which exist in great abundance, do not require an expenditure of labor time in order to satisfy human need and therefore possess no exchange value. Diamonds, which are very difficult to locate, have a high exchange value because the labor cost involved in their discovery is so great. If, reasoned Marx, some easily accessible substance like carbon could be turned into diamonds with only a small amount of labor, then the normal exchange value of diamonds would fall below that of bricks.

As time went by, however, Marx became progressively more troubled over certain other weaknesses in this first version of his theory of value. The result of his search for a more realistic explanation of the valuation process appears, most particularly, in the latter part of volume III of *Das Kapital*. The issues involved in the so-called second and third versions of the theory of value and price will emerge more clearly, however, if they are taken up following our discussion of Marx's theory of wages, surplus value, and profit.

VII·

The Subsistence Wage

Marxist doctrine distinguishes among five general types of production *relations* corresponding to the Marxian stages of social history. The labor situations in question are: (1) "primitive communist" labor, (2) formal slavery, (3) wage-slavery, (4) Socialist labor, and (5) Communist labor. The nature of the first of these has already been set forth. The character of Socialist and Communist labor is considerably beyond the scope of this volume. Our immediate interest is with wage-slavery and with formal slavery as it bears upon it. According to Marxian theory, formal slavery emerged with the end of primitive communism and lasted, with some modifications, until the advent of Capitalism. Wage-slavery is said to have appeared with the emergence of Capitalism and is regarded by Marxists as a distinctive feature of the Capitalist epoch.

Formal slavery, in its Marxian sense, may be defined as that production relation in which the dominant minority owns members of the expropriated majority in the same legal and moral sense as it owns any physical or non-human piece of property. Here no separation is said to exist between the human being thus enslaved and his capacity for labor. Marx calls this capacity for labor—the sum of physical and mental ability to create something of use value—*labor power*. It may be helpful to think of labor power as a "bundle of creative capacities." In the case of formal slavery, according to Marx, labor power does *not* enter the labor market. The slave neither sells his labor power nor does the slave-owner buy it. The trading or buying and selling of slaves, even in highly organized markets, is not regarded as the same thing as labor power alone entering the labor market. Marx defines a wage as the price paid for labor power. In terms of this definition the concept of a wage does not exist when the labor arrangement is that of formal slavery. The slave is forced or motivated to exert himself physically or mentally by the threat of punishment or promise of reward. In either case he receives sustenance rather than a wage payment since the slave does not sell his labor power. His situation is analogous to that of a machine which must be fed some form of energy and kept in good repair as long as required by rational economic considerations. The level of sustenance may differ among slaves much as some machines are costlier to operate or maintain than others.

The reader will recall the Marxist point that a given productive force necessarily results in a corresponding production relation. Marx maintained that the pre-Capitalist productive force—characterized, as it was in the main, by agarian self-sufficiency—made a production relation of formal slavery a logical necessity. The emergence of the Capitalist productive force—defined by Marx in terms of the dominance of commercial-industrial-financial activity and production for unknown markets—made a production relation of wage-slavery equally inevitable. According to Marx, wage-slavery exists when the capitalist-employer buys labor in increments and only as he needs it. The worker is no longer owned in the sense of any other form of property. At the same time the buyer or user of labor has no economic interest in supporting or sustaining a worker whose labor power he does not need within the current production period. The logic of the Capitalist productive force is such, according to Marx, that it is not economically feasible for the capitalist to operate with a fixed labor cost.

Here, certainly, is a case where Marx integrates economic analysis with the economic interpretation of history. Marxist doctrine holds that the working class was not freed from formal slavery because of the independent appearance of a new or different morality on the part of capitalists or bourgeois society in general. The emergence of the "free labor market" is said to have been initiated with a change in the productive force and to have been finally reflected in the morality (superstructure) of bourgeois society. According to Marx's theory of history, the working class has no choice but to suffer through the stages of both formal and wage-slavery before its emancipation under Socialism. Yet Marx could not refrain from moralizing about the "fact" that in a certain sense wage-slavery is an even more callous variant of the production relation than formal slavery. Marx's point here was that, unlike the slave-owner, the capitalist is not forced by economic self-interest to care for or sustain those workers whom he does not need during the immediate production period. Thus, as long as class division remains, the worker is presumed by Marx not to have any real power over his material circumstances. Since Marxist doctrine defines a worker as one who is excluded from the ownership of the means of livelihood it follows that the worker can survive only if he sells his labor power to the capitalist-employer. As Marx put it, "the laborer, instead of being in the position to sell commodities in which his labor is incorporated must be obliged to offer for sale as a commodity that very labor power, which exists only in his living self." Thus, according to Marx, the wage-slave is free only in the sense of the Hobson's choice between accepting the labor terms imposed upon him by the Capitalist system or starving to death (practically speaking, going to the "poor house").

THE WAGE THEORY

Ordinarily one thinks of a labor market as an institutional arrangement whereby the worker sells and the employer buys so many units of labor time (hours, weeks, etc.) of a certain category or level of skill. For example, a firm may be said to employ a carpenter at a wage-rate of $3 an hour or $120 for a 40-hour week. Marx saw the matter in a different light. He introduced a critical distinction between what the capitalist-employer buys (i.e., pays for) and what he actually gets when he employs workers. According to Marx, the following transaction is what really occurs in the Capitalist labor market: In seeking employment the worker offers for sale his "bundle of creative capacities" or labor power. When employing a worker the capitalist-employer buys that labor power for which he pays a wage. It is important to note that the item bought and sold is not labor time or hours in the ordinary sense as above. Suppose, for example, that a worker is employed for a ten-hour period during which he produces (in conjunction with the means of production) a given quantity of some commodity. What the capitalist-employer *buys* or *pays for* is not the value of the commodity thus produced but the *right* to have utilized that worker's labor power during the time interval in question. What that same capitalist-employer *gets,* however, is the exchange value of the resulting output during the ten-hour period.

This difference is but one of several rather ingeniously related distinctions that Marx was forced to make for the sake of logical consistency. The one between labor and labor power—the worker and his "bundle of creative capacities"—has already been noted. It was this separation that enabled Marx to maintain that while labor is the "substance" and the "immanent measure of value" it has no exchange value as such. But it is this next distinction which, according to Marx, gets to the heart of and reveals the true nature of the Capitalist productive process. Labor power, says Marx, is itself a commodity in that it meets both conditions of having use as well as exchange value; yet it differs from all other commodities in one critical respect. It has to do with something that occurs in the $C–M–C$ process of circulation of commodities from production to consumption. In all cases, *except that of labor power,* commodities circulate in this process with only a transfer of commodity ownership, i.e., the exchange value of the commodity in question remains unchanged. All that is involved is the monetization of exchange value. Labor power, as it enters the same process, differs from all other commodities because, in Marx's words, it "*counts as a value* [that is] . . . in the process of production, labor power performs the function of creating value." The capitalist, Marx tells us, is well aware of this unique value-creating feature of labor power as a commodity; which is why, as we shall see in greater detail soon, he is interested in the employment of workers. It is this final distinction, between labor power and all other commodities, that Marx offers as the *raison d'être* of the Capitalist class.

What then, according to Marx, determines the exchange value of labor power? Since he accords labor power the status of a commodity, logic dictates that its exchange value be determined by the same factor that sets the value of any other commodity, be it ships or shoes or sealing wax. Thus Marx maintains that the exchange value of labor power is set by that amount of abstract, socially necessary labor, at each stage of production, which is required to produce that quantity of food, clothing, shelter, etc., essential for sustaining the worker and enabling him (on the average) to reproduce his kind. At the present level of analysis, the same thing may be expressed in monetary terms. Say that a worker receives $10 as the money wage for the sale of a day's labor power to the capitalist. The $10 represents that sum of the standard money behind which there is that quantity of gold or silver which can be produced with an equal amount of labor as that required to produce the worker's subsistence for that day. The worker receives a sub-sistence wage, in other words, which is composed of two elements: (1) It includes an amount which enables him to purchase, at prevailing prices, such consumer goods and services as are necessary to maintain an average level of productive efficiency for his particular skill or job category. (2) The wage must also cover, on the average, the cost of rearing and educating the children, maintaining the family, etc.

Here, "as with all other commodities, so with labor," Marx retains the distinction between market and normal exchange value and price. In the short run, according to Marx, the forces of supply and demand may cause the market wage to deviate from its normal or long-run equilibrium level. Thus at any moment in time a worker may receive a wage which is either above or below the normal subsistence wage. Again, however, Marx main-tained that the short-run fluctuations in the market wage cancel out so that in the long run workers receive a normal wage equal to subsistence; and that it is this latter wage which is analytically significant. The single point, in this connection, which deserves reemphasis is the fact that Marx's so-called subsistence theory of wages is no more than the logical extension of his labor theory of value to a specific commodity.

THE MEANING AND SIGNIFICANCE
OF MARXIAN SUBSISTENCE

Historic controversy surrounds the question of whether Marx held to an absolute or flexible, physical or socio-historical, concept of subsistence as represented by the normal wage. Either view can be shown to be what Marx really had in mind by the particular quotations selected from his and Engels' writings. A perusal of the relevant literature indicates that while non-Marxists tend to favor the absolute or physical interpretations, Marxists lean in the direction of the flexible, socio-historical interpretation. The undeniable secular rise in real wages over the course of Capitalist history may well be the compelling reason for the preference in both cases. Marxists have endeavored to explain the long-term upward movement in real wages by insisting on a flexible definition of subsistence. Some non-Marxists, on the other hand, favor the physical subsistence view because it so obviously leads to the conclusion that the Marxian theory of wages is patent nonsense. There is a third possibility worthy of consideration. The validity of Marx's theory of wages aside, it may be that his concept of subsistence is neither as inconsistent nor as fuzzy as some have made it out to be. The view that Marx's position on subsistence is a combination of the physical and socio-historical standing in a particular relationship to each other is suggested here.

Let us consider first some of the evidence in support of the flexible, socio-historical interpretation of subsistence. As we have already seen, Marx was entirely clear regarding the fact that the subsistence wage includes not merely the requirements of the individual worker but those of the entire family. This is logically necessary, according to Marx, because the Capitalist system must provide for the perpetuation of the race of wage-slaves. More specifically, Marx states that the subsistence wage must cover the cost of training or education required for each level of skill. Thus he accounts for existing wage differentials in terms of the varying amounts of labor required to reproduce, i.e., maintain, train, and educate. Assume that a company physician is paid a salary of $1,000 a month while a floor sweeper employed by that same firm receives $100 for the month. According to Marx, both the physician and floor sweeper receive no more than a subsistence wage. The 10:1 earnings differential is said to result from the fact that it requires ten times as much abstract, socially necessary labor to produce or reproduce a physician as it does a floor sweeper. As noted earlier, Marx relies on market forces to work out all of these complex arrangements. But observe, in passing, the element of circular reasoning which appears here. Marx treats wage differentials as a function of differences in the cost of reproducing the various skills and then regards the existing wage differentials as set in the market as the true measure of what such differences in labor cost are.

To view the matter from a somewhat different angle: Marx makes the categorical statement in *Value, Price and Profit* that the subsistence wage "is not a fixed but a variable magnitude." Elsewhere, in volume I of *Das Kapital*, he defines the subsistence wage as "sufficient to maintain him [the worker] in his normal state as a laboring individual. His natural wants . . . vary according to climatic and other physical conditions of his country. . . . The number and extent of his so-called necessary wants, as also the modes of satisfying them, are themselves the product of historical development, and depend therefore to a great extent on the degree of civilization of a country, more particularly on the conditions under which, and consequently on the habits and degree of comfort in which, the class of free laborers has been formed." In these and numerous other places Marx avers that something more than the physical element enters into the subsistence of the worker. Beyond the physical, the subsistence wage is said to be set by the force of "custom," or "tradition," and to vary with the worker's "station in life," his "country," and the "historical period" in question.

Broadly interpreted, Marx seems to be saying here that a worker's subsistence will include whatever may be regarded by the society in question as necessary in order to enable that worker to maintain an average level of productive efficiency and reproduce his kind. So flexible a reading of Marx has led some critics of Marxism to say that in such a case the worker could demand a great deal more under the guise of necessity and thus realize a high wage indeed. To this a Marxist might reply that such an observation ignores the "fact" that the worker's own idea of what he needs or wants is but a reflection of the character of the Capitalist productive force. Be that as it may, there are several conclusions which may logically be drawn from the above interpretation of subsistence. The subsistence level of workers may, to use some modern examples, very conceivably have to include automobiles if the structure of the Capitalist productive force is such as to require those workers to live a good distance from their place of employment. The subsistence wage of a corporation lawyer may, indeed, have to cover the cost of membership in an exclusive country club if that happens to be the "customary" way of conducting business or the legal affairs of that society.

Still the fact remains that in direct statements and by implication, Marx also conceives of the worker as existing at the physical margin of subsistence. In volume I of *Das Kapital*, while accounting for the existence of wage differentials, Marx also makes the following important parenthetical statement: "In order to modify the human organism, so that it may acquire skill . . . a special education or training is required, and this . . . costs an equivalent in commodities of a greater or less amount. . . . The expenses of this education *(excessively small in the case of ordinary labor power)*, enter *pro tanto* into the total value spent in its production." [Italics mine.] According to Marx, in other words, one of the important factors which raises the level of subsistence for some workers above the purely physical is barely operative in the case of "ordinary" (masses of) workers.

Elsewhere, in that same volume, Marx speaks of the constantly (secular) increasing organic composition of capital and notes its impact on the subsistence wage: "To purchase the labor-power of a family of four workers may, perhaps, cost more than it formerly did to purchase the labor-power of the head of the family, but, in return, four days' labor takes the place of one, and their price falls in proportion to the excess of the surplus-labor of four over the surplus-labor of one. In order that the family may live, four people must now, not only labor, but expend surplus-labor for the capitalist. Thus, we see, that machinery, while augmenting the human material that forms the principal object of capital's exploiting power, at the same time raises the degree of exploitation." Technological improvement and progressively greater reliance on machinery, in other words, force (all other things being equal) family subsistence downward.

Thus it is reasonable to conclude that Marx's view of subsistence is not an either-or proposition and, in that sense, necessarily a contradiction. He was entirely aware of the presence of a labor aristocracy and accounted for its existence. At the same time, Marx saw the dynamics of the Capitalist process operating in such a way that a progressively larger fraction of the labor force would not require more than physical subsistence as a condition of employment. It may well be that Marx applied the flexible, socio-historic, version to the progressively declining segment of the labor force and the physical one to the remaining members of the working class.

THE MARXIAN VERSUS EARLIER CONCEPTS OF SUBSISTENCE

The idea that, in the long run, a worker could never hope to earn more than a subsistence wage did not, of course, originate with Marx. The wages-fund doctrine and the Malthusian theory of population were well known to Marx. He and his followers have, in fact, interpreted these earlier doctrines as a calculated attempt by bourgeois intellectuals to justify or excuse the exploitation of the working class. The paragraph that follows is the way in which a hypothetical Marxist writer on the history of economic thought might interpret these earlier wage theories for his readers.

"The wages-fund doctrine was designed to prove that no amount of effort by workers could result in an improvement of their economic circumstances. The reason offered by bourgeois ideologists was that in the short run the total fund available for payment of wages was necessarily fixed. At best, therefore, trade unions could secure more for organized labor only at the expense of nonunion workers. At first this short-run cause for pessimism was not allowed to interfere with secular optimism. The worker was told that in the long run his real wage would rise as the absolute size of the capital fund grew in response to technical and scientific progress. Then along came Malthus with his infamous proposition that while the means of subsistence does increase over time, it does so only arithmetically; while the number of mouths to be fed increases in geometric progression. The worker was now being told that perforce the future would be quite as dismal as the present. He was assured that Nature in her infinite wisdom made certain that in the end—through overwork and disease, famines and wars—the population would be kept in check with the means of subsistence. Who is to blame? According to Malthus, certainly not the factory owner. Accept it, the worker was told, for it is all a part of Nature's inescapable plan."

Marx, who agreed with the notion that the normal wage tended toward subsistence, took sharp issue that this was all part of Nature's grand and inescapable design. He placed the full blame at the door of a class society, especially one in which the logic of the productive force requires a system of wage-slavery. According to Marx, the working class was doomed to a subsistence wage not forever but only as long as Capitalism lasts. History, said Marx, holds forth great promise for the working class. Once Capitalism comes to an end and Socialism emerges the worker will be paid according to his full productivity and finally, under Communism, in accordance with needs.

VIII·

Surplus Value

ITS ORIGINS AND ESSENCE

What, according to Marx, is surplus value? How, by what process, is surplus value generated within the Capitalist system? Both questions have, in fact, already been answered *implicitly* in the section on Marx's theory of wages. But the role of surplus value in the Marxian economic model is so central that its basic nature, along with its many implications, must be made *explicit*. First, however, it will be useful to summarize certain Marxian key points regarding the institutional arrangements of Capitalist society as they relate to the question of surplus value.

(1) The capitalist-employer is the buyer and the worker is the seller of a commodity known as labor power. (2) The worker, who possesses only his own labor power, has but one of two options: he can either sell his labor power to the capitalist-employer on the latter's terms or remain unemployed—"starve," go to the "poorhouse," etc. (3) The capitalist as such produces nothing of economic value, that is, he neither creates nor adds anything to exchange value; and, in that sense, is outside the valuation process. (4) The capitalist-employer, nevertheless, has the power to direct and holds control over the productive process by virtue of his private ownership of the means of livelihood. It is he, in other words, who brings laborers together and sets them to work in conjunction with the natural agents and the existing instruments of production for the purpose of commodity production. (5) The capitalist's interest in such commodity production is entirely personal, not social. His concern is not with the creation of use value or with meeting the economic needs of society. His single objective is the realization of some personal gain. In popular language, this is the distinction that Marxists draw between "production for use" and "production for profit." (6) The realization of such a gain is made possible by the fact that, *as a class*, the capitalists possess the power to set all the terms of employment in regard to the workers, i.e., wages, hours, working conditions, etc. (Given the assumption of a perfectly competitive market the individual capitalist or firm has no such power and simply takes the market circumstances as given.)

We turn now to an examination of the actual process by which, according to Marx, surplus value is generated within the Capitalist system. Three of the assumptions made by Marx in this portion of his analysis must be made explicit. (1) Marx assumes the existence of a perfectly competitive market, i.e., the absence of any element of monopoly or monopsony in the labor market. (2) Both buyer and seller of labor power view the transaction in the same light as do all other buyers and sellers of all other commodities. (3) Each capitalist-employer and worker regards himself as a "free" agent buying or selling labor power, for a specified period of time, at the existing market-determined price. The principles involved here can be perceived most clearly by tracing the transactions between a single capitalist-employer and worker.

The process begins with the capitalist-employer and worker entering the labor market as characterized above. The capitalist-employer purchases the right to the use value of a worker's "bundle of creative capacities" for a specified time interval, say, one standard work-day. Having thus contracted with the worker, by the offer or payment of a money-wage, the capitalist-employer is now empowered to put that laborer to work. Recall Marx's definition of the act of commodity production as the application of "live" labor, in conjunction with the means of production ("frozen" labor), to the otherwise inert natural agents. Thus labor—and labor alone—is held to be productive or value-creating by the manner in which it transforms the natural agents into items possessing both use and exchange value, namely, commodities. This act of putting the worker to work involves, according to Marx, the redirection of labor power from one to another sphere. Labor power leaves the process of circulation, where value and therefore surplus value is never created, and enters the process of production, which is the sole sphere within which surplus value is generated. Thus when a commodity reenters the process of circulation its exchange value is greater by the amount of labor power expended during the corresponding process of production.

But the key to the origin and nature of surplus value lies in Marx's distinction between what the capitalist-employer *gets* when he employs a worker and what he *pays* for or to that worker. What the capitalist-employer *gets* is the ownership right to all that the worker produces during the time period in question. What he *pays* the worker is his subsistence as earlier defined. The difference is surplus value, which, as we are about to see, may be expressed in a variety of forms. Stated in monetary terms: The capitalist-employer gets the exchange value or price of the commodities produced by the worker during the specified time period. He pays that worker a wage which, in the long run, represents the monetary expression of the normal (subsistence) exchange value or price of labor power. Surplus value is the difference between these two magnitudes. Recall that, according to Marx, the exchange value or price of labor is determined by the amount of "pure and simple," socially necessary labor power required to create (reproduce) that quantity of labor power which the worker has placed at his employer's disposal for the time period in question. Surplus value is, thus, the difference between the money advanced for the purchase of labor power and the money equivalent of the exchange value of the product of labor. Stated in still another way: When employing a worker the capitalist-employer gets the use value of labor but pays only for the exchange value of labor power. The difference between the two is surplus value, which, given the institutional framework of Capitalism, accrues to the capitalist.

The Marxian concept of surplus value emerges at its clearest, however, when expressed in terms of hours of work. The key to its origin lies in the proposition that the Capitalist class normally succeeds in setting the length of the work day *above* the amount of time necessary to make the food, clothing, shelter, etc., which a worker requires in order to be able to do that day's work at average efficiency. Thus surplus value is made possible, according to Marx, by the fact that normally labor possesses the capacity to produce more within a given time interval than is necessary for its subsistence and replacement. Where that is not the case the capitalist would have no reason or incentive to employ labor. Assume the standard work day to be 12 hours. Assume, further, that a worker is able to produce the equivalence of his subsistence in six hours. In this instance, according to Marx, the worker labors six hours for himself and six for his capitalist-employer. The latter six hours constitutes surplus value pocketed by the capitalist.

SOME SPECIAL OBSERVATIONS

According to Marx, the very existence of surplus value, however expressed, proves the presence of exploitation within the Capitalist system. The revolutionary side of Marx could hardly have bypassed the issue of exploitation even if the scholar and theorist in him had so desired. His principal achievement in this regard was to have exposed the shallowness of the ordinary radical's notion of exploitation. Marx was especially intent on showing that exploitation was not an occasional or accidental phenomenon arising from the willful action of an individual capitalist. He sought to prove, instead, that exploitation is an inevitable consequence of the logic of the Capitalist productive force. There are three distinct points in this regard which deserve further comment.

One is that Marx could not remain content with slogans about how the worker is cheated or gouged by employers, landlords, and sellers of products. This is not to say that he denied the existence of such practices or that he refrained from moralizing about the injustices involved. The point is that Marx did not incorporate such petty practices into his theory of Capitalist development nor base his conclusion that Capitalism will destroy itself upon them. Indeed, quite the contrary is true. Given the institutional framework of Capitalist society, Marx conceived of surplus value as something which the capitalist comes by as a legal and legitimate right. He viewed the capitalist as honest and the whole process as unfraudulent in the sense that the product is sold at its "true" or labor value and the worker is paid for his labor power on the identical principle. By classifying labor power as a commodity and extending his general theory of value to wage determination, Marx thus enables surplus value to emerge without violating the laws of exchange.

Secondly, Marx was very careful to point out that surplus value does not emerge out of fluctuations of market price around normal price or of the market wage around the normal wage. Such departures from long-run equilibrium result in short-term windfalls, gains, or losses, which are quite another matter. Marx regarded surplus value, on the other hand, as a "normal" and "permanent" feature of the Capitalist process. Theoretically, of course, one could conceive of surplus value disappearing under one or both of the following circumstances: (1) If the working class could somehow manage to push wages up so far above any realistic concept of subsistence as to leave nothing for the capitalist, i.e., fully absorb surplus value. (2) If the capitalist-employer limited the standard work day to that number of hours required to produce just enough to meet the worker's subsistence needs. But both assumptions are entirely outside the broader logic of the Marxian economic model. In the first instance, Marx could not admit as much as a theoretical possibility that workers could, in any long-run sense, push wages up so as to absorb surplus value. To recognize such a possibility is to render totally meaningless a subsistence theory of wages; and since this theory is but an extension of a general theory of value the dilemma is self-evident. The second assumption contradicts Marx's contention that surplus value is at the heart of the Capitalist system inasmuch as it is held to be the driving force behind production. "The capitalist's aim," wrote Marx, "is to produce not a use value, but a commodity also; not only use value, but value; not only value, *but at the same time surplus plus value* [Italics mine]." What else could Marx have meant but that in a Capitalist society surplus value is the *raison d'être* of all production? What incentive, then, would the Capitalist class have to limit the standard work day to the time required merely to produce the worker's subsistence?

The third and final point is that Marx viewed exploitation in a mechanical rather than a psychological way. The will or intent, the dishonesty or greed, of the capitalist is all beside the point of Marx's economic analysis of Capitalist development. Surplus value is not something which the capitalist volitionally wrenches out of the worker. Its emergence is an inevitable consequence of the economic logic of the Capitalist productive force. The capitalist can exist only as long as he accumulates and he can accumulate only as long as he can realize surplus value. Nor is the extent of a worker's

awareness of exploitation—whether he suffers more or less or not at all—
relevant for Marx the economic theorist. It is the *fact* of exploitation, not
the human suffering normally associated with it, which underlies the process
of Capitalist contradiction. To exaggerate the point but only for the purpose
of emphasis: Take the case of a motion-picture star, a worker by Marxian
definition, who earns a salary of a million dollars in a single year. Or assume
a Capitalist society in which the minimum wage is sufficient to enable all
workers to realize the American dream by way of a living standard. Imagine,
finally, a labor force composed entirely of masochists who, suffering the
worst possible life, enjoy their status of wage-slaves and do not wish to see
the system destroyed. According to Marxian economic logic, not only is
exploitation present in all three cases but its very existence will cause the
ultimate breakdown of the system no matter how the individuals concerned
feel about it or what their actual material circumstances happen to be. To
put it another way: exploitation is said to occur as long as one class which
produces nothing continues to receive some claim against the total social
product created entirely by another class. It is this fact of exploitation—not
the attitudes toward it or the extent of suffering—which, according to Marx,
constitutes the objective circumstance for Capitalism's demise. But viewed
in this light Marx no less than Malthus lifted guilt from the conscience of
the "factory owner."

MEASURING THE DEGREE OF EXPLOITATION:
RATE OF SURPLUS VALUE AND RATE OF PROFIT

Non-Marxian economics has never been overly preoccupied with the
question of classes. Its approach to economic classes has been, in the main,
a functional one. The focus in this regard has been on the traditional division
of economic society into worker, capitalist, landlord, and entrepreneur and
thus on the principles which underlie the distribution of income into its
relative shares: wages, interest, rent, and profit. Marx lacked fundamental
interest in this matter because, in his own words, "Rent, interest, and industrial profit are only different names for different parts of the surplus value
of the commodity, or the unpaid labor realized in it . . . and all of which . . .
are equally derived from this source, and from this source alone." Still the
economic theorist in Marx was not entirely content with ignoring the principles on which the "spoils" wrung from labor are divided up among those
"who do not work." Thus Marx's analysis of interest, rent, and profit determination will be covered, if only briefly, at the appropriate juncture in this
exposition. The fact remains that Marx was far more concerned with finding
a way to measure the degree to which labor was being exploited under the
Capitalist system. And it is to this one of his endeavors that we now turn.

The Marxian equation $C = c + v + s$ is fundamental to an understanding
of the point at hand as well as to much of the material to follow. C represents

the value of the commodity in question. It is equal to the sum of c, v, and s where: (1) c is constant capital, i.e., the value of the instruments of production consumed in the production process; (2) v is variable capital, i.e., the value of the labor power employed in that same process; (3) s is surplus value, i.e., the value created by the labor power thus utilized. There are several reasons why this breakdown of commodity value (C) into its three components is analytically significant. The division of capital into its constant and variable proportions serves to point up Marx's contention that surplus value derives solely from the application of labor power in the productive process. Another reason is that changes in the $c:v:s$ ratios can take place over time without necessarily being reflected in a corresponding variation in the value magnitude of C. Such alterations, which would otherwise be concealed, are important indicators of trends or basic shifts in the structure of the Capitalist economy.

There are two basic approaches to the calculation of the *rate* of surplus value; either of which, according to Marx, is an equally "exact expression for the degree of exploitation of labor-power by capital, or of the laborer by the capitalist." Marx's illustration of the first method, which appears in volume I of *Das Kapital*, is clear enough. In order to simplify he assumes a value magnitude of 90 for v and 90 for s with c equal to zero. Marx writes: "We have now the value produced ($v + s$). Given the new value produced— £180—which sum consequently represents the whole labor expended during the process, then subtracting from it £90, the value of the variable capital, we have remaining £90, the amount of surplus value. This sum of £90 or s expresses the *absolute* quantity of surplus-value produced. The relative quantity produced, or the increase percent of the variable capital, is determined, it is plain, by the ratio of the surplus-value to the variable capital, or is expressed s/v. In our example this ratio is 90/90, which gives an increase of 100 percent. This relative increase in the value of the variable capital, or the relative magnitude of the surplus-value, I call "The *rate* of surplus value" [Italics mine].

The second expression of the rate of surplus value is in terms of the division of the work day. Recall Marx's point that during any given work day a worker labors for a segment of it in order to produce his own subsistence (i.e., the exchange value of his labor power) and for the remainder of that day in order to create surplus value for the capitalist-employer. Marx refers to the subsistence portion of that day as *necessary labor* (nl), and the latter part of the day as *surplus labor* (sl). The rate of surplus value may thus be expressed as nl/sl.

Marx draws a sharp distinction between surplus value and profit and thus between the methods by which the rate of each is to be properly calculated. Recall, as well, Marx's point that surplus value is generated only by the employment of variable (as against constant) capital in the process of production. But neither the division of capital into its constant and variable proportions nor, for that matter, the breakdown of commodity exchange value into its three components $c:v:s$ is really understood by or concerns the capitalist. Marx writes: "The capitalist understands well enough that . . . surplus value seems to arise equally from all its different elements consisting of means of production and labor. . . . all of them add their values, which are advanced as capital, to the value of the product, and they are not distinguished as constant and variable magnitudes." Thus the capitalist, whose single interest in production is the realization of a maximum return on *total* investment, equates surplus value with profit. Against this background, Marx took issue with the traditional approach to calculating the profit rate. He viewed the standard method of expressing the rate of profit as a percentage of total capital investment as an understatement of its true magnitude. There are, according to Marx, two ways by which to calculate the "true" rate of profit. One is $s/c + v$. To illustrate the point: Assume a capital structure of $80c + 20v + 20s$, giving us an exchange value of 120 for the commodity in question. Here the rate of surplus value is 100 percent, i.e., s/v or 20/20. The organic composition of capital is 80 percent, i.e., $c/c + v$ or 80/100. The rate of profit is 20 percent, i.e., $s/c + v$ or 20/100. The alternative formulation is p/k. Here p represents the profit realized and k Marx's notation for the capital advanced in production or what he calls its "cost price." The rate of profit, then, is p/k, which amounts to the same thing as $s/c + v$.[1]

Before proceeding further, that is, taking a second look at that which is divided among the various types of capitalists, we should consider Marx's modifications of his theory of value and price, or the so-called second and third versions of that theory of value.

IX·

Marx's Theory of Value and Price: Second and Third Versions

As time went by Marx became progressively more troubled over certain weaknesses in the first version of his theory of value and price. He was concerned over the failure of the theory to account for what was actually happening to the structure of market prices in his day. He found it difficult to dismiss the fact, for instance, that the prices of at least some commodities deviated from their respective labor content even in the long run. Apparently Marx became aware that something more or other was involved than the forces responsible for the oscillation of market around normal value. The results of his search for a more realistic explanation of the valuation process appear, most particularly, in the latter part of volume III of *Das Kapital*. We turn, therefore, to the modifications that Marx made in his theory of value and price.

THE SECOND VERSION

The crux of the issue is best stated as a question: Is commodity exchange value, in fact, equal to commodity price? Given Marx's *labor* theory of value, in order for exchange values to be equal to prices it is necessary that relative prices exactly reflect the relative quantities of labor embodied in commodities. This can be made to follow by assuming, as Marx did in his first approximation, both an equal rate of surplus value and profit for all spheres of production. This can only be so, however, if the organic composition of capital is also assumed to be identical for every industry and for each firm within an industry. To have assumed the contrary would have been a violation of the internal consistence of Marx's theory of price.

But Marx was well aware of the facts in this case and was much too good a logician to stick to this critical assumption of equality in regard to the organic composition of capital. Thus he was forced to admit that even in the long run—for technical as well as value reasons—the organic composition of capital did vary significantly from one industry or sphere of production to another. However, Marx also made the rate of profit a function of the organic composition of capital; which, by his own account, varies throughout the productive process. To clarify the point using Marx's own example and figures: Take the case of two industries, A and B, with greatly varying technical requirements of production. Say that industry A is highly labor-intensive and B equally highly capital-intensive. Assume, further, an identical advance of capital and a 100 percent rate of surplus for both industries.

Assume, finally, a capital structure of $10c + 90v$ for industry A and $90c + 10v$ for industry B. The commodity exchange value for industry A is then $10c + 90v + 90s$ or 190. In the case of industry B it is $90c + 10v + 10s$ or 110. Employing Marx's method of calculating the rate of profit ($s/c + v$) we arrive at the following figures: a profit rate of 90 percent for industry A and 10 percent for industry B.

Thus, Marx was forced to admit the long-term existence of significant variation in the organic composition of capital; which, as just illustrated, logically results in the emergence and persistence of different rates of profit among the various spheres of production. Yet Marx writes, and there can be little doubt about his meaning here: "A difference in the average rate of profit of the various lines of industry does not exist in reality, and could not exist without abolishing the entire system of capitalist production." This second proposition follows from two basic premises on which, in the first instance, Marx's theory of value rests: (1) A perfectly competitive market structure and (2) the capitalist's single concern with a return on his total investment. In the long run, according to Marx, the force of competition among capitalists thus oriented must result in an equality of profit rates throughout the productive process.

The technical problem confronting Marx, therefore, was how to reconcile the reality of differing organic compositions of capital with the long-run tendency of profit rates toward equality throughout the productive process. The analytic significance of this issue emerges all the clearer when one recalls what it is that Marx sought to prove in this regard. He wanted to show that in the long run, commodity exchange value is equal to commodity price, i.e., that relative prices truly reflect the relative quantities of labor embodied in commodities. In Marx's words: "Whatever may be the way in which the *prices* of the various commodities are first fixed . . . *the law of value always dominates*. . . . If the labor time required for the production of these commodities is reduced, *prices* fall; if it is increased, *prices* rise . . ." [Italics mine.] But, again, this process depends on the assumption of long run equality in the rates of profit. Marx's endeavor at resolution here amounts, in its essence, to the following line of reasoning. He draws a distinction between two kinds of profit and two profit rates. There is the *specific* or *special* rate of profit, as it relates to a particular industry or line of production, and which may or does reflect the deviation of commodity price from its true labor content. There is, as well, an *average* or *general* rate of profit for the productive process as a whole. It is, then, this average profit rate which in Marx's second version appears to satisfy the condition of equality as initially set down.

What Marx does here is clear enough. He transforms an earlier and undifferentiated concept of profit into an average profit and average profit rate, thereby equating commodity exchange value with price of production. What emerges as Marx's second version may be summarized: (1) In the short run, the price of any one or more commodities may deviate from its "true" labor content, i.e., commodity price may not be equal to commodity exchange value. (2) The *special* rate of profit, which is related to the specific organic composition of capital for the given industry, reflects this difference. (3) In the long run there is, in Marx's words, a "center of gravity" or "equilibrium point" around which commodity prices do in fact fluctuate. It is here, according to Marx, that relative prices "approximate" the actual relative quantities of labor embodied in commodities. (4) The initial requirement of equality of profit rates, as a condition for exchange value being equal to price, is met by equality in the *general* or *average* rate of profit as discussed above. Whether or not Marx has really accomplished what he set out to do here or has simply succeeded in shifting ground by redefining profit remains an open and debatable question.

THE THIRD VERSION

Be that as it may, Marx was not content to rest the case there. For argument's sake let us say that Marx had effected the necessary reconciliation and that, in the long run, the exchange value of a commodity is equal to that commodity's price of production. The short run fluctuations of price around this "center of gravity" remain and Marx was concerned with the causal factors involved. Thus we come to the so-called third version of Marx's theory of value and price. Here it will be helpful to recall an earlier distinction between *market* (short-run) and *normal* (long-run) exchange value. Having assumed that at equilibrium normal exchange value is equal to long-run price, we can now speak of market (short-run) and normal (long-run) *price*. According to Marx, therefore, market price is equal to normal price at the point of perfect equilibrium. Marx defines an equilibrium market situation, in turn, as one where the demand for and the supply of the commodity in question are in balance. Time and again Marx refers to this point as "the center of gravity around which the daily market-prices tend to fluctuate and tend to balance one another within definite periods." Marx's interest here centered on the operation of two groups of causal forces: (1) those responsible for the day-to-day fluctuations of market around normal price, and (2) those which accounted for the tendency toward equality at equilibrium. He analyzed these forces, as we are about to see, in terms of the more or less traditional concept of supply and demand with but one significant departure. Marx denied the existence of a functional link between supply and demand, i.e., between the forces underlying the volume of production and those behind aggregate demand.

We turn now to Marx's analysis of the forces that cause market price to deviate from normal price. In his first version, Marx drew no distinction between use value and demand. "So long," wrote Marx, "as we are dealing simply with the individual commodities, we could assume that the demand for any one commodity . . . existed without inquiring into the extent to which this demand required satisfaction." But when, Marx continued, "the product of some entire line of production is placed on one side and the social demand for it on the other . . . it becomes necessary to consider the amount, the quantity of this social demand." It was at the aggregate level, therefore, that Marx came to separate "effective" demand from simple social want and acknowledged the existence of a particular functional relationship between amount demanded and price. Marx found, to be specific, that aggregate demand "is essentially conditioned on the mutual relations of the different economic classes and their relative economic positions," and that the amount demanded is often "very elastic and changing." Thus, according to Marx, workers and capitalists alike are bound by this law of demand. In the case of the worker, he writes, "If the means of subsistence were cheaper, or money-wages higher . . . a greater 'social demand' would be manifested." Elsewhere, citing the repeal of the corn laws in England as evidence, Marx insists, "It is a mistake to say that the consumption of necessities of life does not grow with their cheapening." So it is for the capitalists, says Marx, that "if cotton were cheaper the demand of the capitalist for it would increase." In still another place Marx notes, "If the market-value [market price as used here] is changed, then there will also be a change in the conditions under which the total quantity of commodities can be sold." It appears, therefore, that Marx had in mind not only shifts in the supply and demand curve but movements along a curve.

The following, then, is Marx's account of the mechanics of fluctuation of market around normal price. As a point of departure, let us assume a market at perfect equilibrium. Here the amount of a commodity demanded is just equal to the amount of it supplied at the prevailing market price; which by definition, is equal to normal price. Marx views the state of demand at this point of equilibrium as standard or in balance. In the short run, however, the forces just mentioned may cause the market price of a commodity to rise above or fall below that commodity's normal price. Marx characterized the state of demand, in relation to supply, as substandard in the first and above standard in the second instance. There is yet another and more basic or long-run force which, according to Marx, tends to drive market price back to equality with normal price. Recall that Marx reasons all of this out within the theoretical framework of a perfectly competitive economy. Deviation of market from normal price is said by Marx to cause at least some firms within a given industry to realize something more than or less than the ordinary magnitude of surplus value or profit. The presence of such a windfall gain, where market price is above normal price, causes certain existing firms to expand output or new firms to enter that industry or both. The result, in either or both cases, is an outward shift of the industry supply curve, a fall in market price, and the tendency toward the restoration of equilibrium in that market. The reverse path toward equilibrium is followed, of course, where market price falls below normal price.

MARX'S THEORY OF PRICE: A SUMMARY

As we have just observed, Marx's theorizing in regard to the determinants of value and price passed through three distinct stages. It would be a mistake, however, to conclude from this that the third approximation represents the final version of Marx's theory of price or that it is central to the Marxian economic model. But it was in this last stage, as found in volume III of *Das Kapital,* that Marx concerned himself most particularly with the part played by the forces of supply and demand in the pricing process. It was here, as well, that he came dangerously close to recognizing the role of utility in the valuation process. He flirted with it and then ran away by refusing to cross the line between the short and the long run. It is equally clear that Marx did not rest his case on the first or crude version of his labor theory of value. He did not, as we have observed, ignore the question of the relationship between exchange value and price (with all that this implies by way of assumptions) or fail to distinguish between use value and effective aggregate demand. What remains is that Marx made the second or prices-of-production version central not only to his analysis of Capitalism but to post-Capitalist economies as well. The real issue, of course, is not a *labor* theory of value as such. It is that of a cost of production as against a utility approach to a theory of value and price; a point which many post-Marxian economists made convincingly clear. Indeed, the views of such economists as William Stanley Jevens, Carl Menger, Eugen von Böhm-Bawerk, John Bates Clark and Alfred Marshal regarding utility as the determinant in the valuation process is so well known and so generally accepted as to require no belaboring.

X·

Surplus Value: A Second Look
at That Which is Divided

Technically speaking, Marx distinguished between profit and surplus value and in the method of calculating the rate of each. But he also treated the two terms as synonyms in another and more general sense. He does so in reference to that element of total value which goes to the capitalists *as a class,* i.e., the *s* in $C = c + v + s$. Since Marx characterized Capitalist society as composed of only two basic and antagonistic classes, his primary concern was with the principle underlying the division of the total produce between the two classes. But Marx also recognized the existence of subgroups within each class and was aware of conflicts of interests at that level. Thus he speaks of merchant, industrial, money, and landowning capitalists. Our present concern, therefore, is with that part of Marx's economic analysis which endeavors to explain the basis on which, to paraphrase Marx, the various kinds of capitalist exploiters divide up the loot wrung from the productive labors of the working classes. The approach here will be, first, to take a somewhat closer look at the genesis, nature, and magnitude of the total pool of surplus value or profit. Marx's views on interest and rent, as shares going to specific types of capitalists, will be examined in chapter 11.

THE NATURE AND ORIGIN OF SURPLUS VALUE

One point in regard to the genesis of surplus value deserves special emphasis. According to Marx, economic value and therefore surplus value are generated only within the sphere of production and not at all in the process of circulation. In volume I of *Das Kapital* Marx states: "Circulation, or the exchange of commodities, begets no value." He repeats and expands on this in volume III: "Merchant's capital is simply capital performing its function in the sphere of circulation . . . But no value is produced in the process of circulation, and therefore, no surplus value. . . . In fact, nothing occurs there but the metamorphosis of commodities and this has nothing to do with either the creation or with the transformation of values." This is not to say, however, that Marx denies a return to mercantile capital. He simply views such a return as the merchant capitalist's share of the surplus value which is generated solely within the sphere of production. In essence, as we shall see, Marx takes this same position in regard to money and landowning capital.

But this profit or surplus value, Marx then tells us, is not a uniquely Capitalist phenomenon. A surplus as such is said to have existed during the Slave period and will continue to exist under Socialism and Communism. Indeed, all other things being equal, the absolute size of the Socialist surplus must be larger than that under Capitalism. Both of these points follow from two far more general Marxian propositions. One is Marx's definition of surplus value or profit as that magnitude which results when the level of the productive force is such that workers can, or are forced to, produce more goods within a given time period than are required for their subsistence for that same time interval. The second is that a Socialist productive force, since it appears at a later stage of historical development, is superior to the Capitalist productive force. "Capital has not invented surplus value," is the way Marx sums up this point.

Thus, as we have seen, all economic value is said to be created by labor employed in the process of production. This fact, says Marx, is entirely independent of the stage of historical development or the society in question. The real issue, according to Marx, is whether all that is produced returns, directly or indirectly, to those who have produced it or whether there exists a class which creates no economic value yet receives a share of the total social product. This depends on the nature of existing property relations, which, in turn, determine the class character of society. The critical factor here is whether the means of production are privately or collectively owned. "Whenever a part of society possesses the monopoly of the means of production," writes Marx, "the laborer, free or not free, must add to the working time necessary for his own maintenance an extra working time in order to produce the means of subsistence for the owners of the means of production." And that remains true, Marx goes on to say, "whether the proprietor be the Athenian, . . . Etruscan theocrat, civis Romanus, Norman baron, American slave owner, Wallachian Boyard, modern landlord, or capitalist." The only difference, among societies where the means of production are privately owned, is in the technical mechanism by which the surplus is "extracted" from the workers. Recall, in this connection, Marx's views on and distinction between the production relations of formal and wage-slavery. Our concern, of course, is with Marx's analysis of how this mechanism operates within the institutional framework of Capitalist society.

Marx was particularly insistent, for reasons we are about to see, that the capitalist's "right" to a share in the total social product is a property "right" and no more. It is private ownership of the means of production—guaranteed by bourgeois law and protected by the bourgeois state—that enables the Capitalist class to direct the economic process and pocket the profit generated within the sphere of production. How did the bourgeoisie ever arrive at this position of dominance? In essence, says Marx, by the same means as did all earlier ruling classes. The bourgeoisie emerged first as economically dominant, writes Marx, through "conquest, enslavement, robbery, murder, briefly force." The process of primitive accumulation "was accomplished with merciless vandalism, and under the stimulus of passion, the most infamous, the most sordid, the pettiest, the most meanly odious." Following economic dominance, the bourgeoisie gained political dominance and thus "the law itself" became "the instrument of the theft." "And the history of this, this expropriation," Marx tells us, "is written in the annals of mankind in letters of blood and fire." It is here that Marx employs some of those "white-hot phrases" mentioned in an earlier chapter. It is here, as well, in his related dismissal of alternative theories of profit and interest that Marx is at his ironic and sarcastic best. These are also two of the areas, it must be added, where Marx the economist appears at his weakest. For, as many students of Marxism have observed, Marx's theory of primitive accumulation amounts to little more than the long since exploded robber-baron approach to this aspect of history.

Marx was equally vague in regard to such related questions as the nature of the entrepreneurial function, who the entrepreneur really is, where he comes from, and his precise relationship to the capitalist. As best as can be made out—especially in regard to innovation—Marx maintained that the logic of the Capitalist system generates its own body of innovators. Toward the end of volume III of *Das Kapital,* Marx pays some brief attention to the question of the original source of such innovating talent. Here he draws an interesting analogy between the medieval church and Capitalism. The "Catholic Church in the Middle Ages," writes Marx, "formed its hierarchy out of the best brains of the people without regard to estate, birth, or wealth . . . [as] the principal means of fortifying priest rule and suppressing the laity." And so it is with Capitalism, says Marx, "that a man without wealth, but with energy, solidity, ability and business sense may become a capitalist. . . . Although this circumstance continually brings an unwelcome number of new soldiers of fortune into the field and into competition with the already existing individual capitalists, it also secures the supremacy of capital itself, expands its basis, and enables it to recruit ever new forces for itself out of the lower layers of society." Unfortunately, on the point of interest here, Marx ends up by revealing something of far greater political interest than the amount of light he sheds on the genesis of innovation and innovators. For, Marx concludes, "The more a ruling class is able to assimilate the most prominent men of a ruled class, the more solid and dangerous is its rule."

Holding to the above views, Marx was thus able to dismiss as bourgeois ideology the then prevailing economic orthodoxy in regard to profit, interest, and rent as earned shares of the total social product. It is here that he first drew the distinction between the money capitalist and the industrial capitalist. He defined the former as the owner and lender of the capital fund used in production and the latter, who borrows money capital, as the one who owns and directs the process of production. Following this distinction, Marx challenges both the industrial capitalist's claim to profit as a return for services rendered and that of the money capitalist for the sacrifice ininvolved in the act of saving. Marx was fully aware, of course, that men and machines do not come together accidentally or without purpose. What he does, however, is to separate the decision-making function from the industrial capitalist as such. According to Marx, this function is performed by highly skilled workers whose wage corresponds to that level of skill and whose labor power does, indeed, enter into the valuation process. Marx calls these workers "industrial managers" and refers to them as "the souls of our industrial system." This leaves the industrial capitalist, as such, with no other basis for the profits that he receives than the property relations mentioned in the first instance.

Marx disposes of the money capitalist's claim, which takes the form of interest as a reward for necessary abstinence, with particular sarcasm. He finds, first of all, little if any functional relationship between consumption and capital accumulation. If anything this functional relationship is held to be positive rather than negative. The capitalist's consumption, says Marx, tends to rise as his capital accumulates. The notion that production and economic growth hinge on the capitalist's self-denial struck Marx as ludicrous. So much so, in fact, as to have caused him to make the following widely quoted comment in volume I of *Das Kapital:* "The simple dictates of humanity therefore plainly enjoin the release of the capitalist from martyrdom and temptation, in the same way that the Georgian slaveowner was lately delivered, by the abolition of slavery, from the painful dilemma, whether to squander the surplus-product lashed out of his niggers, entirely in champagne, or whether to reconvert a part of it, into more niggers and more land."

In a more serious vein, Marx returns to the point with which he began. Profit or surplus, which is the single source of capital accumulation, is generated solely by the employment of labor in the sphere of production. All that occurs following that is the division of this surplus among the various types of capitalists. And all the best efforts of the "vulgar economists" to deny this, to justify the capitalist's claim, cannot save this "last illusion of the capitalist system," concludes Marx. So much for the source of surplus value or profit. We turn now to Marx's analysis of the factors which determine the magnitude of this surplus value.

THE MAGNITUDE OF SURPLUS VALUE

According to Marx, the magnitude of surplus value is a function of two variables: (1) The length of the normal work day, and (2) the exchange value of labor power. A change in either or both will, in turn, cause a corresponding change in the amount of surplus available for division among capitalists. Marx introduces a distinction here between two categories of surplus value: absolute and relative. The former results from changes in the length of the work day and the latter from changes in the exchange value of labor power. We shall consider the question of absolute surplus first even though Marx clearly attaches considerably more significance to relative surplus.

What, according to Marx, sets the length of the Capitalist work day; which, in turn, determines the magnitude of absolute surplus value? Unfortunately, this is one of those areas where Marx distinguishes himself by his vagueness. He conceives of the standard work day as a range rather than a fixed number of hours. Depending upon certain factors, it can be as short as eight or as long as eighteen hours a day. Some of these factors are obvious and need only to be mentioned. At one end of the 24-hour scale, workers require some time during which to sleep, rest, eat, etc. At the opposite end of the scale, laborers must work a given number of hours a day in order to produce their daily subsistence. They are also obliged to work an additional part of the day in order to produce a *minimum* surplus value; for, otherwise, the capitalists would have no incentive to employ them. The standard work day establishes itself somewhere within this range. Marx is indeed vague as to the actual number of hours per day that are required for the regeneration of the worker and the production of subsistence. He is equally indefinite as to the precise division between minimum and above-minimum surplus value.

The manner in which, once again, Marx interweaves sociology and economics is of greater interest. He credits the Capitalist class with economic rationality in that it seeks to impose whatever standard work day will maximize long-run aggregate surplus value. But he makes rationality, in this case, a function of such nonquantifiable factors as: (1) the historical stage of development, (2) national and cultural differences, and (3) the "politics" of the situation. Thus what is rational for one variant of production relations is not necessarily rational for another. Given a slave economy, "blessed" with "teeming preserves," it is the height of rationality, wrote Marx, "to take out of the human chattel in the shortest space of time the utmost of exertion it is capable of putting forth." Marx did not find this to be so for Capitalism. In the case of wage-slavery, economic rationality dictates that the length of the standard work day be limited, as well, by the cost of a too-rapid depletion of the labor supply.

More generally, Marx makes class struggle an integral part of the operation of the Capitalist productive force. He views the struggle between capital and labor over the length of the work day as continuous. This enabled Marx to point out another of those "capitalist contradictions" that he was so fond of exposing. Recall that Marx assumes a perfectly competitive labor market in this portion of his analysis, i.e., the single firm within an industry faces a given labor supply. Thus the issue of depletion of the total labor supply does not enter into the rational calculations of the single firm. The individual capitalist-employer is entirely rational, therefore, in his endeavor to maximize the surplus value of the firm by pressing for a longer standard work day than that which will maximize surplus value for the capitalist class as a whole. So it is that the individual capitalist-employer contrives, by every means possible, to stretch the length of the work day. Every extra "moment" of work squeezed out of the worker, says Marx, means that much more "profit" to his employer. The technique for lengthening the work day may be direct or indirect, obvious or subtle. A worker may be required to stand at his machine before the official work day begins. A few minutes, here and there, may be stolen from the lunch hour. Control over visits to the rest room may be imposed. A factory clock which runs a few minutes late each day because of a mechanical defect may remain unadjusted. The tempo of a machine may be speeded up. The capitalists behave as they must. But, adds Marx, so do the workers. The proletariat (the most politically advanced segment of the working class) takes advantage of the existing conflict of interests among capitalists and thereby exacts a certain amount of protective legislation from the bourgeois state. This, according to Marx, is what explains the ten-hour day, the child labor laws, etc. "Hence it is," Marx concludes, "that . . . the determination of what is a working day, presents itself as the result of a struggle, a struggle between collective capital . . . and collective labor." Somewhere, within the range mentioned above, the standard work day is set by the forces of this class struggle.

We turn now to the second category of surplus value. What, according to Marx, are the causal factors behind the variation in the exchange value of labor power and thus in the magnitude of relative surplus value? The single most important factor given is the movement of the Capitalist productive force toward a higher order of the organic composition of capital, i.e., a progressively greater reliance on machinery in the productive process. Marx draws an interesting distinction here between the proposition that constant capital is not value-creating and the fact that labor productivity rises as progressively more machinery is employed in the process of production. The critical division in this case is between that portion of the standard work day during which the laborer works to produce his own subsistence and that segment during which he works for the capitalist. An illustration will help to clarify Marx's argument. Taking a point in time, let us assume: (1) a standard work day of twelve hours; (2) a given order of the organic composition of capital; (3) a corresponding labor productivity such that six hours are required to produce the worker's subsistence and the other six hours the surplus value going to his employer. Moving to a later point in time, let us now assume: (1) a standard work day remaining at twelve hours; (2) a higher order of organic composition of capital; (3) a corresponding rise in labor productivity such that a worker can produce his subsistence in four instead of six hours.

The significance of this change in the ratio of subsistence to surplus-value time from 6:6 to 4:8 may be expressed in any one of several ways. It means a fall in the amount of socially necessary labor required to produce a *given* output. It means a decline in the exchange value of labor power. It means a fall in the cost of production (Marx's second version) and thus a corresponding drop in commodity price. Since, in the long run, the worker is assumed to receive only a subsistence wage, it follows that the value of all additional output resulting from the rise in labor productivity goes to the capitalist. This is what Marx had in mind by relative surplus value. There is nothing in this portion of his analysis which implies an absolute decline in the worker's material living standard as labor productivity rises, i.e., as the exchange value of labor power falls. If, as some interpret Marx, the workers suffer a secular deterioration in their material circumstances, it is for a different set of reasons which have yet to be discussed. Still what does happen, according to Marx, is that the rate of exploitation of labor increases with rising labor productivity; for it is only the capitalist who benefits, in the form of an increase in relative surplus value, from a higher order of the organic composition of capital. The only point that the capitalist must consider, in this regard, is that the increase in relative surplus value be at least equal to the direct labor cost involved in the creation of the machinery. Concretely, Marx appears to have been exceptionally taken with the extent to which rapid technological change under Capitalism was causing labor productivity to rise and thus constantly increasing the rate of exploitation of the working class.

Marx viewed the mechanization of production as the single most important but certainly not the only determinant of the magnitude of surplus value in its relative sense. Change in the organizational structure of the Capitalist productive force is another. Recall all that Marx subsumes in his concept of the productive force. The following are but some of the interdependent elements which are connected with the social organization of production and which, according to Marx, bear on the level of labor productivity and thus on the magnitude of relative surplus value: (1) the extent to which there is a combining of capital stock and therefore cooperation among capitalists in a given line of production; (2) the existing size and locational distribution of the labor force; (3) the number of laborers working under one roof; (4) the spreading of managerial labor cost as a function of the length of the standard work day; (5) the existing degree of division of labor and specialization; (6) the technical-efficiency relationship of man to machine; and so forth.

Marx suggests certain other, less direct, factors which also affect the magnitude of relative surplus value. One is the progressive substitution of female and child labor for that of the male adult. The greater the level of mechanization, the more sophisticated the process, the less is the need for the kind of physical strength normally associated with the male breadwinner. As brought out earlier, Marx's notion of subsistence is that of family subsistence. Thus when more than one member of a family is employed the exchange value of labor power falls and relative surplus value increases. The family may or may not be worse off, in an absolute sense, depending upon the extent to which the use of female and child labor causes heads of households to become unemployed. Marx's notion of subsistence also includes the "necessary labor time required for the reproduction of labor power." To the extent, therefore, that the introduction of machinery and improvement in the social organization of production enables the substitution of unskilled for skilled labor, there occurs a decline in the exchange value of labor power and a corresponding increase in relative surplus value. Another such factor is a change, for whatever reason, in the mix of consumption goods making up a worker's subsistence. Any cheapening in the quality, composition, or price of workers' goods means a drop in the exchange value of labor power and hence a rise in relative surplus value. Finally, Marx considers the same question from a purely monetary standpoint and finds that certain monetary changes offer the capitalists a very special "opportunity for defrauding the workman." The circumstance envisaged by Marx is one where, because of an increase in the gold supply or the depreciation of the currency by the state, there would result a general increase in the price level without a corresponding increase in money wages. This would, in real terms, cause the exchange value of labor power to fall and relative surplus value to rise. This is clearly not a case which contradicts Marx's basic proposition that money is neutral in regard to the valuation process.

The capitalist *qua* capitalist, as we have seen, has but a single concern: the realization of the highest possible rate of return on investment. He is presumed to be unaware of, or at best, uninterested in such Marxian distinctions as those between: (1) constant and variable capital, (2) surplus value and profit, (3) absolute and relative surplus value, (4) normal and supernormal profit, (5) the short and the long run, etc. Nevertheless there are certain forces at work within the Capitalist system, according to Marx, which can only be correctly understood in the above terms and with the aid of such distinctions.

Why, for instance, is the capitalist-employer under a constant pressure to lengthen the work day? According to Marx, a major factor in this regard is the cost of capital depreciation as it relates to the magnitude of surplus value. Marx breaks capital depreciation down into three distinct categories: (1) circulating, (2) non-use and (3) technological. The first of these results from the direct consumption of constant capital in the process of production, i.e., using up of raw materials, etc. The second stems from the inability (for reasons yet to be discussed) to utilize all of the existing machinery and equipment during a given production period. The third and most significant has to do with the innovating process, which, according to Marx, is so characteristic of the Capitalist productive force. He has in mind here the factor of obsolescence due to either or both of these circumstances: (1) a fall in the socially necessary labor required for the reproduction of the existing type of machinery; (2) the introduction of improved, that is, technologically superior, machinery. The capitalist is aware, according to Marx, of the inverse relationship between the cost of capital depreciation and the magnitude of surplus value. He seeks, therefore, to keep this cost at its minimum by the most rapid utilization of constant capital in the productive process. Two of the three forms of capital depreciation are not really at issue here. The first or circulating capital depreciation varies directly with the length of the standard work day and that is that. The second or "idleness" form of capital depreciation varies inversely with the length of the work day but is, nevertheless, beyond the control of the individual capitalist-employer. What the capitalist-employer can and does endeavor to minimize is the cost associated with the third or obsolescence form of capital depreciation which also varies inversely with the length of the work day. Marx's point here may also be stated in the following way. The rapidity with which existing constant capital is absorbed in the production process varies directly with the length of the working day. Thus the longer the period, all other things being equal, the lower is the obsolescence cost of capital depreciation and the greater is the magnitude of surplus value. This, then, is why capitalists strive to stretch the work day and why there is a tendency to organize production in shifts so as to keep machines operating as nearly around the clock as possible.

The particular basis of the distinction between normal and less than or more than normal profit, between the short and long run, is another characteristically Marxian point about the behavior of the Capitalist economy. We may recall in the second version of Marx's theory of value, that the long-run price of a commodity is set by the amount of *socially necessary* labor time required for its production. The long-run equilibrium situation is one, therefore, where the commodity price of each firm is equal to the market price as set by whatever constitutes socially necessary labor as an average or for the industry as a whole. In this case each firm will realize just its normal profit. But this equilibrium situation will not prevail, in the short run, if: (1) the labor requirement of one or more firms within an industry is above or below that which is socially necessary as an average for the industry, or (2) market supply and demand are not in balance. Marx's reasoning here is as follows: Where a given firm is more than normally efficient, i.e., uses less labor than is socially necessary for the industry as a whole, that firm will realize something more than normal profit. This is so because while that firm's commodity price, which is equal to its cost of production, is below the market price the firm can sell the commodity at the market price. Where the opposite situation prevails the firm will realize something less than normal profit. If, according to Marx, "the market cannot stomach the whole quantity at the normal price . . . this proves that too great a portion of the total labor of the community has been expended. . . . The effect is the same as if each individual . . . had expended more labor-time upon his particular product than is socially necessary."

Marx's analysis of the self-generating and cumulative aspect of the innovative process is of particular interest here. Assuming an initial source and supply of innovators, Marx is quite explicit about the intraindustry and interindustry forces which operate so as to perpetuate the stream of innovations. Indeed, Marx not only found the genesis of innovation in the very logic of the Capitalist productive force but saw the innovating process as one that feeds upon itself and thus as highly cumulative.

In the intraindustry case the process is said to operate as follows. Assume an initial change in the design of an existing machine or, for that matter, the introduction of a new machine. Marx found the cost of the first change of innovation to be quite high relative to the cost of producing subsequent units of that same general type of machine. According to Marx, competition among producers within an industry necessarily results in both cost reduction and further improvements in the design of that general type of machine. The original innovator is thus forced, in an effort to maintain his position, to innovate again; and so on in an endless chain of cause and effect. But the cost of the first change or the initial model is so high, Marx tells us, that its introduction may well ruin the innovating firm. "It has been estimated, roughly," Marx writes, "that the first individual of a newly invented machine will cost about five times as much as the construction of the second. . . . [thus] the first leaders in a new enterprise are generally bankrupted, and only those who later buy the buildings, machinery, etc., cheaper, make money out of it." Marx concludes this point on a typically ironic note that has little to do with the economic logic or analysis at issue: "It is, therefore, generally the most worthless and miserable sort of money-capitalists who draw the greatest benefits out of the universal labor of the human mind and its cooperative application in society."

The following, as it appears in volume I of *Das Kapital*, is self-explanatory as it relates to the interindustry case: "The revolution in cotton spinning calls forth the invention of the gin, for separating the seeds from the cotton fibre; it was only by means of this invention, that the production of cotton became possible on the enormous scale at the present required. But more especially, the revolution in the modes of production of industry and agriculture made necessary a revolution in the general conditions of the social process of production, i.e., in the means of communication and of transport."

One point, which underlies the analysis to follow, deserves special attention. Given the analytic framework of Marx's theory of value, all effective innovation is necessarily labor-saving. This is not to say, however, that all innovations have identical effects on the capital structure of the Capitalist firm. The introduction of a given innovation may, theoretically, generate one of three results in regard to the order of the organic composition of capital: (1) a higher order if the labor-saving is in the variable component of capital; (2) a lower order if the labor-saving is in the constant component; (3) no change if the labor-saving occurs in both parts so as to leave the ratio of variable to constant capital the same. The net effect, in any case, is a reduction in the socially necessary labor requirement as a result of innovation. Practically, Marx's interest centered on the process by which the introduction of machinery generated a higher order in the organic composition of capital, with the resulting consequence in regard to normal commodity price and surplus value or profit.

The path of Marx's analysis in this regard may best be followed by recalling the (nearly) perfectly competitive market structure within which he reasons here and by assuming, as a point of departure, a given industry at perfect equilibrium. In fact, let us go further and specify about the industry in question that: (1) all firms are identical in respect to magnitude of the capital fund, state of technology, size of labor force, order of the organic composition of capital, and share of the commodity market; (2) market supply and demand are in balance; (3) firm commodity price is equal to social commodity price; (4) market price is equal to normal price; (5) all firms realize just normal surplus value or profit. These specifications are made for the sake of simplicity. Recognition is taken of the fact that certain of these conditions imply and/or follow from others and that not all are, strictly speaking, necessary to the state of equilibrium Marx had in mind.

Thus we have the *initial situation,* i.e., perfect equilibrium, as specified above. The *transitional situation,* that which transpires in the short run, is as follows. Assume that some one firm within an industry comes into possession of a new machine, process, or technique which it introduces into the productive process. Marx's point that such innovation constitutes a *net* (taking into account the labor cost of, say, the new machine) reduction in the labor time required to produce a given quantity of the commodity has already been established. Here, then, Marx considers two possibilities. (1) An innovating firm, having thereby cut its labor cost, "could continue to sell . . . at the old market price," as determined by what is still socially necessary for the industry as a whole. In this instance the firm's share of the commodity market remains unchanged. But now, since its cost of production has fallen, the innovating firm realizes something more than just normal surplus value or profit. (2) An innovating firm lowers its individual commodity price below the prevailing market price in order to gain a larger share of the market. Marx regarded this as the more realistic case based, apparently, on direct observation of what actually happens in the Capitalist economy. This, of course, constitutes somewhat of a departure from the standard assumptions in terms of which a perfectly competitive market structure is characterized. Marx describes the behavior of the Capitalist firm which innovates: "But in the same measure in which his production has expanded, his *need to sell* also increases. The more powerful and costly means of production that he has called into life *enable* him, indeed, to sell his commodities more cheaply, they *compel* him, however, to sell more commodities, to conquer a much larger market for his commodities; consequently our capitalist will sell . . . more cheaply than his competitors . . . [but] he attains the object he wishes to attain, if he puts the price of the goods only a small percentage lower than that of his competitors. He drives them from the field, then wrests from them at least part of their sales by underselling them." Thus the innovating firm reaps an extraordinary gain but only as long as it can retain its monopoly over the new method of production.

The *final situation,* the new long-run equilibrium, comes about and is characterized by Marx: The majority of firms within the industry cannot simply stand by while the one firm gains a progressively larger share of the commodity market through price cutting. The force of such competition compels most firms to follow suit; in Marx's words, "to introduce the new method of production under which the proportion of the variable to the constant capital has been reduced." Thus it is that the innovating firm's extraordinary gain, which is a function of its short-term monopoly position, is wiped out in the final analysis. The new long-run equilibrium for the industry is identical with the *initial situation* in these respects: (1) Market supply and demand are again in balance; (2) firm commodity price is equal to social commodity price; (3) market price is equal to normal price; (4) all firms realize just normal surplus value or profit. The critical difference between the *initial* and *final situation* is that the order of the organic composition of capital is now higher for the industry as a whole. There is a drop, in other words, in the average socially necessary labor requirement in the case of that industry. All other things being equal, this means a fall in the normal exchange value or price of the commodity and a corresponding impact on surplus value or profit. The speed with which all of this occurs depends, according to Marx, on such factors as: (1) The state of the patent laws, (2) the extent to which the new method of production causes market supply to increase relative to demand, and (3) general frictions or rigidities which characterize that particular market.

XI ·

Division of the Surplus:
Interest and Rent

INTEREST

INTEREST

Just how subsidiary a role in the economic process Marx assigns to interest and its rate may well be surmised from his initial proposition that, except for a given institutional arrangement, interest need not necessarily exist in or characterize the Capitalist economy. "If all capital were in the hands of the industrial capitalist," writes Marx, "there would be no interest and no rate of interest." But this was not the path, according to Marx, along which Capitalism had developed. The phenomenon of interest payment is said to owe its existence to the presence of more than one variant of capitalist. (The same is true in regard to the payment of rent.) Two earlier Marxian propositions have special relevance here. One is that surplus value or profit is generated solely within the sphere of production. The other is that three conceptually distinct species of capitalists emerge over the course of capitalist development: the *industrial* capitalist, the *money* capitalist, the *landowning* capitalist. (The merchant or mercantile capital is yet another matter.) An industrial capitalist is one who owns the actual productive process—the textile mill, the glass-making concern, the iron foundry, etc. Ownership, in this case, really means the legal right to the revenue derived from the sale of the output in question. A money capitalist is one who owns money capital; a commodity, according to Marx, without which the productive process cannot be activated. A landowning capitalist is one who owns the land and the natural agents necessary to any act of production. Thus the basis of Marx's distinctions here is in terms of that which is owned.

What, then, does Marx tell us about the genesis of money capitalists? His account, presented in its most general terms, runs along the following lines. The logic of the Capitalist productive force generates two basic but related founts of money capital: (1) a class of wealthy people, and (2) the development of a system of banking and credit. In reference to the first, Marx writes: "As a people progresses in the development of wealth, there arises and grows more and more of a class of people, who find themselves possessed of funds through the labors of their ancestors." Theoretically, members of this class have three options open to them. (1) They can live off or squander the "social capital" in their possession. A relative few may, in fact, do so. But this is not the dominant pattern of economic behavior since the very logic of being a capitalist dictates otherwise. (2) They may invest their funds directly in the sphere of production and thereby become industrial capitalists. This option is most likely to be selected during the pre-Capitalist stage or the earlier stages of Capitalist development. (3) They may elect to have others, i.e., industrial capitalists, invest their funds and thereby become money capitalists. As Capitalism matures, this option becomes more dominant. "In old and rich countries," writes Marx, "that portion of the national capital, whose owners do not care to invest it themselves, makes up a larger proportion of the total productive capital of society than in newly settled and poor countries."

But the supply of money capital does not depend solely on the relative few who inherit or accumulate wealth. The logic of the Capitalist productive force also requires the continuous development and sophistication of the banking and credit system. Many people save, regardless of class, if only in small amounts or for short durations. Now and then the business community finds itself with idle funds. Both constitute bank deposits which in the aggregate become money capital or, in Marx's words, turn into "money power." Beyond this banks extend credit on promissory notes, "bills of exchange," backed by collateral. Thus we have the sum of individual and business saving plus credit as the second source of money capital; with banks or bankers as money capitalists.

Thus, in a purely functional sense, Marx speaks of two species of capitalists: money capitalists who lend and industrial capitalists who borrow the money capital required in the productive process. Interest is what the borrower pays and the lender receives for the use of money capital in the sphere of production. In his discussions on interest, Marx laid considerable stress on two propositions: (1) that the money capitalist cannot exist independently of the existence of and the role played by the industrial capitalists; (2) that money capital, while required in the productive process, is nevertheless not value-creating. The lengths to which Marx went in this regard are evident from the fine lines of distinction that he was forced to draw. Money and money capital are not one and the same since the latter has the additional property of being necessary to the act of production. But while Marx thus accorded money capital the status of a commodity, he insisted that interest is not properly its price. The explanation given is that price is simply the monetary expression of value and the value of *money* capital is therefore its price. Since interest is not the price of money capital, and does not represent a return for the value-creating power of such capital. what is it? An interest payment, according to Marx, is "but the outcome of a specific legal agreement between buyer and seller."

Here, once more, Marx links sociology and economic analysis. The interests of all three species of capitalists are said to coincide in one very fundamental regard. Surplus value or profit, derived entirely from the sphere of production, is the common pool from which industrial profits, interest, and rent payments come. The larger the absolute magnitude of surplus value or profit, i.e., the higher the rate of exploitation of labor, the more there is for division among the three species of capitalists. Recall, however, that aspect of Marx's theory of social class which admits of conflict of interest among subgroups *within* a class. The narrower financial interests of money and industrial capitalists stand opposed to one another in that industrial profits and interest payments come out of the same source. This brings us to the final question concerning the antagonistic relationship between the money and the industrial capitalist. On what basis does this division of surplus value into industrial profit and interest occur? More specifically, what factors or forces set the market rate of interest?

First, however, Marx's particular formulation in regard to the magnitude and rate of interest should be noted. (The numerical example presented here is intended solely for illustrative purposes and implies nothing more about the actual complexities involved.) Let us assume the following circumstances and transactions. (1) Money capitalist A lends and industrial capitalist B borrows, for the period of one year, a sum of money capital equal to $10,000. (2) B possesses no money capital of his own—that is, the sum lent by A to B is equal to the sum of money capital now under the control of B. (3) B invests the $10,000 of money capital in the sphere of production; as a result of which, at the end of that production period, he realizes an absolute profit of $3,000. (4) As due, under the existing legal arrangements, B repays A the principal plus interest totaling (say) $12,000. B is thereby able to retain only $1,000 of the $3,000 profit realized within the sphere of production. This $1,000, which accrues to the industrial capitalist, Marx calls industrial profit. The remaining $2,000, coming out of the same pool, is the interest payment made by the industrial to the money capitalist. The market rate of interest, in this case, is simply:

$$\frac{A_{1r} - A_1}{A_1} \quad \text{or} \quad \frac{\$12,000 - \$10,000}{\$10,000} \quad \text{or} \quad 20 \quad \text{percent};$$

where A_{1r} is the principal plus interest received by A at the end of the period and A_1 is the amount of the loan at the beginning of the period. Thus, according to Marx, "do the exploiters divide up the loot wrung from the labors of the working class."

The point is often made that Marx really had no theory of interest or interest rate determination. There are several reasons why, strictly speaking, this is true. The most significant is that, even when viewed within the framework of his own economic analysis, Marx does not draw the standard distinction between the "normal" and "market" concept in regard to the rate of interest. This follows from his earlier proposition that the factors that set the rate of interest, unlike the forces which determine commodity price as well as surplus value or profit, lie outside the sphere of commodity production. Marx's approach to interest rate determination is, in fact, somewhat analogous to the so-called "bargaining theory of wages" which had some currency during the early 1950's. Marx theorizes about an upper and lower absolute limit in this regard. The interest rate would, in the absence of a money capitalist class, be zero. But in reality the rate of interest cannot fall to zero since, as already observed, Marx viewed the emergence of a money capitalist class as part of the laws of Capitalist development. Neither can the rate rise so high as to swallow up all surplus value or profit; for Marx also recognized the dependence of Capitalist commodity production, its direction and magnitude, on the existence of industrial capitalists. Thus, the actual range in which movement occurs is narrowed, and at any given point in time, the market rate of interest will be set somewhere within this narrower range depending on the relative bargaining power of borrower and lender. The "objective circumstances" which, according to Marx, determines such relative strength will be set forth shortly.

Marx's recognition that a link exists between interest and the growth rate of the economy is clearly discernible and the implication is equally clear. The higher the return to the money capitalist (necessarily at the expense of the industrial capitalist) the stronger, *ceteris paribus*, is the dampening effect on the growth rate of the Capitalist economy. But there is very little more of any real significance on this. At one point Marx touches on the relationship of risk to interest but veers away from any meaningful economic analysis in this instance. He admits that the money capitalist, the "usurer . . . at least risks his own capital" as against the landowner who does not. This, to Marx's mind, explains why "the rate of interest at which ground rent is bought is generally lower than that of other investments." But, again, this hardly constitutes a serious concern with interest rate differentials, their relationship to alternative forms of investment, or the more general link between interest and resource allocation. The very limited and unrelated nature of Marx's observations or contributions in regard to such fundamental economic relationships is another reason why it is said that there really is no Marxian theory of interest.

We return, therefore, to the question: What factors determine the rate of interest within the narrower range as set forth above? Given the rate of surplus value or profit for the economy, the market rate of interest is set, according to Marx, by the existing relationship between the demand for and the supply of loanable funds. Having said this much Marx then proceeds, typically, to ignore the demand side and to focus most of his attention on the factors behind the supply of money capital. He does this, inferentially, by simply taking the demand for loanable funds as given. This is understandable quite apart from his general shyness toward the demand side in any part of his economic analysis. Had Marx seriously considered the factors underlying the demand for loanable funds, he would have been forced, in his analysis of interest, to return to the sphere of commodity production with all that this implies. Most of the factors cited by Marx as bearing on the supply of loanable funds have already been mentioned earlier in this discussion. That which follows, therefore, constitutes a summary and a tying together of Marx's analysis of interest and interest rate determination.

Marx's most general proposition may be stated as follows: Given the demand for loanable funds, the rate of interest will vary inversely with the availability of loanable funds. The supply of such funds is a function, first of all, of how large the class of money capitalists is at the given stage of Capitalist development. It is, secondly, a matter of the particular savings habits, the customs and traditions, of the community in question. The degree of development and sophistication of the banking and credit system is another, and particularly important, factor on the supply side. In part, of course, this involves or depends upon such other considerations as the direction of the world flow of gold and silver, the existing character of banking and credit legislation, etc.

What, finally, does Marx tell us about the movement of the general rate of interest over time? Here he does consider the short and the long run; but not, it must be noted, in the "market" and "normal" sense as in the case of commodity prices or wages. Marx recognizes short-term fluctuations in the interest rate and accounts for such movements in terms of shifts in the direction of the world movement of the precious metals, changes in existing banking and credit laws, and certain other minor institutional factors. The movement of the long-term interest rate, on the other hand, is downward. This is bound to occur since, according to Marx, the supply of loanable funds (relative to demand) increases over the course of Capitalist development. A society becomes wealthier. The savings of all classes increases. The relative size of the money capitalist class grows. With the progressive development of the banking and credit system more money capital becomes available. Marx takes note of a possible offset to this decline in the interest rate—one which involves the government in certain longer-run monetary policies—but concludes that such "artificial maneuvers . . . become from year to year more difficult for it."

The fact that all of this does not, strictly speaking, constitute a theory of interest has already been acknowledged. What, then, can be said on the positive side of Marx's approach to this question? As in a number of other instances, his analysis of interest has served well to point up the errors or weaknesses in earlier or prevailing views on this subject. Marx challenged, and his approach to interest acted as an antidote to, such earlier notions behind the theory as thrift, sacrifice, abstinence, etc. Marx's contribution here is assessed by Schumpeter: "He contemptuously rejects the bourgeois nursery tale *(Kinderfibel)* that some people rather than others became . . . capitalists by superior intelligence and energy in working and saving. Now he was well advised to sneer at that story about the good boys. . . . It is true that one does not ordinarily attain the status of capitalist . . . by saving from a wage or salary. . . . The bulk of accumulation comes from profits and hence presupposes profits. . . . The means required in order to start enterprise are typically provided by borrowing other people's savings, the presence of which in many small puddles is easy to explain or the deposits which banks create for the use of the would-be entrepreneur. . . . As a matter of economic theory, therefore, Marx had a real case—though he overstated it—when he denied to saving the role that the classical authors attributed to it. Only his inference does not follow."[1]

RENT

Marx's analysis of rent and rent determination need detain us only briefly. One reason is his view that rent, like interest payment, merely represents the further division of the "spoils"; all of which is generated solely within the sphere of production. Another is that many of the institutional arrangements discussed in connection with interest apply equally in the case of rent and thus need only to be recalled. Thirdly, the relevance of Marx's theorizing on rent determination to modern economics or present-day Capitalism is all too marginal to justify attention to its fine details. The emphasis, therefore, is on the basic issues and Marx's general conclusions.

Marx begins by recognizing the obvious fact that land (or, more accurately, parcels thereof) is privately owned by one segment of the Capitalist class. He calls those in possession of this particular form of property "land-owning capitalists." These capitalists have the standard legal right to use or, more important, to allow the use of their land in the sphere of production. They have an equal right, of course, to withhold its use if that be in their interest. In his analysis of rent, Marx draws no qualitative distinction within the productive sphere between agricultural and nonagricultural production. Both yield a commodity and the application of variable capital in either case generates surplus value. The functional distinctions that Marx does make in his discussion of rent parallel those in the case of interest. The parallelism is as follows:

INTEREST		RENT	
Class	Payment received by	Class	Payment received by
Money capitalist	Interest	Landowning capitalist	Rent
Industrial capitalist	Profits	Agricultural capitalist	Profits
Industrial worker	Wage	Agricultural worker	Wage

In regard to land and rent, therefore, there is, first, the landowning capitalist who allows his land to be used for purposes of commodity production. There is, secondly, the agricultural capitalist who elects to enter the field of farming rather than industrial production. The decision by this species of capitalist to invest in agricultural production rather than, say, manufacturing is said to be culturally determined. There are still some, according to Marx, who seek the security and vestigial status associated with the landed aristocracy and its way of life. The price paid for this, Marx asserts, is that the return to such capital tends to be below the average realized in nonagricultural production. There is, finally, the agricultural worker who, like his industrial counterpart, has been divorced from the ownership of the means of livelihood. He is thereby forced to till the soil for a subsistence wage. The resulting surplus value goes, in the first instance, to the agricultural capitalist. Given the existing institutional arrangements, however, the capitalist is required to share this profit with the landowner who allows his land to be used in commodity production. The contractual sum paid periodically by the former to the latter is ground rent. In Marx's words: "This renting capitalist pays to the landowner . . . a sum of money at definite periods fixed by contract . . . for the permission to invest his capital in this particular sphere of production. This sum of money is called *ground rent*, no matter whether it is paid for agricultural soil, building lots, mines, fishing grounds, forests, etc."

Marx was careful to point out, however, that this ground rent normally includes an element of interest along with a return for the right to exploit the unimproved land. He arrived at this proposition by showing the relationship of the prevailing system of land tenure to permanent land improvement resulting from the application of capital to land. Since at the termination of a contract the ownership of land improvement passes from the agricultural to the landowning capitalist, Marx reasoned, an element of interest is necessarily present in ground rent. Here, once more, Marx takes note of a subclass conflict. The agricultural capitalist is interested in the longest-term and the landowner in the shortest-term rental contract.

So much for who receives ground rent and why. We turn to Marx's views regarding the character of this rent and its determination. Here—and this is the heart of the issue—the earlier parallel between the agricultural and the nonagricultural sector ends. The element of monopoly, as we shall see, turns out to be the critical variable in Marx's analysis of rent determination. First, however, it is necessary to note that for purposes of analysis Marx distinguishes between *differential* and *absolute* ground rent. His further division of differential rent into that resulting from *extensive* and *intensive* application of land capital is fairly standard and adds little of analytic significance. Practically speaking, of course, the actual payment received by the landlord is held to include differential and absolute rent as well as the element of interest related to land improvement.

The following partial analogy should help to convey the essence of Marx's views about the nature of differential rent and its determination. The reader is reminded of the Marxian distinction between normal (long-run) and extraordinary (short-run) profit. Recall that a given firm can, by introducing a labor-saving technique, lower its cost below that which remains socially necessary for the industry. For a time this firm will continue to sell its output at (or slightly below) the prevailing market price; one that equals the, as yet, unchanged industry cost of production rather than its own lower cost. The innovating firm will, therefore, realize something over and above a normal profit. But this extraordinary gain is a short-run phenomenon. The lure of extraordinary gain and/or fear of losing a share of the market—in short, the force of competition—makes itself felt. In the long run other firms within the industry will introduce the same or similar labor-saving techniques with a resulting drop in that industry's cost and, therefore, price. Thus extraordinary profit disappears in the long run. To put it another way: Extraordinary profit or loss is a function of the deviation of individual cost-price from social cost-price. In the long run, assuming perfect competition, individual cost-price is equal to social cost-price and extraordinary profit or loss is zero.

But this analogy was purposefully qualified as *partial* precisely because Marx drops the assumption of perfect competition in the case of agriculture. In regard to land, taken in its broadest sense, Marx writes: "It is a *monopolized* natural power which . . . is only at the command of those who can avail themselves of particular pieces of the globe and its opportunities." He takes the case of a waterfall, as an example of such "a *monopolized* natural power," and generalizes from this to differences in fertility of the various soils. The presence of such a natural power is what, according to Marx, raises labor productivity in that sphere of commodity production. This, in turn, causes the deviation of individual cost-price from social cost-price and the emergence of something like extraordinary profit. The crucial issue here is that, by definition, "natural power" is nonreproducible. The extraordinary profit resulting from the spread between individual and social cost-price need not disappear even in the long run. The fact that such natural power is "monopolized," i.e., privately owned, is why this form of long-run extraordinary profit accrues as ground rent to the landowner. Differential rent is thus a function of differences in output yield of a given area of land to which equal amounts of labor and land capital are applied. And since, as already observed, such rent is the difference between market and individual cost-price, differential rent is price-determined rather than price-determining.

Marx pressed his analysis of differential rent much further, of course. He recognized that variation in agricultural output per unit of land results not only from differences in the natural fertility but from the application of land capital to unimproved soil as well as from the locational factor. Marx took issue with, in his words, "the primitive misconception of differential rent still found among men like West, Malthus, Ricardo" based on the proposition that the best land is always the first to be cultivated. The sequence in which land is placed under cultivation depends, according to Marx, on the precise relationship existing between the fertility and locational factors; the significance of the latter being, in turn, a function of the state of development of the transportation network, markets, etc. As a consequence, Marx offers (in volume III of *Das Kapital*) an unnecessarily elaborate and extraordinarily dull set of arithmetical calculations showing the emergence of differential rent beginning with the best as well as beginning with the worst piece of land. The only analytically significant difference between the two cases appears to be that in the first the price of agricultural commodities rises with mounting pressure of population while in the second price holds constant. Marx examined such other aspects of differential rent as the impact of land improvement on existing productivity differentials and the consequence of the continued extension of cultivation of the land.

Marx went to considerable length, finally, in his analysis of intensive land cultivation. He did so because, in his words, it was "the rule for Europe" and because he wanted to account "for the woes of the landlords from Scotland to Italy, and from Southern France to Eastern Prussia." More particularly, Marx wanted to expose those forces at work which, sooner or later, would "ruin all the great landlords of Europe and the small ones into the bargain." In his theoretical analysis, Marx examines all the possible consequences in regard to the magnitude of money rent resulting from intensive cultivation of various qualities of soil. Intensive land cultivation could improve the fortunes of the landowner but only under the following set of circumstances: (1) increasing, as against falling, agricultural productivity per unit of capital investment; (2) an increase in the demand for the product such that the fall in its market price (due to the increased supply) is, relatively speaking, less than the rise in agricultural productivity. In this case money rent will rise. But Marx found precisely the opposite set of circumstances prevailing in the Europe of his day. European agriculture was characterized, according to Marx, by "falling prices and falling productivity of the additional investment of capital." None of this alters Marx's fundamental proposition, however, that differential rent associated with intensive land cultivation is no different in its basic character than that resulting from extensive cultivation.

Total ground rent received by the landowner consists not only of differential rent but a constant which Marx calls absolute rent. The latter element necessarily emerges and must be paid whenever the institutional arrangement is that of private landownership. A fundamental distinction in Marx's rent analysis appears at this point. Recall that differential rent is said to be price-determined in that it represents the differences between cost-price of the least and the progressively better grades of land. Absolute rent, on the other hand, is held to be price-determining. The market price of agricultural commodities is higher, in other words, by an amount equal to the magnitude of this absolute rent. Two premises underlie this proposition. (1) The natural endowment of the land, coupled with its improvement by the application of science and technology, is such that surplus value generated within the agricultural sector is above the average for the economy as a whole. (2) The force of competition, which normally works toward an equalization of short-run differences in rates of return, is not fully operative even in the long run in this case. The fact, in other words, that land is privately owned introduces a crucial element of monopoly within the agricultural sector of the economy. The flow of capital between the agricultural and nonagricultural sectors—which would otherwise occur and thus tend to equalize the disparate rates of return between the two spheres—is checked by the existence of private landownership. Recall that the institutional arrangement is such that the difference between the agricultural profit and that which is average for the economy as a whole goes to the landowning rather than to the agricultural capitalist. This then is the "foreign power," as Marx refers to it, which capital meets and which (for lack of incentive) impedes its flow between the two sectors. Thus it is that absolute rent enters into the price of agricultural commodities, is borne by the consumer, and ends up as a portion of the total money rent received by the landowning capitalist. Note should be taken of the fact that since this absolute rent is a constant it in no way distorts the level or relationships in regard to differential rent. Very special note should be taken of this final fact: Marx neither asserts nor assumes that the actual amount of absolute rent going to the landlord equals the full difference between surplus value in agriculture and the average profit in the economy. This differential represents no more than the upper limit. Other factors such as consumer demand, the supply of uncultivated land, etc., set the actual magnitude of absolute rent at any given point in time. But Marx's economic analysis is especially weak here and on the matter of absolute rent in general. In any case, the whole matter of rent lies outside the mainstream of the Marxian laws of Capitalist development.

XII·

Capital Flow and Capital Accumulation

Marx's general theory of Capitalist development is a theory of secular growth and decline, of expansion and contraction, of life and death. It is more. It is the heart of Marx's thesis, the essence of *Das Kapital,* that these forces are linked in a very special way. Thus the *ultimate* conclusion (the sum of a myriad of specific predictions) is best stated as two related propositions. (1) Capitalism must, because of the contradictions inherent in its productive force, inevitably destroy itself. (2) The very economic logic by which such destruction occurs lays the necessary foundation for the emergence of the Socialist system to follow.

This, of course, is why Marx was primarily interested in investigating the existing relationships among economic aggregates and less so in the behavior of the individual economic unit. He endeavored, above all, to explain the general process of commodity value creation, hence the emergence and disposition of aggregate surplus value, and thereby to expose the forces of Capitalist contradiction. This, too, is why at a certain point in his analysis Marx was forced to inject the time variable into his economic model. But it would be inaccurate (though some of the literature on this subject refers to it as such) to speak therefore of a dynamic model; for the necessary technical conditions—for example, equilibrium—are not to be found.

Marx's views on capital form an integral, indeed the critical, part of his general theory. His analysis of capital flow serves as the vehicle by means of which the process of general commodity valuation and aggregate surplus value formation is exposed. It constitutes, as well, the theoretical framework within which Marx's observations regarding innovation, changes in the organic composition of capital, the falling rate of profit, and short-term crisis must be understood. Marx's capital accumulation model is equally essential to the comprehension of his propositions pertaining to the economy's secular growth and decline, the precise nature of the instability inherent in the Capitalist productive force, and all that follows.

CAPITAL FLOW

We turn first, therefore, to Marx's analysis of capital flow. He had in mind here the rotation of capital through the total exchange process; which, for purposes of analysis, is divided into the sphere of production and the sphere of circulation. It is especially important, in this connection, to recall Marx's point that commodity and thus surplus value are generated solely within the productive sphere. The fact remains that capital flows through both spheres and involves the element of time. It is more meaningful, therefore, to conceive of this process in a temporal sense: as the total *period* of production consisting of the *time* of production and the *time* of circulation. The former is that interval during which the commodity is actually produced. The latter is the remaining time during which (because the resulting output is sold for money) the money capital for the next round of production is generated.

Thus far the term "capital" has been intentionally left unqualified with but one exception: the earlier noted distinction between the money (and landowning) capitalist and the industrial capitalist. Our concern now is entirely with industrial capital and the several transformations which, according to Marx, this capital undergoes as it circulates through the total period of production. Industrial capital, as it enters and subsequently leaves the process, takes the form of *money* capital. This is simply Marx's way of denoting the monetary fund which is in the hands of the industrial capitalist before and following the completion of an act of production. Capital serves a second special function, called *commodity* capital, at another stage in the process. It takes the form of the inputs—labor and the means of production—as well as the final but as yet unsold output. At yet another and the narrowest stage, commodity capital takes the form of *productive* capital. It is called that during the interval when the inputs are in the process of being shaped into the finished product. The important point to recognize here is that these stages do not represent entirely different or mutually exclusive categories of capital; rather, they are different terms which Marx attaches to the general class of industrial capital as it circulates.

Assuming, for the moment, that there are no impediments to the movement of industrial capital, Marx distinguishes between the case of "simple" and "progressive" capital flow. Here, again, the purpose is primarily analytic. The difference hinges on what the industrial capitalist is assumed to do in respect to the monetized value of the resulting surplus product. Simple reproduction occurs where the capitalist spends the full sum of this surplus money capital on personal consumption. Thus the amount of industrial capital available for circulation remains unchanged between one and another total period of production. Progressive reproduction occurs where the capitalist retains a portion of the surplus for purposes of investment. In this instance the amount of industrial capital available for circulation increases between one and the next total period of production. The latter is, of course, what Marx tells us actually occurs as dicated by the logic of the Capitalist productive force. The capitalist must accumulate, says Marx, for how else did he become a capitalist, how else can he remain one, or hope to become an even larger capitalist?

Continuity and/or growth of Capitalist production, hence the uninterrupted movement of capital through the process, is held to be a function of three related variables. (1) The most important and general of these is the existing relationship between the supply of and the demand for commodities. Marx's categorical rejection of Say's law, that supply generates its own demand, is well known. Thus the flow of capital is said to be impeded whenever market demand proves to be insufficient relative to the existing volume of production. Marx refers to the resulting idleness of commodity capital as a "glut." (2) The second is the state of the capital-goods market. Industrial capitalists will be forced to "hoard" (to use Marx's terminology) a portion of their money capital in the face of an existing shortage in the requisite means of production. (3) The final variable relates to the purely technical character of the production function. The magnitude of that part of the realized surplus money capital which the industrial capitalist has and wishes to plow back into the process may, for any one period, be sufficient in terms of the technical requirements of production. That part of the surplus which, therefore, is held out over several periods of production Marx calls "latent" capital. These in sum are the three factors which operate in such a way, according to Marx, as to obstruct the smooth and continuous circulation of capital through or from one to another total period of production.

A major objective of this aspect of Marx's analysis is to show the particular relationship existing between capital circulation and the magnitude of surplus value. In this case the prime variables are (1) the *ratio* of the time of production to the time of circulation and (2) capital *turnover time*. In order to develop this side of Marx's argument it is necessary to delve somewhat deeper into his concept of the total period of production; especially its second or time-of-circulation component. First, however, recall that by the time of production Marx meant the period during which the physical goods are actually being created. It is that portion of the total period when "live" labor, working in conjunction with natural agents and the means of production, generates commodity value and thus surplus value. It is, as well, the sum of the working days required for the completion of a given stock of output. The industrial capitalist must, of course, expend the necessary capital to finance this time of production, i.e., pay wages to labor, purchase the requisite material inputs, etc. The length of the time span involved is clearly an element in determining the magnitude of the capital required for a specified time of production. What then, according to Marx, sets the particular time of production associated with a given expenditure of capital?

It is said to be a function of three factors: (1) technology, (2) banking and credit, and (3) marketing facilities. Thus the more advanced the level of technology, the higher the order of the organic composition of capital, the shorter *(ceteris paribus)* is the time span in question. The same, in essence, is held to be true in regard to the state of development of credit and marketing facilities. In the case of the time of production, finally, the full amount of the socially necessary labor embodied in such production is a cost and therefore enters into the normal price of the commodity.

Let us take a closer look now at Marx's propositions regarding the time of circulation. Industrial capital, though it necessarily circulates through the entire process, is nonproductive as it flows through the time-of-circulation segment of the total period of production. To be more specific: Marx defines this component as the time during which capital is employed for such purposes as the storing of inputs and the finished product, transportation to markets, and the more general elements associated with the sale of commodities. In none of these cases, however, does such capital generate commodity or surplus value. But this is not to say that Marx overlooked certain of the costs involved in this case or that he ignored the relationship of mercantile to industrial capital. He considered two general classes of costs: (1) expenses arising during the time of production, and (2) expenses associated with the time of circulation. The former enter, without qualification, into the normal price of commodities.

The matter is not quite as clear cut in regard to the expenses of circulation. The following terminology (not Marx's but consistent with his analysis) may be helpful in conveying the point at hand. Capital may be said to be productive, unproductive, or nonproductive. It is unproductive when used up in making something which has no use value. It is productive when its use results in the generation of commodity and therefore surplus value. It is nonproductive when its employment is essential to the total process of production but where such capital does not of itself result in the creation of commodities and thus a surplus. Marx accorded mercantile capital the status of being nonproductive, though, unfortunately, he used the word unproductive. In any case, his was the classic notion that services—be they those of doctors, teachers, or merchants—are necessary but not productive in the sense that they add nothing to the size of the total physical product.

Two of the three categories of expenses of circulation are, nevertheless, viewed by Marx to be price-determining. Recall that it is the second or cost-of-production version of his theory of price which is central to the Marxian economic model. The rationale for excluding one such category of expense while including the other two in the pricing process is to be found in the further distinction between fixed and variable cost. Marx argues along the following lines. There are certain resource-using operations such as clerical work, bookkeeping, merchandising, etc., involved in the sphere of circulation. The costs arising from such operations not only are relatively fixed in the short run, but, because of improving technology, decline over the course of Capitalist development. These cost elements do *not*, therefore, enter into the price of commodities. But costs associated with holding (inputs as well as output) inventory and transporting goods to market vary with the scale of production; or, more generally, with the stage of Capitalist development. Thus the value equivalent of the labor power embodied in the construction and maintenance of warehouses, transport facilities, etc., enters into commodity price.

The immediate relevance of the exposition above lies, first, in the significance of the relationship between the ratio Tp/Tc (time of production/time of circulation) to surplus value. All other things being equal, the amount of surplus value that a specified industrial capital can generate in a given time period is a function of the existing ratio Tp/Tc. The principal factors determining the time span in each case have already been noted. Since capital is productive only in the time of production, however, the shorter the circulation time the greater is the amount of surplus value realized by the given capital.

Surplus value is also a function, as noted earlier, of the number of times the capital which is advanced circulates through the entire period of production. Here, for purposes of analysis, Marx equates the year (as the temporal unit) with the total period of production and both with what he calls the time of capital turnover. The question can then be put: How many times does a given amount of capital turn over during the year as it rotates through the total period of production? Suppose we take the hypothetical figure 3 as the number of capital turnovers. In this case a given amount of industrial capital is used or serves to complete 3 rounds of production and sale of a specified commodity during 1 year. Thus (and even before we delve into the further complexities involved) it is clear that a direct relationship exists between the number of such turnovers, the amount of capital available to be advanced, and the magnitude and rate of surplus value.

One of the complexities has to do with the fact that the capital advanced for the year is not all used up during any one round of commodity production. Marx recognized, of course, that in the long view any specified unit of capital is finally exhausted. The issue is that in the short run some part of the annual capital is used up and some portion is not. For purposes of analysis, therefore, Marx distinguishes between two types of such capital: (1) that which is consumed in a given round of commodity production or *circulating* capital; (2) that which remains in its factor form or *fixed* capital. This distinction enables Marx to make the critical point that the fraction of the yearly capital advanced which is available for employment in the actual production of commodities is a function of the ratio of circulating to fixed capital. The point is critical precisely because of the familiar Marxian prop-

osition that commodity and therefore surplus value is generated only
within the sphere of production. The particular relevance of the above to
the question under consideration, that is, the relationship of capital turnover
to surplus value, may be stated in one of two Marxian forms. (1) The greater
the portion of the annual capital advanced which is used up (i.e., the higher
the fraction of circulating capital to total), the greater the number of capital
turnovers for the year, the larger is the magnitude of the annual surplus
value generated by a given advance of industrial capital. (2) Recalling the
earlier concept of the organic composition of capital: Surplus value is
generated solely by the employment of variable, as against constant, capital.
The annual volume of surplus value is thus determined by the amount of
variable capital employed in production; which, in turn, is a function of
the number of capital turnovers within the year.

That which follows is, in the main, a summary of Marx's views on capital
circulation. Marx was primarily concerned here with the process by which
industrial capital reproduces itself over the course of Capitalist development.
He dismisses simple reproduction as uncharacteristic of the system and
concentrates on the progressive case which involves the reinvestment of a
fraction of surplus value as industrial capital. He employs as an analytic
device the total period of production through which industrial capital flows.
Injecting the time variable, Marx divides the total period into time of production and time of circulation. Industrial capital necessarily circulates
through both components but generates commodity and surplus value
solely within the time of production. Capital assumes different forms (industrial, money, commodity, and productive) *seriatim* as it rotates within
the total period of production. But the character of the Capitalist productive
force is such that, in reality, the movement of such capital is not necessarily
continuous. Factor shortages arise (hoard), aggregate supply and demand
do not coincide (glut), and the technical requirements of scale (latent capital)
obstruct the smooth flow of capital through the total period of production.
In regard to the valuation process: Commodity price is equal to the cost
of production which, in turn, includes all expenses associated with the
time of production and those of storage and transportation associated
with the time of circulation.

The focus of Marx's analysis of capital circulation is on the relationship
between this flow, most particularly capital turnover, and surplus value.
Here there are three basic propositions. (Since Marx was intent on devising
a measure for the degree of Capitalist exploitation, where possible the
relationships involved will be expressed in terms of the *rate* rather than the
absolute magnitude of surplus value. Recall that the annual rate of surplus
value is the absolute amount of such surplus generated during the year/the
value of the *variable* capital *advanced* for that same time interval.) (1) The
annual rate of surplus value is a function, first of the ratio of the time of

production to the time of circulation. The shorter the circulation time, therefore, the higher the rate of surplus value. (2) The annual rate of surplus value is also a function of the number of capital turnovers during the year. Thus the greater the number of such turnovers during the total period of production the higher the annual rate of surplus value. (3) Marx maintained, finally, that as the Capitalist productive force develops both time spans— that of production as well as that of circulation—shorten. From this it follows that the number of capital turnovers increases and thus, *ceteris paribus,* the amount of surplus value also rises. But, as the saying goes, *ceteris* is not always *paribus,* as we are about to see in our investigation of the Marxian model of capital accumulation.

CAPITAL ACCUMULATION

The fact that the totality of Marx's economic model contains both the element of positive economic growth *and* crises, leading to ultimate collapse, does not and need not constitute a contradiction. The point may well be obvious to most students of Marxian economics. It is mentioned only in order to dispel the vague and popular notion still persisting that somehow the laws of Capitalist contradiction necessarily imply the secular shrinkage of all or most of the economic magnitudes over the course of Capitalist development. The real issue, as it concerns us here, is what determines the rate at which the Capitalist economy grows even as it finally contradicts itself out of existence.

According to Marx, the growth rate of the Capitalist economy is a function of two variables. (1) One is the absolute size of the surplus generated by the economy as a whole. Recall, taking the macro view, that the absolute amount of surplus value for a given time period is the difference between the total value of the output and the total cost of production. (2) The second variable is what the capitalists, as a class, actually do with that surplus. The answer, at least in first approximation, is quite simple. Marx tells us in a particularly famous passage in volume I of *Das Kapital:* "Accumulate, accumulate! save, save, i.e., reconvert the greatest possible portion of surplus-value, or surplus product into capital! Accumulation for accumulation's sake, production for production's sake ... [is] ... the historical mission of the bourgeoisie." Marx meant nothing more by this than that capitalists are driven by the logic of their class position to reinvest or turn a portion of their surplus value into industrial capital; with the aim, of course, of earning still more surplus value and so on. We turn, therefore, to a somewhat more detailed examination of Marx's views regarding capital formation. In doing so we take as given Marx's premises both as to the nature of Capitalist property relations and the technical character of the production function.

In this portion of his analysis, therefore, Marx does two things. (1) He divides the economy into two generalized sectors or "departments." Department I produces only capital goods and Department II only consumer goods. In the latter Marx distinguishes further between the production of worker-type goods and luxury items purchased by capitalists. This division is consistent with one of the many assumptions underlying his analysis of capital formation. In this instance it is that all workers receive a normal or subsistence wage. (2) Marx examines the process of capital formation in two different models. Many of the assumptions, as we shall see, are common to both models but a few differ. The critical difference between the "simple" and "progressive" reproduction model has already been noted. Recall that in the first the capitalist is assumed to spend his entire surplus value on items of personal consumption. In the second, the realistic case, he saves, that is, turns a portion of the surplus value into industrial capital.

We begin with a brief account of the simple reproduction model which Marx worked out solely for purposes of analysis. Here Marx assumes a given magnitude of total output which is the sum of all that is produced by Departments I and II. Each department requires, of course, a given amount of constant and variable capital for that level of output; the latter amount determining the magnitude of surplus value resulting from such production. The total value of that produced by each department, hence the value of the output for the economy, is equal to the familiar Marxian $c + v + s$. In the simple reproduction model Marx assumes that the order of the organic composition of capital, therefore the rate of profit, is the same not only within but between the two departments. He assumes, finally, that price relationships and the state of technology remain unchanged.

The fact that in the second case, in violation of his own earlier logic, Marx assumes a different order of the organic composition of capital and rate of profit as between Department I and II seriously affects the internal consistency of his progressive reproduction model. This issue arises because in version two of his value-price theory—the one central to the entire economic analysis—Marx insists that at long-run equilibrium the rate of profit must be equal throughout the economy. At no time, however, does he relinquish the proposition that the rate of profit is a function of the organic composition of capital.

Be that as it may, Marx first proceeds to trace the nature of the exchange relationships in the case of simple reproduction. Recall that Department II produces only consumer goods and Department I only capital goods. The exchange relationships involved are as follows. (1) Capitalists of Department I spend the full amount of their surplus value on the purchase of consumer goods produced by Department II. (2) Workers of Department I spend the full sum of their wage incomes on the purchase of consumer goods produced by Department II. (3) Capitalists of Department II purchase the requisite amount of capital goods from Department I. (4) Capitalists and workers of Department II spend the entire amount of their surplus and wage incomes, respectively, on the purchase of consumer goods from Department II.

Marx's prime purpose here was to point out the basic exchange condition necessary for the stability of the Capitalist system. Stability is defined, in this case, as the period-to-period reproduction of a given magnitude of capital and hence total output. This implies, of course, neither economic growth nor decline. The stability condition may be expressed in a variety of ways. Two of the briefest are: that the constant capital requirements of Department II be equal to the difference between the total output and the constant capital needs of Department I; or that there be an exchange of value equivalences such that the value of the capital goods sold by Department I to Department II is equal to the value of the consumer goods sold by Department II to Department I. But it was precisely Marx's intent to establish the fact that the above "premise of simple reproduction is irreconcilable with capitalist production"—in a word, that this is not actually the way in which capitalists behave or the manner in which the Capitalist system operates.

Thus Marx came to elaborate a progressive reproduction model in order to reveal the "true" nature and consequence of the Capitalist process of capital accumulation. Since this case is somewhat more complex than the first, Marx's exact example, including his arithmetic, will be relied upon here. The introduction of additional or changes in assumptions will be pointed out as necessary. This growth model is a two-sector model (as is the simple reproduction one), with Department I representing the capital goods and Department II the consumer goods industries.

Marx begins by positing the following initial situation and hypothetical figures: a total output, for a fixed time period, of 9,000 units of which Department I produces 6,000 and Department II 3,000 units. The capital composition of Department I is given as $4,000c + 1,000v + 1,000s$ and that of Department II as $1,500c + 750v + 750s$. Note that while the rate of *surplus value* is the same both within and between the two departments, the rate of *profit* is assumed to be equal only within each department and to differ as between Department I and II. Thus, in reference to the figures above, the rate of surplus value (s/v) is 100 percent for both departments. But the organic composition of capital ($c/c + v$) of Department I is 80 percent and that of Department II 66⅔ percent. The rate of profit ($s/c + v$) of Department I, therefore, is 20 percent while that of Department II is 33⅓ percent. Marx assumes next that the capitalists of Department I wish to spend one half the 1,000 surplus on items of personal consumption and to accumulate, i.e., turn into industrial capital, the remaining one half. Note, once more, the following points in connection with this particular illustration. (1) The process of capital accumulation *initiates* within Department I and, as we shall see, compels accumulation out of surplus within Department II. (2) Both the state of technology and the rate of accumulation for Department I, 50 percent in this illustration, are held as constants. Given all the above it is now possible to follow the process by which, in Marx's words, "accumulation resolves itself into the reproduction of capital on a progressively increasing scale."

This portion of Marx's analysis starts with the proposition that the capitalists of Department I decide to invest 500 of the 1,000 surplus in such a way as to add 400 to the existing 4,000 of constant and 100 to the 1,000 of variable capital. In one particular, however, the behavior of Department I's capitalists remains qualitatively the same as that posited in the simple reproduction model. They seek to exchange that quantity of producer's goods, equal to Department I's $v + s$, for an equal value of consumer goods produced by Department II. Following the initial act of accumulation, therefore, Department I wishes to sell a quantity of producer goods represented by the figure 1,600 ($1,100v + 500s$) in exchange for its value equivalence in consumer goods. The immediate problem arising, however, is that Department II's constant capital requirement remains unchanged at $1,500c$.

Thus—if this exchange process is to continue—the capitalists of Department II are forced to make the necessary adaptation. The adjustment takes the form of a cut in personal consumption equal to the difference between Department I's initial $1,000v$ and its current $1,100v$. But this can only come out of Department II's surplus and thereby reduces the existing surplus from $750s$ to $650s$. The fact that the magnitude of Department II's constant capital is thus increased from 1,500 to 1,600 necessitates a second adjustment. Technological considerations compel Department II to increase, accordingly, the amount of its variable capital (in this case by $50v$). Again, however, this can only be met out of existing surplus, which is thereby reduced still further to $600s$. But note now that the sum of $c + v$ for both departments has risen from 5,000 to 5,500 for Department I and from 2,250 to 2,400 for Department II. Thus we see the first consequence of the initial act of accumulation: an increase in the value of the total capital, for the economy as a whole, by 650.

A larger capital fund with which to enter the next time period means, of course, a corresponding increase in total output. Assuming, as before, that the rate of exploitation is the same or 100 percent: Department I will show a surplus of 1,100 and Department II a surplus of 800. Looking now at the capital structure of both departments, we see that the total output for this time period is 9,800, or 800 above that of the initial round of production. Total output for the next round of production (based on the same assumptions and using the identical method of calculation) would then rise from 9,800 to 10,780 or by 980; and so on progressively with no theoretically determinable end. Thus Marx considers not only the simple process of capital formation but, by injecting a rate of accumulation as the independent variable, accounts for Capitalism's economic growth.

Wherein, then, does the problem lie? The answer in this case is complicated by two special factors. The first is that there is more than one capital accumulation model in this portion of Marx's capital theory. The difference hinges, in the main, on whether constancy or variability is assumed in regard to the rate of accumulation and/or technology. Practically speaking, however, there is no doubt but that Marx regarded secular improvement in technology and a progressively increasing rate of accumulation as most representative of the real world of Capitalism. The other factor, as we shall see, is that both the clarity and validity of Marx's argument here are damaged by certain errors in his analysis. Be that as it may, it will be helpful to begin by recalling those elements of the institutional framework and those propositions on the basis of which Marx reasoned in the current context.

The following, highly generalized, statements are all that appear necessary for the purpose at hand:

1. There are two and only two classes in society, namely, workers and capitalists;
2. Class membership, hence economic behavior, is determined solely on the basis of ownership versus exclusion from ownership of the means of livelihood;
3. Possession of money capital, as against land, is dominant at this stage of historical development;
4. The system results in the distribution or division of the value of the total social product into two basic parts—wages to labor and surplus value to capitalists;
5. The propensity to consume of the working class (subsistence wage) is unity and that of the capitalist class something less than unity;
6. Economic growth, its rate and sustaining power, is a function of *net* investment. (Marx assumes the necessary conditions such as a corresponding growth of labor force, provision for depreciation, etc.).

Given the institutional arrangement, as above, it follows that the net investment necessary for economic growth must be made, can only come, out of surplus. To put it somewhat differently: If economic growth is to occur it is the capitalists, as a class, who must spend less than the full amount of their income (surplus) on personal consumption. How and why capitalists behave as they do in regard to the disposition of this surplus, its division between consumption and investment, is thus the crucial question of the moment. Of course, capitalists must first "eat." Consumption is, nevertheless, treated as the dependent variable in this analysis. For, according to Marx, the fraction of any given surplus thus spent on consumption is a function of two interacting variables: (1) the rate of accumulation, and (2) the organic composition of capital.

In reference to the rate of accumulation, Marx writes: "At the historical dawn of capitalist production . . . avarice, desire to get rich, are the ruling passions. . . . When a certain stage of development has been reached, a conventional degree of prodigality . . . becomes a business necessity to the 'unfortunate' capitalist." As Capitalism matures, in other words, accumulation becomes a habit, deeply ingrained in the logic of class position. Moreover, Marx tells us, once this process gets under way the rate of accumulation tends to increase. Two causal factors are suggested here: (1) an interaction between accumulation and the organic composition of capital, and (2) concentration and centralization of capital. Marx's reasoning in regard to the first of these is as follows. Accumulation increases the absolute amount of available capital and thus the scale of production. Larger scale, a more capitalist mode of production, stimulates a higher order of the organic composition of capital, more surplus, and thus still more accumulation and so on progressively. Marx's endeavor to establish such a relationship, as we shall soon see, turns out to be tenuous at best and a case of faulty economic logic at its worst. His reasoning in regard to the second of these two forces is more perceptive. The entire process, as described above, is said to result in the amassing of progressively greater magnitudes of capital into fewer and fewer capitalist hands. Marx refers to this as the process of capital *concentration*. Marx was well aware that the laws of capitalist inheritance served as a countervailing force in this regard. He found, however, that the resulting capital dispersion was more than neutralized by yet another force called *centralization*. Larger capitalists acquire, by virtue of size, certain competitive advantages over smaller ones. The larger, the more financially secure the firm the better are the terms and the more easily is credit attainable. This makes possible further expansion of scale, still more credit, and so on in an upward spiral. At the same time, larger capitalists are in a better position to introduce improved technology (i.e., to innovate in pursuit of short-run extraordinary gain) as well as to survive periods of general crisis. Under a variety of circumstances, for instance, they engage in short-term price cutting in order to expand their own market. All of this is, naturally, at the expense of the smaller capitalists who are thereby "swallowed up" by the "giants." More and more capital is thus amassed into progressively fewer hands with a resulting increase in the rate of capital accumulation.

It is at this point in Marx's account of the basic cause of the capital problem that his purpose in having presented the simple reproduction model emerges at its clearest. Recall that here stability, the simple reproduction of capital, is attained because capitalists are assumed to spend the full amount of the surplus on personal consumption. In this case, of course, there is no net investment and thus no economic growth. Recall, as well, the technical condition for such stability as set down by Marx: that the sum of the value of Department I's variable capital and surplus be equal to the value of Department II's constant capital requirement. The problem arises in Marx's version of the real world of Capitalism because progressive accumulation takes place. Driven by the desire (more accurately by economic necessity) for surplus value, and still more surplus value, capitalists accumulate to the point of a critical imbalance. The fundamental cause of the imbalance is that the very fact of progressive accumulation denies, at least fails to guarantee, the stability condition given above.

A somewhat less formal, yet reasonably correct, summary of the situation may be:

1. The working class (given a propensity to consume of unity) in any circumstance spends all of its wage income on consumption;
2. This leaves the decision regarding the division of the surplus between investment and consumption entirely to the capitalists;
3. Progressive accumulation of capital results in a corresponding increase in productive capacity;
4. The critical imbalance occurs at the nodal point where, for a specified capital outlay, the fraction of the surplus that capitalists accumulate exceeds that which they consume;
5. Thus the capitalists do not and the workers cannot make up the necessary difference.

SOME CONCLUDING COMMENTS ON MARX'S
APPROACH TO CAPITAL

What Marx set out to do here was, in essence, "to embrace the whole process of reproduction" with the aid of an analytical device simulating François Quesnay's famed *Tableau économique*. But certain weaknesses in this endeavor become apparent even if most of Marx's basic premises and propositions about the institutional setting and the laws of Capitalist development remain unchallenged. Marx makes certain assumptions, shifts others, and asserts particular causal relationships which are either unwarranted, violate consistency, or, at best, are not convincingly established. At the base of these deficiencies, or so it seems to this writer, lies the now familiar value-price problem. It is an issue, one might add, which not only troubled Marx but remains to plague many who try to follow his economic reasoning. The following points, therefore, are deserving of special note.

1. Recall, once more, that it is the second (the exchange value = cost of production = price) version of Marx's value theory which is central to his general model of the Capitalist economy. Logical consistency would seem to dictate, therefore, that his analysis of departmental exchanges in both the simple and accumulation models should have been expressed in the form

of price. Instead, as we have observed, the analysis in both two-sector models is in terms of value rather than price equivalences. The difficulty that confronted Marx in this case is not hard to surmise. The use of price rather than value in the simple reproduction model would not have enabled him to arrive at the neat equilibrium solution which otherwise emerges. But having once used value in the first instance he could not, with any logic, have shifted to price in a growth model.

2. In his simple reproduction model Marx assumes an identity in the organic composition of capital and thus in the rates of profit as between the two departments. By assuming the opposite in the case of his growth model, however, Marx leaves himself open to the following inconsistency. A difference in the organic composition of capital as between Department I and II necessarily means a disparity in the rates of profits between the two sectors in the growth model. Yet, as we have already observed, Marx insisted with some force that Capitalism could never function or survive unless profit rates tended toward equality in the long run and for the economy as a whole.

3. It is perfectly apparent that Marx saw the real world of Capitalism as one of continually improving technology, a progressively increasing rate of capital accumulation and, therefore, economic growth; even as, taking the very long view, Capitalism was contradicting itself out of existence. But the extent to which he succeeded in correctly establishing the functional relationships and interactions among the relevant variables in the above regard is open to serious question. Specifically, these variables are: (1) the utility functions of the two classes, (2) the organic composition of capital, (3) the rate of exploitation, (4) the rate of profit, (5) technology, (6) the rate of accumulation, (7) concentration and centralization of capital, and (8) the rate of economic growth. Only a few of the issues involved here can be touched upon in the present context. Marx does little more than assert a causal relationship and interaction between the rate of capital accumulation and improvement in technology. Assuming the most realistic case of an increasing rate of accumulation and improvement in technology, Marx is altogether too vague as to what this really means in regard to the growth rate of the economy. Concentration and centralization of capital are offered as important factors leading to a continuous improvement in technology. At the same time, according to Marx, as the order of the organic composition of capital rises the rate of profit must decline. What, then, in the face of a declining rate of profit can be known about the growth rate of the economy? Marx's views on capital leave many other questions unanswered; to say nothing of the basic premises and propositions mentioned above.

Taken as such, therefore, Marx's analysis of the role of capital in the economic process is not particularly interesting. It appears all the less so when viewed in relation to present-day capital theory. More important, as we have seen, it is weak by the theoretical standards of Marx's own day. It falls short in logical consistency and predictive value even as compared with numerous other parts of Marxian economic theory.

Part III

XIII·

An Introduction to the Process of Capital Contradiction

Time and again, because the point is so crucial, it has been observed that the central purpose of Marx's economic analysis was to offer an ailing world the "scientific proof" (hence assurance of salvation) of Capitalism's inevitable if not imminent demise. The material presented thus far in Part II of this volume constitutes no more than the necessary theoretical framework within and on the basis of which Marx reasoned to his final conclusions. We are now ready to follow along these last paths of Marxian economic logic. What, in other words, did Marx maintain would occur over the course of Capitalist development? What, to be more specific, is the precise nature of the contradictions that Marx found to be inherent in the Capitalist productive force and on the basis of which he prognosticated doom for the existing system?

In all that follows there are several points that should be kept in mind.

1. The time element, i.e., the various stages of Capitalist development, plays a considerably greater and more significant role in this portion of Marxian analysis than heretofore.

2. Many forces are at work, many things occur and interact simultaneously. The rate of profit is said to fall, the size of the industrial reserve army grows, international markets expand, the interest rate declines, to mention but a few of the factors. The mechanics of exposition makes it necessary, of course, to focus on a limited number of factors and interactions at a time.

3. It is also well to note the presence in this part of Marx's analysis of certain "leads and lags" at the same point in historical time. According to Marx, for example, the agricultural side of the productive force is measurably less developed than the industrial side *at all stages* of Capitalist development. This is why peasant political consciousness is said always to lag behind that of the industrial proletariat.

4. It is of particular interest to observe the manner in which Marx links the process of Capitalist contradiction with the emergence of Socialism. Capitalism, in Marx's view, not only destroys itself but in that very process generates the necessary conditions for the emergence of the next main stage

of history. The following Marxian reasoning should suffice to illustrate the point. It is part of the logic of the Capitalist productive force that over time more and more workers are employed under a single factory roof, crowded into urban slums, etc. It is equally the case that such workers will communicate with one another, form associations, and thereby develop the necessary class consciousness. Concentration of capital in progressively fewer hands causes a literate or educated element to be spun off into the working class. There will thus emerge a segment within the working class which will be able not only to lead the revolution but manage the affairs of a Socialist society once it appears.

5. Observe, too, Marx's endeavor to relate changes in the economic base with corresponding changes in the social and political superstructure of Capitalist society. The role played by the state, the revolutionary rather than the economic role of the trade union, the appearance of the Communist party, are all cases in point.

6. Note, finally, that there are critical segments of this portion of Marx's analysis where his meaning, point, or prediction is unclear, capable of varying interpretation or, indeed, in direct contradiction to a view taken elsewhere. This represents a glaring shortcoming and, perhaps, also the mark of a prophet. As far as possible an endeavor is made, in that which follows, to throw some additional light on these penumbric areas of Marxian analysis.

With these points in mind we turn now to an examination of Marx's views on the major forces of Capitalist contradictions.

XIV·

The Secular Decline in the General Rate of Profit

THE BASIC ISSUE
Marx's prediction that in the long run the general rate of profit must decline is well known. The importance that he attached to this phenomenon is equally well recognized. The primary concern of this chapter is with the analytic path along which Marx arrived at this conclusion. The basic cause behind the fall in the rate of profit is given as the "necessity" on the part of capitalists to innovate. The consequence of this is said to be reflected in the entire fabric of Capitalist society. "The bourgeoisie cannot exist," reads one of the classic statements in the *Communist Manifesto*, "without constantly revolutionizing the instruments of production, and thereby the relations of production, and with them the whole relations of society."

A note regarding Marx's general position on innovation before discussing its ascribed role within the Capitalist system. Innovation as such is neither undesirable nor even a necessary cause of economic instability. The innovating process *per se* is independent of the existing system. New ideas and methods of production result from the general development of science and technology. Indeed, a Socialist productive force, once unfettered by Capitalist property relations and contradictions, will cause science and technology to flourish to a degree as yet unknown in human history. It is quite another matter as long as Capitalism continues to exist. At the same time, as we shall see below, Marx carefully absolved the innovating capitalist of making a positive contribution.

Recall Marx's dictum that as a class the bourgeoisie can only exist as long as profits and still more profits are forthcoming. Thus the capitalist's single concern, in this context, is with his *rate* of profit. Recall, as well, that by the rate of profit Marx meant the net return accruing to that capital which is advanced for the production and marketing of commodities ($p = s/c + v$). The capitalist, Marx tells us, behaves as he must being driven by the economic logic of his class position. Capitalists spring into existence by an initial ("primitive") act of capital accumulation and are thereafter compelled, as a condition of survival, to accumulate at a progressively greater rate in a constant pursuit of a higher rate of profit. That same logic equally compels them to react in a given pattern in the face of the secular decline in the profit rate.

But Marx was not content to rest his case with the ordinary proposition that capitalists are somehow motivated to innovate or that innovations are simply disruptive. He sought to establish the fact that they have no other choice even though, in the long run, this necessarily causes the rate of profit to fall still further. His intent, quite clearly, was to point to this as one of the important contradictions inherent in the Capitalist productive force. The initial reasoning in this case need not detain us long since most of it follows from material already covered in some detail. Very briefly, then, Marx maintained that the capitalist's continuous search for higher profits drives him to seek means by which to produce more cheaply. In this case the cost reduction is the result of some technological improvement, i.e., a higher order of the organic composition of capital. For the sake of analysis, therefore, let us take a given industry and assume an initial act of cost reduction by one of its firms. The innovating firm thereby realizes an extraordinary gain, that is, something over and above normal profit. This is so because the labor time required for the production of a given output for the innovating firm has fallen relative to that which remains "socially necessary" for the industry. Three factors, however, assure that the other firms within the industry will follow suit: (1) common knowledge that the commodity in question can be produced more cheaply; (2) the lure of extraordinary profits resulting from such cost reduction; (3) the fear of losing or the desire to gain a larger share of the market. In a word, the force of competition is at work. Invariably, however, a point is reached where the bulk of the firms within that industry also come to employ the same or even superior technology. As a consequence the "socially necessary" labor time for the industry as a whole falls, and, therefore, normal price must decline correspondingly. Thus it is, Marx concluded, that the fiercest of competition among capitalists is always at work to wipe out the extraordinary profits resulting from acts of innovation. This being so, says Marx, there is no alternative open to the capitalists but to innovate again and again, to seek further cost reduction, with the same long-run consequence. The necessity to innovate regardless of final outcome is thus given as the prime cause of the secular fall in the rate of profit.

Marx suggests a contributory factor which deserves brief mention. It concerns the specific cost associated with technological change. Capital obsolescence can be assigned a value, according to Marx. With the introduction of technological change, the worth of the existing technology depreciates by an amount equal to the difference between the constant capital value of the "old" and the "new" technique of production. The "true" rate of profit is less by the amount of this charge for capital depreciation. Consistent with an earlier position, Marx argued that both the rate of technological change and the complexity of the physical capital progressively increase over the course of Capitalist development. The resulting rise in the cost of capital obsolescence, Marx concluded, thus serves to depress the rate of profit beyond the prime cause of its decline.

It is one thing to say, as Marx did, that the Capitalist innovating process is self-generating. It is quite another to establish as a "law" the proposition that as a direct consequence of the innovating process the long-term rate of profit must necessarily decline. This, as well, Marx had set himself to do. Several points should be recognized in advance of following through Marx's more detailed argument here. In the final analysis, Marx avoided the easy arithmetic proof of the "law" of falling profits which can be made to follow from the erroneous assumption of an unchanging rate of surplus value. He admitted the fact and coped with the problem that technological improvement means a higher order of the organic composition of capital; which, in turn, causes the rate of surplus value to vary. The fuller implication of this to the "law" of profits will be brought out shortly. Marx's use of the word "law" in relation to the predicted fall in the general profit rate carries with it an element of poetic license. He admitted as much, as we shall see, implicitly if not explicitly. However firmly Marx the slogan-maker may have declared a fall in the rate of profit to be inevitable, a scientific law, Marx the economist was considerably more cautious and modest in his prediction. He distinguished, first of all, between short- and long-term movements in the normal profit rate. More importantly, he observed that a multitude of interacting variables bore on the movement of the general rate of profit. The force of some, he said, causes the rate of profit to fall. The force of certain others explains the upward movement in the profit rate. The most important of these forces will be specified below. The main point of the moment is that in this conflict of opposing forces—on balance and in the long run—the forces causing the rate of profit to fall win out over those which cause it to rise. We are now prepared to take a somewhat more systematic look at what, according to Marx, lies behind this *tendency* of the general profit rate to decline over the course of Capitalist development.

FACTORS BEHIND THE TENDENCY
OF THE PROFIT RATE TO DECLINE

The observation has already been made that Marx avoided the glaring inconsistency that results from the assumption of a constant rate of surplus value in the face of a higher order of the organic composition of capital. A somewhat different problem therefore emerges. Marx was the first to admit that Capitalism is characterized by a high rate of technological change which "raises the productiveness of labor to an extraordinary degree." Each such advance in labor productivity, to follow Marx's reasoning, reduces the fraction of the standard work day required for worker subsistence. Recall that the *normal* wage is always held equal to subsistence. Thus an increase in labor productivity necessarily raises the absolute sum of surplus and thereby the rate of surplus value. The higher the order of the organic composition of capital the greater is the rate of exploitation of the working class.

But if all value resulting from increases in labor productivity ends up as surplus why, even on balance, should the rate of profit fall? Marx's answer, in its essence, is that the rate of surplus value varies directly *but not even proportionately* with increases in labor productivity. He offered the following numerical example: *"Two laborers, each working twelve hours daily, cannot produce the same mass of surplus value as twenty-four laborers, each working only two hours,* even if they could live on air and did not have to work for themselves at all." [Italics mine]. Thus Marx arrived at this falling rate of profit prediction by injecting a dampening factor into the admittedly positive functional relationship between changes in the organic composition of capital and the rate of surplus value.

Did Marx really have any other choice, given his earlier premises and propositions, but to conclude that the long-term rate of profit must decline? True enough, the profit *rate* is measured in terms of the total capital advanced. But only the variable component is value-generating and surplus value is the single source of all capitalist income. How then could the rate of profit (which is dependent on the available "mass of surplus value") fail to decline in the face of the constant, if relative, shrinkage in the value-creating component of capital? What Marx did endeavor to show was why the rate of profit did not fall even faster or more precipitously. Thus we come to those factors which are said to counteract the basic force behind the tendency of the profit rate to fall.

Capitalists, as we have seen, are assumed always to be seeking means by which to realize a higher rate of surplus value. The tendency of the profit rate to fall only serves to intensify this interest. Raising the degree of exploitation, whenever and however possible, is given by Marx as the most obvious and direct means to this end. There are, according to Marx, several ways by which capitalists can increase the rate of exploitation without directly affecting the organic composition of capital. The working day can be extended not only directly but indirectly. Some of the indirect measures mentioned by Marx are: (1) cutting or eliminating rest periods; (2) shortening the lunch or dinner hour; (3) strictly enforcing starting and ending times; (4) setting or allowing the factory clock to run behind the correct time. Assuming a given work day, capitalists can squeeze more out of the same number of workers. They can force them to work harder, more efficiently, or in time with speeded-up machinery. The labor market may be such, at any point in time, as to enable employers to pay a wage below the normal value of labor power. In all of these cases Marx assumes that the resulting value goes to the capitalists as surplus. Thus each of these measures serves to check the decline in the profit rate. Marx cites a complex of other forces which also work to retard this decline. Most of these, however, are more or less directly related to changes in the organic composition of capital. The more important of these are discussed below.

Marx maintained (for reasons yet to be more fully explored) that over the course of its development a Capitalist economy will experience a significant growth in its volume of trade and capital investment with colonies and other areas of the less-developed world. Recall the Marxian proposition that, in the first instance, the rate of profit is inversely related to the organic composition of capital. Further, that the order of the organic composition of capital is higher in the capitalist and lower in the colonial or underdeveloped economies. Therefore in the cases of both foreign trade and capital investment the capital thus advanced is said to yield a higher rate of profit than that realized domestically. The general rate of profit of a Capitalist economy will, therefore, be higher to the extent of such foreign trade and capital investment.

Marx found the same general principle at work within the Capitalist economy. As one case in point, he maintained that as Capitalism matures the mix between worker and capitalist-type consumer goods production shifts in favor of the latter. There are forces at work on both the factor supply and consumer demand sides. The displacement of labor associated with a higher order of the organic composition of capital in general increases the supply of labor available for the production of luxury items. In an absolute sense (thereby not contravening the increasing rate of accumulation proposition) the consumption of those who remain capitalists becomes progressively more conspicious. Thus relatively more capital tends to be invested in the production of luxury items. According to Marx, the production of capitalist-type goods is associated with a relatively low order of the organic composition of capital and thus a higher than average rate of profit. To this extent, therefore, the fall in the general rate of profit is said to be dampened. The precise basis for Marx's assertion that the production of luxury items is associated with a lower than average order of the organic composition of capital is unclear. One can only surmise that Marx had some notion that luxury goods were, in the main, handmade.

The fact that the rate of profit is measured in terms of the total (constant and variable) capital advanced caused Marx to consider the following and longer-run counteracting force to falling profits. The natural agents used in production constitute a significant element in the constant capital component of commodity value. Marx offered two basic propositions in this connection. (1) The higher the order of the organic composition of capital the greater is the relative importance of the natural agents in the process of production. (2) A change in the price of natural agents is inversely related to a change in the profit rate. What will, in fact, occur? Will the price of the natural agents rise and the rate of profit fall correspondingly? Or will the price of the natural agents fall and thus cause the rate of profit to rise by that amount? That depends, Marx tells us, on whether we consider the short or the long term. Marx correctly views the supply of the natural agents as relatively inelastic in the short run. In this case any increase in production will cause the price of the natural agents to rise and the rate of profit to fall correspondingly. Taking the longer view, Marx incorporated into his analysis here some of the broader consequences of Capitalist development. He considered the impact of science and technology on the supply of the natural agents. Fresh sources are discovered. New uses for or a more efficient utilization of the natural agents are found. Transportation facilities are extended or improved and the cost is thereby reduced. Thus over time the supply of natural agents is bound to increase. Implicit in this part of Marx's analysis is that the supply of the natural agents will increase faster than the demand for them. For Marx contends that, in the long run, the price of natural agents will decline and thereby cause the rate of profit to rise to that extent.

Another long-term force working to counteract the basic tendency of the profit rate to fall has to do with changes in the time period of production. The logic of the Capitalist productive force is such, according to Marx, that the *total* period of production (the period of production as well as circulation) becomes progressively shortened over time. That is to say, the number of times a given capital turns over annually increases from year to year. Marx had such causal factors in mind as improvements in transport facilities, further division of labor and specialization, mechanization, urbanization, etc. He commented, most particularly, on the extent to which the time of circulation was being cut by the growing separation between industrial and mercantile capital, i.e., the development of a merchant class specializing in the marketing of commodities. Recall, therefore, the earlier mentioned proposition that the more times a given capital turns over within a year the greater is the resulting annual surplus value. The fact that the yearly rate of profit on the capital advanced is thus increased serves to hold back the tendency of that rate of profit to decline.

Marx considered the causal relationship between technological improvement and changes in the value of labor power a particularly important counterforce to the falling rate of profit. In his view, the shift from a lower to a higher order of the organic composition of capital involves something more than the simple substitution of machinery for labor or the resultant technological unemployment. It also changes the existing relationship of employed workers to the productive process. The higher the degree of mechanization the less essential is the traditional skill and strength of the laborer. Muscle-power is replaced by some other form of energy and existing skills are often rendered obsolete. The process finally comes to a point where the worker, in Marx's words, "becomes an appendage of the machine, and it is only the most simple, most monotonous, and most easily acquired knack that is required of him." The specific consequences of mechanization are: (1) The labor requirements of industry shift in favor of workers with a lower level of skill; (2) women and children, who earlier lacked the necessary physical strength, can now be utilized as tenders of the machine. Recall that the price paid for labor power is held to reflect not only the level of skill but the cost of reproducing the necessary labor supply. Thus the unit value of labor power falls and, to that extent, relative surplus value and hence the rate of profit rise. Marx's comments, his moralizing, on the social consequences of these developments will be given some attention in the section on the increasing misery of the working class.

The final set of forces to be discussed in the present connection requires separate treatment because these forces cannot simply be classified as causing the general rate of profit either to rise or fall. The point at issue is the impact of changes in the division of income among the various categories of capitalists on the *general* rate of profit. Marx left no doubt about the fact that, in the final analysis, *all* capitalists must suffer a drop in their respective rates of return. What else could follow from the earlier proposition that the long-term rate of profit must decline? At the same time Marx recognized that the various rates of return—interest, rent, and industrial profit—need not necessarily move at the same pace or even, in one case, in the same direction. He had forecast, as we know, the near extinction of the *rentier* classes as Capitalism approaches the end. The causal factor here is economic and not at all political, that is, the secular decline in both the rate of interest and the rate of return on land capital. But what of the industrial rate of profit which, according to Marx, is the most directly related to the rate at which capital accumulation occurs and thus to the general rate of profit? If, Marx reasoned, the rates of return to the *rentier* classes fall faster than the average rate of profit then the industrial rate of profit could rise even in the longer run. To this extent the fall in the general rate of profit would be counteracted. Unfortunately, however, Marx was less than specific about the relative rates of change of the various forms of return to capitalists. More generally, he failed to tie up all of the loose ends of this portion of his analysis.

XV·

The Fundamental Cause of Capitalist Contradiction and Forces That Aggravate It

SOME CLARIFYING OBSERVATIONS

Our concern now is with Marx's analysis of the fundamental causes underlying the longest-term instability of the Capitalist system. All too often this aspect of the analysis is clouded by more than an ordinary amount of ambiguity. Marx is largely but not entirely at fault in this case. The following clarifying observations, therefore, are best made at the very outset.

1. Self-generating innovation, as we have just seen, does play a key role in the tendency of the profit rate to fall and is thereby an important variable in the secular instability of the system. But this is not to say that Marx accorded technology or its rate of change the status of the fundamental cause behind the long-term instability of the Capitalist economy.

2. Much of the ambiguity surrounding this portion of the analysis stems from the casual way in which Marx used the word "crisis." Depending upon the context (which is not always easily discernible in Marx's writings) the term "crisis" may have one of several meanings. It may refer to a specific, historically based, panic, i.e., the panic of 1825 or 1847. It may refer to the breakdown of a particular segment of the economy such as the credit system, banking operations, the process of innovation, etc. It may also refer to one of the five phases of the industrial cycle as classified by Marx. It may, finally, refer to the long-run process and ultimate collapse of the Capitalist system. Our immediate interest is in this last category which, for lack of a better designation, we shall call the "basic" crisis.

3. Marx was one of the first economists to draw attention to cyclical phenomena (as against a simple breakdown or financial panic) as a feature unique to Capitalism. His insights and observations on the industrial cycle are universally recognized to have been important and of lasting interest. The fact remains that Marx did not have a theory of the business cycle in any real or technical sense. Moreover, the link between the sum of his observations on the cycle and his theory of the basic crisis of Capitalism is at most tangential. Marx's contributions to the field of business cycles will, therefore, be treated in a separate section of this chapter.

What explanation did Marx offer as to the basic cause of the instability of the Capitalist system? What, to be more precise, is the exact nature of the contradiction inherent in the Capitalist productive force on the basis of which Marx made his *pro futuro* declaration of death? As a first approximation, the case may be stated in any one of the following ways. (1) The basic crisis results from the inevitable emergence of a disequilibrium between aggregate supply and aggregate demand. (2) The crisis appears when, as it must, the productive capacity of the economy outruns the capacity of the market to absorb that level of output. (3) In direct reference to Marx's two-sector model: The basic crisis is a function of disproportionality between the circumstances of supply and demand in the case of the two departments *and* the related disproportionality between the amount of capitalist consumption and accumulation.

Whichever way it is expressed, this particular structural imbalance—and nothing more—constitutes in the Marxian system the necessary and sufficient condition for the basic instability of Capitalism. The other factors, yet to be mentioned, only serve to intensify or aggravate the situation. It is interesting to note, in this connection, that Marx did not insist on the simultaneous appearance of such disproportionality throughout the economy. He credited the Capitalist economy with such complexity and interdependence as to maintain that a general crisis can initiate in any one or more vital lines of production and spread to all of the others. But the question of why such a structural disequilibrium occurs in the first instance remains to be answered.

Marx's analysis here is best understood if we follow his own approach in terms of the two-sector model as set forth in an earlier chapter. Recall, most specifically, the condition that Marx set down for the stability of the economy. It is that the demand of each department (Departments I and II) for the output of the other department is just and always equal to the net output of each department. Thus, for example, Department I must always be able to sell its *net* output of capital goods to Department II and Department II must always be able to sell its *net* output of consumer goods to Department I. (In the case of Department I, net output is the total production of capital goods minus its own capital goods requirements. In the case of Department II, net output is the total production of consumer goods minus the consumer goods absorbed by its own capitalists and workers.)

According to Marx, there are two related reasons why the stability condition given above cannot be sustained in the real world of Capitalism. One focuses on a technical feature of the production process. The other has to do with the division of surplus between consumption and accumulation. We turn to the first of these reasons. The organic composition of capital is continuously changing over the course of Capitalist development. But there is nothing inherent in the existing production process, in Marx's view, that automatically generates or sustains the necessary interdepartmental proportionality required for stability. The key to this point lies in Marx's assertion that the changes which necessarily occur in the organic composition of capital within the two departments are entirely independent of each other. That being the case there is no reason to assume that the circumstances of interdepartmental supply and demand will match; except, of course, as a matter of simple coincidence.

Thus let us say, once Department II's capital goods requirement falls below Department I's net output the first condition of crisis exists. Unable now to dispose of its entire net output, Department I has no choice but to cut production, lay off the requisite number of workers, and correspondingly reduce its purchases of consumer goods from Department II. Assuming, as Marx did, that the capitalists and workers of Department II are buying all that they want or can of consumer goods, Department II now finds itself unable to market its entire net output. And thus it goes. To repeat an earlier statement: The crisis appears when, as it must, the productive capacity of the economy outruns the capacity of the market to absorb that level of output.

What, one might ask, prevents capitalists from buying up any such crisis-causing excess in the form of luxury goods? (By Marxian premise, of course, the workers are already buying consumer goods to the full amount of their purchasing power.) Recall that a rising order of the organic composition of capital means a higher level of productivity and hence a greater volume of commodity production. But here, again, Marx denies the existence of the necessary stability-link between the supply and demand of consumer goods. The key, in this case, lies in his view regarding the consumption-accumulation behavior pattern of the capitalist. It is important to recognize in this connection that Marx was concerned not with absolutes but with relatives. Recall the point that capitalists are driven not simply to accumulate out of surplus but to do so at a progressively higher rate over the course of Capitalist development. Over time the individual capitalist may well experience a higher, more luxurious, living standard in an absolute sense. But this is entirely independent of the disequilibrium resulting from the fact that as the capacity to produce consumer goods increases so does the rate of accumulation, as against capitalist consumption, out of surplus. What really matters, in other words, is what happens in regard to the relative rates of consumption and accumulation out of surplus. These, then are the two causal factors behind the basic crisis of the Capitalist economy.

FORCES OF CONTRADICTION BEYOND THE BASIC CRISIS

The growing complexity of the Capitalist economy is such, said Marx, as to generate certain forces of contradiction beyond those responsible for the basic crisis. He had in mind here such features as: (1) The progressive monetization of the economy; (2) the heightening degree of interdependence among the various lines of production and sectors of the economy; (3) the constantly higher order of the organic composition of capital; (4) the growing separation of commodity production from its marketing. In the main, according to Marx, such developments only tend to intensify or aggravate the basic crisis. In several instances, with only the weakest of explanations as to why, Marx opened the possibility that one or another of these developments might be the initial cause of a general crisis. In either case let us now take a somewhat closer look at the most important of these forces of contradiction.

One of Marx's most fundamental criticisms of the Capitalist system was its highly competitive and planless character. The fact, he writes, that the fiercest of competition among capitalists results in "the introduction . . . on a large social scale . . . of new machinery before the old is worn out," is enough cause for a crisis. A precipitous fall in commodity price and the rate of profit, due to the rapid rate of technological change, will not only upset the basis of profit rate calculation but may well deflate capital values to a point of crisis. Depending upon the importance of the sector where such a "catastrophe" strikes, it could spark a general crisis. And should the rate of profit fall below the required incentive level, for this or any other reason, that of itself would result in a cutback of production with all of its implications. So Marx reasoned.

The unstabilizing impact resulting from the progressive monetization of the economy is offered as the most important of these forces of contradiction. Marx maintained, as noted earlier, that the degree to which the productive process becomes dependent on or involved with money, banking, and credit parallels the course of Capitalist development. Several factors combine to cause a growing reliance on credit for the financing of commodity production and sale. The faster the pace of innovation the more new capital is sought. The higher the order of the organic composition of capital the larger is the capital requirement. The further the distance from the market the more financing becomes necessary. There are parallel developments, i.e., sources of credit, to meet these capital needs. The class of money capitalists evolves still further. Banks and banking facilities multiply. As the volume and complexity of production increase the advantages of specialization become all the more apparent. The resulting separation of production from marketing stimulates the growth of a merchant class. The time required by the industrialist capitalist for the reproduction of money capital is thereby shortened. An expansion of bank credit occurs involving the discounting of notes or bills of exchange generated by transactions between industrial and mercantile capitalists. Thus, writes Marx, "Credit must grow in volume with the growing volume of value in production. . . . A mutual interaction takes place here. The development of the process of production extends the credit, the credit leads to an extension of industrial and commercial operations." Most of this, Marx added, occurs during the upswing phase of the cycle.

The initial difficulty manifests itself when merchants find the commodity market "so slow and meager" as to be unable to move their stock except at markedly reduced prices and, therefore, at the sacrifice of profits. Thus they enter a period of financial reverses. Pressured by banks for payment, finding it difficult to secure new credit, fearing or facing insolvency, merchants fail to reorder and the crisis begins. Since, as we have noted, the economy has become tied to the monetary and banking institutions, the entire credit structure crumbles. But this tells us only why the vicissitudes of the money market have such an impact on the general level of economic activity. The reason why, at a certain point, merchants find the commodity market "so slow and meager" follows. The basic crisis aside, Marx maintained that this financial crisis occurs precisely because of an earlier mentioned separation of producer from the consumer. The emergence and multiplication of a whole system of middlemen serve only to widen still more the gap between what is produced and what the market can absorb. The very fact of a credit system, according to Marx, enables industrial capitalists to produce and merchants to buy commodities "for no other immediate reason than that of obtaining advances of money on them." Thus it is the proliferation of (in Marx's words) "bogus checks" and "fraudulent bills of exchange" that "leads inevitably to an overcrowding of the market and to a crash." The occurrence and recurrence of these financial crises is assured, Marx concluded, since "The effects of mistaken banking legislation can intensify a monetary crisis, but no legislation can abolish it."

THE INDUSTRIAL CYCLE

"Marx's performance in the field of business cycles," according to Schumpeter, ". . . consists of dozens of observations and comments, most of them of a casual nature, which are scattered over almost all his writings. . . . The fact is that he had no simple theory of business cycles. And none can be made to follow logically from his 'laws' of the capitalist process."[1] Marx's observations and insights on the industrial cycle are, nevertheless, interesting enough to deserve our attention. The business cycle, as Marx conceived of it, is not something apart but simply the manifestation of all the causal factors behind the basic crisis and those forces which intensify it. As long as Capitalism exists, therefore, the industrial cycle is held to be inescapable since all crises are declared inevitable.

Marx was much too vague in his characterization of the various phases of the cycle to enable us to attach to them the standard labels of prosperity, recession, depression, and recovery. Let us simply begin, therefore, at that point of a given cycle where the general level of economic activity is at its peak. This period of prosperity, for reasons already noted, must come to an end. The turning point is signaled by the inability of the market to absorb at existing prices all that has or can be produced. Thus overproduction results. The economy thereupon enters a phase during which most of the economic indices are in a process of decline. Merchants reduce or fail to renew their orders. The number of unemployed rises and excess productive capacity appears as industrial capitalists cut back on production. In the face of a shrinking market the struggle among capitalists becomes fierce. Market prices, wages, capital values, and profits take a downward turn. The collapse of the credit structure only makes matters worse. The forces of centralization and concentration of capital are most actively at work during this phase of the cycle.

There follows a period of relative economic inactivity. The general level of production reaches its lowest point during this phase of the cycle. Those capitalists who had managed to survive are now even larger for having swallowed up, at sacrifice values, the production facilities of the smaller or weaker firms. Input prices (the natural agents, machinery and equipment, labor) are at their lowest point of the cycle. Unemployment is at its highest, labor discipline is at its stiffest, the working day is at its longest, and the market wage may even have fallen below the normal value of labor power. But Marx also viewed the course of Capitalist development as characterized by a series of industrial cycles of increasing severity. He had, therefore, to account for an intracycle revival of economic activity leading to the next cycle of greater intensity and duration.

The very circumstances prevailing during the period above, according to Marx, generate the necessary conditions for recovery and thus a temporary return to prosperity. The low level to which raw-material prices have fallen acts as one inducement for a resumption of production. More important, at this point the labor market is said to be most conducive for the exploitation of labor. Commodity capital is by this time well depleted. As a consequence of the centralization and concentration of capital, the rate of profit is higher to the extent of the deflation of capital values. Given a period of stagnation, and following the collapse of the credit structure, the supply of loanable funds again increases. The rate of interest is low and credit transactions are resumed. In light of these developments the earlier pessimism in regard to investment gradually gives way to optimism. Most specifically, the relatively low level of all factor prices serves to rekindle interest in the innovative process. Capitalists begin anew to seek out different products, fresh markets, and improved processes of production. Thus the race for extraordinary profits resumes. Rising expectations—reflecting current increases in production, prices, wages and profits—culminate in new investments and so on back to the point of prosperity.

That this prosperity will not last, that the cycle "must periodically reproduce itself," we already know. Waxing almost poetic, toward the end of the first volume of *Das Kapital,* Marx writes: "As the heavenly bodies, once thrown into a certain definite motion, always repeat this, so it is with the social production as soon as it is once thrown into this movement of alternate expansion and contraction." But why each cycle, which "paves the way" for the next, is necessarily "more intense and more destructive" remains to be explained. The basic reason, according to Marx, has to do with the growth that occurs in the scale of production and the general level of economic activity. The more gigantic the means of production, the greater the degree of interdependence, the higher the level of all economic magnitudes, the further is the fall.

There are several specific causal factors, subsumed under the above generalization, to which Marx attached special weight. One is that the intensity and duration of the cycle varies directly with the lengthening of the lifespan of the fixed capital component of the capital advanced for production.[2] Another is that the progressive expansion of the credit system only serves to make each succeeding cycle that much more severe. A third factor is the ultimate contraction of the world market which counteracts an earlier cause for recovery. A final force is the centralization of production and finance which, as we have seen, is an important factor in the growth of large-scale production. More will be said about the last two points in another connection.

According to Marx, economic imperialism is a major factor in the temporary revival from a given crisis. By economic imperialism Marx meant the secular expansion in the volume of both foreign capital investment and commodity trade as between Capitalist nations and the underdeveloped or colonial parts of the world. The chapter that follows is concerned with Marx's analysis of the causal factors behind economic imperialism as well as its impact on the total character of world civilization.

XVI·

Economic Imperialism

Colonialism, nationalism, war, struggles for independence, stages of conflict and development, co-existence, and liberation movements are but some of the subjects normally associated with the word imperialism. Much of what has and continues to be said regarding these facets of imperialism is, strictly speaking, more Leninist than Marxist. Even so, Marx had something to say about many of these matters as they pertained to his own historical period. He expressed views and took positions on such specific questions as: (1) the American Civil War and its causes; (2) British colonialism in Ireland, Australia, India, etc.; (3) European trade with the Orient; (4) the growing economic rivalry between England and the United States; (5) differences in the relative economic development of Western European nations; (6) Russian economic development as a special case and problem. Interesting as many of these observations may be, they are beyond the scope and purpose of this chapter. Our concern must remain with the mainstream of Marx's economic analysis as it now extends beyond the national boundaries.

THE NATURE AND CAUSES OF INTERNATIONAL
ECONOMIC ACTIVITY

The laws of Capitalist development work in such a way, Marx tells us, as to alter finally the character of the productive force and thus the superstructure of all nations or societies of the world. The *Communist Manifesto* states: "It [Capitalism] must nestle everywhere, settle everywhere, establish connections everywhere. . . . The bourgeoisie . . . draws all, even the most barbarian, nations into civilization." Marx was aware, of course, that significant differences existed in the degree of economic development not only among Capitalist nations but within the underdeveloped areas of the world. The purpose of this portion of the analysis will, nevertheless, best be served if we assume only two types of economies: Capitalist and underdeveloped. Two questions immediately present themselves in this connection. (1) By what process or mechanism do Capitalist nations draw all other societies into bourgeois civilization? (2) What are the consequences, positive and negative, of such internationalization for both the Capitalist and underdeveloped nations of the world?

Capitalism, Marx tells us, "draws all, even the most barbarian, nations into [its] civilization" through foreign capital investment and commodity trade. "The need of a constantly expanding market for its products," according to the *Communist Manifesto*, is what "chases the bourgeoisie over the whole surface of the globe." The need for foreign markets is, indeed, one of a number of fáctors mentioned by Marx in this connection. Taken alone, however, the above statement is a bit misleading. It tends to divert attention from the central force which Marx actually regards as responsible for Capitalism's expansion beyond its national boundaries. The real force behind the growth of foreign economic activity is given as the existence of differentials in the average rate of profit, reflecting differences in the order of the organic composition of capital, as between Capitalist and underdeveloped economies. Let us take a somewhat closer look at this question from both the capital movement and commodity trade side.

As noted earlier, Marx held that the volume of international economic activity was bound to grow over the course of Capitalist development. His view regarding the growth of foreign investments by Capitalist nations rests, in the first instance, on three now familiar propositions: (1) The capitalist is interested in realizing the highest possible rate of return on the total capital advanced for the production and sale of commodities; (2) the rate of profit is inversely related to the order of the organic composition of capital; (3) the average organic composition of capital is at its lowest order in the least developed and at its highest order in the most developed economy. All other things being equal, therefore, the average rate of profit is higher in the underdeveloped and lower in the developed economies. As long as this disparity persists there will be a tendency on the part of capital to flow from the Capitalist to the underdeveloped areas, and the more capitalists are driven to innovate, (the higher the order of the organic composition of capital), the stronger is this tendency. When, under what circumstance, will this process come to an end? When, as a result of this capital flow, the average order of the organic composition of capital and thus the average rate of profit are the same for all economies.

According to Marx, the capitalist's quest for a higher rate of profit is also the underlying factor in the long-term expansion of foreign commodity trade. The content and direction of this trade are given as follows. The imports of a developed economy consist of raw materials and those capitalist-type consumer goods which are indigenous to the underdeveloped area in question. The unavailability of certain raw materials at home and the advantage, in other cases, of lower raw-material prices from abroad is self-evident. The reason for the growing volume of imports from "distant lands and climes" of "silk and spice and everything nice" for the capitalist's table has already been given. The exports of a developed economy consist, in the main, of the articles of its manufacture which are unavailable or prohibitively expensive to produce in the backward areas of the world. The question at this point is why and under what circumstances capitalists find it more profitable to sell their wares in the underdeveloped markets rather than domestically.

In that connection it is necessary to refer, once again, to Marx's theory of price. At long-run equilibrium, a commodity sells at its cost of production. The cost is, in turn, a function of the order of the organic composition of capital. The long-term consequence of the innovative process, i.e., the progressively higher order of the organic composition of capital, is to lower the cost of production and thus commodity price. In order to illustrate simply Marx's point in this case let us assume that capitalist firm A in country B produces Commodity C at cost X. Let us further assume that commodity C can be marketed either in country B or underdeveloped economy D. Assume, finally, that economy D could produce commodity C at a cost of $X + x$. Firm A of country B could, therefore, do one of two things. It could sell commodity C in the domestic market at cost X (= price) and thereby realize a normal profit. It could sell Commodity C in market D at cost $X + x$ (corresponding to the lower order of the organic composition of capital in economy D) and thereby realize an amount over and above its normal profit as measured by the price differential between market B and D. Firm A will, of course, follow the latter course as long as this differential exists. A difference in the level of technological development between economy B and D is thus the basic causal factor involved in the growth of the volume of foreign commodity trade. Marx mentions certain other factors which contribute to (but are not, even in sum, a prime cause of) the expansion in the volume of foreign commodity trade. The principal ones are: (1) striking technological progress in the means of communication and transportation; (2) expansion of credit facilities; (3) periodic need for fresh foreign markets during periods of crisis.

THE CONSEQUENCES OF INTERNATIONALIZATION

We turn now to an examination of the consequences of internationalization. The growth of foreign economic activity means, first of all, the progressive application of the principle of division of labor and specialization on a world scale. The logical culmination of this development is the division of the globe into two basic types of economies: industrial and agricultural, i.e., food and raw-material supplying. According to Marx, this process is self-generating and cumulative over most of the course of Capitalist development. The more advanced the technology of an industrial economy, the greater is its competitive edge in foreign economic activity, the more industrialized that economy becomes, and so on. The opposite is the case, of course, for an agricultural economy. But let us go behind the simple mechanics of foreign economic activity.

What Marx really tells us here is that the growth of international economic activity causes a particular and predictable change in the character of both the Capitalist and underdeveloped productive force, and in turn, corresponding changes in the superstructure of the two basic types of societies. In the context of Marx's emphasis, the impact of internationalization appears at its most dramatic in the backward areas of the world. Recall the point about the flow of capital from the industrial to the backward areas. According to Marx, the resulting application of advanced technology to specific lines of economic activity, i.e., food and raw-material production, will generate the necessary labor supply including the assortment of skills required by such technology. European business managers and technicians will follow the flow of capital into backward nations. Native workers will be broken to industrial discipline and taught the requisite skills. The appearance of European articles of manufacture changes the existing consumption pattern of the underdeveloped economy. Native handicraft loses out in competition with factory organized machine-made goods. Corresponding changes occur in the social, political, religious traditions and institutions of the backward societies. This, again, is what Marx meant by the statement that Capitalism "draws all, even the most barbarian, nations into [its] civilization."

The impact of internationalization on a developed nation is just as real, though perhaps not quite as fundamental. The volume of luxury items for the pleasure of the Capitalist class increases. Periodically the underdeveloped economies provide Capitalist ones with a necessary outlet both for their surplus product and population. Finally, and most important, the impact of internationalization is to make a developed economy still more industrialized and capitalistic; to the point, in fact, where the level of agricultural activity and thus the position of the landowning capitalist decline.

Taking the longest view, however, Marx also noted the process by which the developments mentioned above play themselves out. As observed earlier, the ultimate consequence of capital migration is the equalization of the average organic composition of capital between the two basic types of economies. In regard to foreign commodity trade, Marx foresaw, first of all, the rise of protectionism on the part of the underdeveloped nations. Once a backward nation finds itself in possession of modern technology a spirit of protectionism is bound to emerge. Free trade is, after all, only the freedom of monopoly Capitalism to exploit its colonies. Thus Marx reasoned. More significant is his view that the basic forces of Capitalist contradiction remain unchecked by the expanding volume of foreign economic activity. In the short run a Capitalist economy can "export its crisis," so to speak, by selling its surplus product abroad. But the long-run consequence of internationalization is to force the development of Capitalism in the underdeveloped parts of the world. The more capitalistic an initially backward economy becomes the more it will exhibit the same basic instability inherent in the Capitalist productive force. Moreover, the more economies are bound together by foreign economic activity the more likely it is that any crisis originating in one economy will spread to all other economies. Indeed, according to Marx, a crisis as it occurs or spreads to a developing economy is even more intense than in an industrial economy alone. This view is based on the proposition that prices of the natural agents fluctuate more violently than commodity prices with disastrous results on the marginal food and raw-material supplying areas of the globe. The economic logic of all of these developments, finally, works itself out to this: Geographically speaking there are just so many places in the world where the bourgeoisie can "nestle . . . settle . . . establish connections. . . ." A point is reached where the advanced Capitalist nations necessarily clash over the control and availability of such markets as exist. This struggle over markets is aggravated to the extent that the developing economies themselves become subject to the basic contradiction inherent in the Capitalist productive force. To go much beyond this would involve a move away from Marx and toward the contributions of Rosa Luxenburg, V. I. Lenin, and many others.

XVII·

The Increasing Misery
of the Working Class

THE SIGNIFICANCE OF THE IMMISERIZATION[1] PROPHECY

What, according to Marxian prophecy, do the masses have to look forward to over the course of Capitalist development? A secular decline in real wage rates and the living standard, wrote Marx the economist. Misery, oppression, slavery, degradation, and exploitation, said Marx the slogan-maker and revolutionary. Either way, the statement represents the essence of Marx's theory of the increasing misery of the working class.

The relevant passage in volume I of *Das Kapital* reads: "Hand in hand with this centralization . . . the entanglement of all nations in the net of the world market . . . with the constantly diminishing number of magnates of capital . . . [there] grows the mass of misery, oppression, slavery, degradation, exploitation; but with this too grows the revolt of the working class . . . disciplined, united, organized by the very mechanism of the process of capitalist production itself." What is of special interest here is the manner in which Marx's theory of immiserization connects the Capitalist productive force with the corresponding elements of the superstructure. To be specific: The unfolding of the contradictions inherent in the productive force necessarily intensifies the misery of the working class; which, with equal necessity, leads the working class toward revolt. At the same time the process of Capitalist development also generates the material circumstances requisite for the emergence and growth of working-class identity, solidarity, political awareness, discipline, and organization. The theory of immiserization is clearly the analytic link between the economic and the political—between the (economic) laws of Capitalist development and political action—in the Marxian system. Increasing misery is a necessary though not sufficient condition for the inevitable awakening of working-class consciousness, class struggle, revolution, the end of Capitalism, and the emergence of Socialism. As such it cannot be brushed aside as another of Marx's comments that is either casual or merely tangential to the main lines of the Marxian system. Let us examine, therefore, the basis of Marx's theory of immiserization, its underlying assumptions, and some of the concrete consequences that presumably follow from it.

THE INDUSTRIAL RESERVE ARMY

Marx's theory of the increasing misery of the working class rests primarily on his theory of the industrial reserve army, namely, that segment of the labor force which is unemployed. The following points in regard to the theory of the industrial reserve army are not at issue. (1) The Capitalist productive force necessarily creates and recreates an industrial reserve army. (2) In the short run, depending on the phase of the cycle, this pool of unemployed may either expand or contract. (3) A specified laborer who is thrown out of work need not necessarily remain unemployed for the remainder of his work life.

Several aspects of Marx's theory of the industrial reserve army do present immediate problems of interpretation and are best mentioned at this point. One is that Marx limited his theoretical analysis of what generates the industrial reserve army to the single factor of technological change and thus membership in the reserve army to the technologically unemployed. At the same time he recognized the existence of cyclical and structural unemployment and included such unemployed as, perhaps, the more important elements in the composition of the reserve army. A second aspect arises in connection with Marx's predicted secular increase in the size of the industrial reserve army. For purposes of this portion of his analysis, at least, Marx took the population variable as given. This is not to say that he completely ignored the reality of population growth or the relationship of the growth rate to the supply of labor. He was more concerned, however, with avoiding any possible Malthusian implication as a causal factor in his theory of immiserization. In Marx's purely analytic scheme, therefore, it appears that the predicted increase in the reserve army is relative rather than absolute in the sense that the secularly expanding pool of unemployed represents an increasingly larger fraction of a given total labor force.

What are the details of the process by which the industrial reserve army is generated? According to Marx, as we have seen, incessant technological change is a basic feature of Capitalist development. In this connection it is necessary to recall, as well, a second Marxian proposition. A higher order of the organic composition of capital means a rise in labor productivity resulting in more profits as a basis for additional capital accumulation. All of this has a dual effect on the demand for labor. Mechanization, as such, causes the demand for labor to decline. Accumulation out of increased profits adds to the demand for labor. The crucial question, as it bears on the industrial reserve army, is what precise relationship is assumed to exist between these two forces. Here Marx distinguishes between what *may*, in fact, happen in the short run and what *must* occur in the long run. In the short run (depending, again, on the phase of the cycle), the *net* demand for labor may decrease, increase, or remain the same. Thus, but only as a short-term phenomenon, the size of the reserve army may grow, contract, or remain unchanged. In the long run, however, the Capitalist productive force necessarily operates in such a way as to cause a *net* decline in the demand for labor, a *net* displacement of workers, and thus a secular increase in the industrial reserve army.

Marx's predicted increase in the industrial reserve army is based primarily on the proposition that the decline in the demand for labor *due to mechanization* is necessarily greater than the increase in the demand for labor arising out of the related additional capital accumulation. First and foremost, therefore, the growth of the reserve army means an increase in technological unemployment. Marx also considered the following, but clearly secondary, factors as contributing to the secular expansion of the reserve army. (1) Recalling Marx's prediction regarding the fate of the money capitalist class: The reserve army grows to the extent that the long-term fall in the interest rate causes the smaller money capitalists to enter the ranks of the working class. Unable to live off a shrinking income, lacking the requisite labor skills, the smaller *rentiers* end up in the industrial reserve army. (2) Recalling Marx's analysis of the process of centralization of capital: As the bigger capitalists swallow up the smaller ones, as the subsequent scale of production and thus labor productivity rises, additional workers as well as former smaller industrial capitalists tend to fall into that same pool of unemployed. (3) Marx recognized but, for the reason suggested earlier, minimized population growth as a factor in the expansion of the industrial reserve army.

Marx sums up his argument in this case, toward the end of volume I of *Das Kapital:* "Since the demand for labor is determined not by the amount of capital as a whole, but by its variable constituent alone, that demand falls progressively with the increase of the total capital. . . . It falls relatively to the magnitude of the total capital, and at an accelerated rate, as this magnitude increases. With the growth of the total capital, its variable constituent or the labor incorporated in it, also does increase, but in a constantly diminishing proportion . . . [thus] a population of greater extent than suffices for the average needs of the self-expansion of capital, and therefore a surplus-population [results]."

It is at this juncture that one aspect of the tenuousness of Marx's theory of increasing misery best be made explicit. This forecast hinges, as we have seen, on the secular expansion of the reserve army; which, in turn, rests mainly on the net growth of technological unemployment. Existing economic literature regarding the impact of mechanization on net employment is vast, complex, and, even to the present, largely inconclusive. The point here is that on this issue, most particularly, a return to the words of Marx is least rewarding. Marx offers little if any substantive evidence or proof that the labor absorbed by additional capital accumulation is necessarily less— and progressively so—than that which is displaced through mechanization. Just why the profits resulting from a technologically caused rise in labor productivity could not be equal to or more than enough to absorb the technologically unemployed remains a mystery. The inclusion of secondary factors, those contributing to the growth of the reserve army, does nothing to resolve the issue. The impoverished *rentiers* constitute, at most, a marginal element in the reserve army. The rate of population growth is, as we have noted, essentially ignored. As for capital concentration, the basic question remains: Why should the additional profits resulting therefrom necessarily be insufficient to absorb the labor thus displaced?

The fact remains that, for his purposes, Marx needed an industrial reserve army and one that would expand as Capitalism matured. Recall that Marx assumed a competitive labor market (on the demand as well as supply side) throughout his analysis. The market wage could, therefore, rise above or fall below subsistence depending on the existing relationship between the demand for and the supply of labor. Remember, as well, that the Marxian normal or subsistence wage is not the Malthusian one. Recall, finally, that in Marx's analysis the general level of subsistence falls over the course of Capitalist development. (It does not matter at this moment in the analysis whether the secular decline in subsistence is interpreted as being absolute or relative.) The point is that Marx had to find some force other than population pressure in order to establish not only that the normal wage tends toward subsistence but that such subsistence tends to fall over the long run. The industrial reserve army (and its secular expansion) is that other force in the Marxian system. Given a competitive labor market, what better means for driving down the real wage rate than an expanding pool of unemployed howling outside the factory gate? Note, most particularly, that this pool of unemployed is not (as is the case with the rate of population growth) a factor exogenous to the Marxian system. In Marx's analysis, the industrial reserve army emerges and grows as a necessary consequence of the very logic of the Capitalist productive force.

THE QUALITATIVE DIMENSIONS
OF INCREASING MISERY

But Marxian increasing misery is not only a quantitative phenomenon. It involves something more than numerical increase in the pool of unemployed, or a decline in the real wage rate. Immiserization has various qualitative dimensions many of which Marx described—some of which he documented—in the most vivid of terms. It is not our purpose here to reproduce the "white-hot phrases" employed by Marx in his indictment of Capitalism. The point at hand will be served well enough by simply mentioning the principal qualitative features associated with the growing misery of the working class.

One such feature, perhaps the most important, is the change that is said to occur in the composition of the labor force. As a direct consequence of mechanization, the labor of men is progressively displaced by that of women and children. According to Marx, as the reader will recall, the real value of labor power is set by the subsistence requirement of the family as a unit. In this sense the value of labor power does, indeed, fall as women and children are employed. There is the added but nonmeasurable suffering associated with a situation in which the male head of the household becomes unemployed while his wife and children work in order to maintain the family. Marx's views on what all of this does to the moral fabric of the working-class family—in fact to the whole institution of the bourgeois family—is too well known to require repetition here.

A second qualitative consequence of mechanization is the extent to which it dehumanizes the work process for all laborers. Marx makes the point both in the *Communist Manifesto* and in *Das Kapital*. Men, women, and children alike become mere appendages of the machine. As work loses its individual character, as the need for special skills disappears, the work process becomes progressively more monotonous, distasteful, and, in one sense, more arduous. Working becomes, finally, a matter of sheer economic necessity. Add to this the impact on the industrial workers of the change that occurs in the organizational structure of production. The factory system means not only the extension of supervision over the workers and the tightening of labor discipline but the concentration of such workers in urban slums with all that these things imply: poverty, disease, squalor, moral and intellectual degradation, etc. Thus it is, declares the *Communist Manifesto,* that "The modern laborer, on the contrary, instead of rising with the progress of industry, sinks deeper and deeper below the conditions of existence of his own class. He becomes a pauper, and pauperism develops more rapidly than population and wealth." Only the agricultural worker or peasant, says Marx, fares even worse.

Joseph Schumpeter, with fact and logic on his side, offers the following assessment of Marx's theory of immiserization: "As a prediction, this was of course singularly infelicitous and Marxists of all types have been hard put to it to make the best of the clearly adverse evidence that confronted them . . . the real trouble is that Marx's theoretical structure is anything but trustworthy in that sector: along with the vision, the analytical groundwork is there at fault . . . both analysis and vision fail beyond remedy."[2] So telling a criticism of Marx's theory of immiserization is, one is forced to admit, particularly damaging to the inevitability feature of the Marxian system.

SOME EFFORTS TO SAVE THE THEORY
OF IMMISERIZATION

The trouble is that neither wage statistics nor even a casual glance at what has actually happened to the condition of the working class supports

Marx's theory of increasing misery. It does not matter, in this instance, whether Marx is read as having had absolute or relative misery in mind. The issue of relativity first arose because Marxists were finally forced to admit what all the statistical time series showed: that neither the rates of real wages nor the absolute share going to labor had any tendency to decline. If anything, of course, the precise opposite has been the case. But Marx had said just enough about the purely psychological side of misery, the decline in relative wages, the flexibility of subsistence, and the fall in the relative social position of the working class to have provided his followers with a second line of defense.

It came to be argued that by increasing misery Marx had really meant one or more of the following: (1) a widening of income differentials; (2) the failure of wages to keep pace with increases in labor productivity or profits; (3) a worsening in the relative social position of the working class; (4) a decline in the relative share of labor incomes in total income. Again, however, the empirical evidence did not support the Marxian conclusion. The division of total income between labor and capital has tended to remain strikingly constant over time. The relative share going to labor has, just as clearly, failed to decline. Present-day Marxists, having discovered yet another set of clues in Marx's writings, were thus able to go on to a third line of defense.

The third argument, stated as briefly as possible, runs along the following lines. Increasing misery is, without question, inherent in the laws of Capitalist development. Its failure to have shown up in the statistical time series is simply due to the counteracting force of economic imperialism. The extent of international economic activity, the degree to which colonial labor has been exploited, during the past century has been greater than even that which Marx had visualized. The "law" of increasing misery has thus been "paralyzed," but only temporarily, in the case of mature Capitalist economies. This "law" will reassert its primacy, show itself in wage statistics, as the underdeveloped nations of the world gain economic and political independence.

The question of "paralysis" of a socio-economic law—of any law for that matter—appears to this writer to border on the metaphysical and should best be left at that. The real issue, as it concerns us, is that the logic of Marx's economic analysis necessitates an absolute increase in the misery of the working class *as a whole*. Specifically, as Schumpeter points out, "Marx's main conclusions presuppose that the *absolute* per capita share of labor should fall or, at the very least, not increase."[3] What else could Marx have possibly meant in regard to the pressure of a growing reserve army on wages, the cheapening of labor power, the fall in family subsistence, etc.? An absolute decline in the real wage rate need not, of course, preclude any of the qualitative aspects of increasing misery or deny the relative nature of some as cited by Marx.

Two final and related points remain in order to complete this survey of Marx's analysis of the laws of Capitalist development. One concerns the particular nature of the relationship which, according to Marxian analysis, exists between the economic logic of the Capitalist productive force and the increasing misery of the working class. The other has to do with the manner in which Marx linked economic causation with political action leading to revolution. Both points are considered in the concluding chapter.

XVIII·

The Objective Circumstances
for Revolution

The year 1848 was the historic moment when, in the *Communist Manifesto*, Marx and Engels declared: "A spectre is haunting Europe—the spectre of Communism. . . . Let the ruling classes tremble at a Communist Revolution." This proclamation was based on Marx's then firm conviction that Capitalism had run its full course. He saw the "objective conditions" for both the Communist Revolution and the emergence of Socialism all around him. Marx and Engels were not only ready but offered themselves as leaders of that revolution. Marx explained the failure of the Revolution of 1848 by admitting that the "objective conditions" for the Communist Revolution had not yet fully materialized. He estimated that Capitalism had yet another decade, at most two, before finally contradicting itself out of existence. The reader is reminded of these facts because they bear so directly on the final two points under consideration.

Exactly what did Marx have in mind by the "objective conditions" for the Communist Revolution? His meaning can be found in the answer to a second question: What is the essential nature of Marx's serious economic writings? *Das Kapital*, which stands at the center of such works, is primarily an analysis of the laws of capitalist development. It is neither a blueprint for post-Capitalist societies nor, in the main, a treatise on history, philosophy, politics, or the art of revolution. The fact that, on analysis, Marx found the laws of Capitalist development to be in contradiction only brings us back to the main point with which we began this survey on Marxian economics. It may, indeed, be useful at this point to recall the essence of what was stated at the outset.

Marx the social philosopher was mainly concerned with unearthing the universal law of historical change. As a Hegelian, he began with the philosophical proposition that all social systems (except the final and thus perfect one) must, by force of the dialectic, contradict themselves out of existence. In his theory of history, Marx maintained that all social change initiates dialectically within the production force and that such change is, though with a time lag, necessarily reflected in the superstructure of the social universe. But it is one thing to say that each productive force harbors the seeds of its own contradiction. It is quite another to expose the laws of contradiction unique to a particular productive force. According to Marx, the specific forces of contradiction within the productive force that once put an end to Slavery or Feudalism are not the same as those which operate with equal dialectic inevitability to assure the demise of Capitalism. This is why Marx the economist set himself the task of investigating the particular character of the contradictions inherent in the productive force of his day. It was along these lines and on this basis that he was then able to predict the equally inevitable end of the Capitalist system.

By the objective condition for the Communist Revolution Marx meant, therefore, that point in the long course of Capitalist development when the productive force breaks down by its own contradictions; thereby causing "the capitalist integument [shell, superstructure]" to burst. There comes a point, in other words, when the Capitalist productive force simply ceases to function in the sense that it can no longer meet even the basic economic requirements of society. Immiserization (with all that this connotes) is not, therefore, the actual cause of the Communist Revolution and the collapse of Capitalism. The increasing misery of the working class is but a reflection or consequence of the laws of Capitalism as the contradictions inherent in the productive force manifest themselves over time. What is at issue here, of course, is Marxian inevitability. The Communist Revolution will necessarily succeed, according to Marx, but only if it occurs at that point in historical time when the Capitalist productive force has broken down of its own accord. How do we know when that point is reached? According to Marxist doctrine, when in fact the revolution succeeds. Marx suggested a certain flexibility here when he wrote about the possibility of shortening or lengthening the birth pangs associated with the emergence of the next social order. What some of Marx's followers have made of this, especially in connection with bypassing stages of development, is quite another matter. As for the nature of the basic contradictions inherent in the Capitalist productive force: that, of course, is what this survey of Marxian economics has been all about.

The manner in which Marx linked economic causation with political action remains. According to Marx, the same laws of Capitalist development that finally manifest themselves in the breakdown of the productive force also set the preconditions for the Communist Revolution and Socialism. What better way to make the final point, and thus bring this survey to an end, than in the words of Karl Marx? Toward the very end of volume I of Das Kapital: "As soon as this process has sufficiently decomposed the old society from top to bottom, as soon as the labourers are turned into proletarians, their means of labour into capital, as soon as the capitalist mode of production stands on its own feet, then the further socialisation of labour and further transformation of the land and other means of production into ... common means of production take a new form. .... *This expropriation is accomplished by the action of the immanent laws of capitalistic production itself,* by the centralisation of capital. .... Hand in hand with this centralisation ... develop, on an ever extending scale, the co-operative form of the labour-process, the conscious technical application of science, the methodical cultivation of the soil, the transformation of the instruments of labour into instruments of labour only usuable in common ... the entanglement of all peoples in the net of the world market. .... Along with the constantly diminishing number of magnates of capital ... grows the mass of misery, oppression, slavery, degradation, exploitation; but with this too grows the revolt of the working class, a class always increasing in numbers, and disciplined, united, *organized by the very mechanism of the process of capitalist production itself.* The monopoly of capital becomes a fetter upon the mode of production, which has sprung up and flourished along with, and under it. Centralisation of the means of production and socialism of labour at last reach a point where they become incompatible with their capitalist integument. This integument is burst asunder. The knell of capitalist private property sounds. The expropriators are expropriated." [Italics mine].

Appendix

The more objective studies and biographies of Marx see him as a unique composite of social philosopher, scientist, scholar, teacher, agitator, economist, revolutionary, and prophet. The problem is that decided differences persist as to which of these elements dominates. How should Marx be regarded on balance? Was he, in essence, a slogan-maker or scholar, social philosopher or agitator, economist or prophet? The final judgment must remain with the reader. This sketch can only hope to provide some of the factual and circumstantial evidence as a basis for reaching such a judgment. Whatever it may be, however, let us record at the outset that Karl Marx was a brilliant intellect and a very learned man.

THE ACADEMIC SIDE OF KARL MARX

Karl Marx was born in 1818 in a southwestern German town called Treves. There he received his elementary education along with special instruction both from his father, a lawyer and his future father-in-law. At the age of seventeen Karl Marx acquiesced to his father's wish by entering the University of Bonn in order to study law. By the end of his first year there Marx made it quite clear that he lacked enthusiasm for the study of law and for following his father's footsteps into the legal profession. He decided instead to enroll at the University of Berlin where, for four years, he studied history, the arts, literature, and philosophy. Philosophy became his first love and it was in this field that Marx subsequently received a doctorate from the University of Jena.

The seriousness and intensity with which Marx approached his studies is striking. He was absorbed with the academic side of life to the exclusion of nearly all other interests and activities. Marx joined only that university "club" which had as its primary purpose the discussion of philosophical issues. He sought out mainly the company of those who were intellectually stimulating or controversial enough to challenge him. More often Marx preferred solitude. It is known, for instance, that he would shut himself in his room for days at a time in order to understand or work out entire philosophical systems.

Marx's searching, restless, quarrelsome mind netted him a small core of friends and a much larger number of enemies. Early in his career as a graduate student Marx made it known that he aspired to an academic post. Upon receipt of his doctorate he tried, indeed, to secure an appointment at the University of Bonn. Failing there he tried other German universities but with no more success. It is generally held that the door of the academic world was closed to Marx because of his nonconformist views aggravated by a Jewish ancestry.

The qualities of mind which distinguished Marx as a student remained with him throughout his life. Unable to secure an academic post he was forced, under the lash of economic necessity, into a sporadic career of journalism. The decade of the 1840's is acknowledged to have been his most active revolutionary period. But even then, while moving about Europe, Marx spent more time and energy gathering evidence for and crystallizing his social philosophy than in conspiring to overthrow governments or social systems. This period, moreover, was only the prelude to the decade that followed, during which Marx virtually buried himself in the archives of the British Museum.

Karl Marx was, of course, strongly influenced both by his cultural heritage and the particular circumstances of his day. Only a few of the more important of these factors can be touched upon here. One was his ancestry. He was born a Jew, descended from a Dutch (on the maternal side) and a German (on the paternal side) rabbinical family. When he was six his father embraced the Protestant faith. The real reason or reasons for the conversion to Christianity remain a matter for conjecture. Some of Marx's biographers note the desire on the part of the elder Marx to rid himself of Judaism as a particular fetter to professional success. Others see the reason as much more deeply rooted in philosophical issues. Be that as it may, at first glance, it may seem that neither Marx's birth as a Jew nor his family's conversion to Christianity really matters since Karl Marx declared himself to be an atheist and dismissed religion as an "opiate.'" It is also well known that Marx disassociated himself from what, for lack of a better term, might be called Jewishness or Jewish culture. He, in fact, evidenced a peculiar kind of contempt for certain aspects often associated with Jewish culture or tradition. But not all students of Marxism cancel Marx's ancestry quite so readily. R. N. Carew Hunt, for instance, tells us "His [Marx's] rabbinical ancestry is important for two reasons. First, he derived from it his peculiar sense of authority; and, secondly, it was responsible for that messianic element which plays so important a part in Jewish thought. For Jewish thought has never been 'other-worldly' . . . it has always insisted upon the duty of establishing an era of peace and happiness in this present world. It is no accident that so many of the communist leaders from Marx's day onwards have been Jews."[1]

In any case the fact remains that whether Marx regarded himself as a Jew or not, the world did and does. Marx's Jewish ancestry has doubtless colored his view of the world as well as the world's view of Marx.

Other major factors have been noted by V. I. Lenin, who once observed that Marx had been influenced by three distinct cultures: French, German, and English. The French influence was the dominant revolutionary element. The German provided Marx with his philosophical base. The English tradition set the framework for Marx's economic analysis.

Marx was born and raised in the Rhineland where French thought and culture pervaded. Guided by his father and his future father-in-law, young Marx became familiar with the mainstream of eighteenth- and early nineteenth-century French liberal and radical thought. During and following his years of formal schooling Marx developed an independent curiosity about the European socialist movement. Material critical of the existing institutions was already plentiful and Marx read much of it. During the 1840's he made a special point of becoming personally acquainted with some of the leading socialists and social critics who had made Paris their center. The result of this French influence was a pronounced inclination on the part of Marx toward socialism but not, of course, of the utopian variety.

In regard to the German influence, the seriousness with which Marx approached the study of philosophy at the university is not quite as exceptional as it may appear. Marx had exactly the kind of mind to which philosophy, especially of the Germanic type, would appeal. The German universities of Marx's day were passing through a period of great philosophical controversy and ferment. The eye of this intellectual storm was the philosophical system of Georg Wilhelm Friedrich Hegel. Hegelianism was, indeed, all the fashion at that time. Thus it was only natural that Marx took an intense interest in Hegelian philosophy and came to understand it as well as any of his contemporaries. Ultimately, Marx declared himself to be a Hegelian; not, however, without first rejecting some aspects of it and reversing others. When Marx entered the university there already existed a generation of German students who regarded themselves as neo-Hegelians. Their quarrel with the existing philosophical orthodoxy centered around two fundamental issues. Neo-Hegelians saw in their master's concept of the universe a rational directing force or Providence. They found themselves unable to accept such an abstraction along with its theological implications. Neo-Hegelians were also unwilling to accept and support certain conservative, even totalitarian, political views and policies which could be drived from orthodox Hegelianism. As a neo-Hegelian, therefore, Marx took Hegel's construction and method as the philosophical framework for his own system of thought.

The English may, if they wish, claim double credit in regard to Marx. The relative liberality of the British political climate provided Marx with both his final place of residence and the facilities for continuing study. Secondly, Marx the economist is most heavily indebted to the English Classical school. By the time he settled in London Marx was already familiar with the ideas of the leading economists of his day. But it was with the doctrines and method of the English school—David Ricardo most particularly—that Marx really became intimate. He leaned most heavily on the methodology of the English economists, retained many of the same theoretical assumptions, and began his investigation into the laws of Capitalist development by asking the same central question concerning value and price. For more than a decade, following his move to England, Marx immersed himself in the archives of the British Museum, studying the history of the world and its institutions. There he amassed much of the empirical material that appears in *Das Kapital* and subsequent works. This so-called Micawberish period of his life, as we shall soon see, was thus more the result of self-imposed demands of scholarship than the consequence of Marx's direct revolutionary involvement.

The fact that Marx had been so strongly influenced by so many forces and currents of thought has led some to the view that there is really nothing new or original in the Marxian system of thought. The extent of Marx's borrowing, the cross-cultural and interdisciplinary nature of his system, is undeniable and by this mode of reasoning the above view is correct enough. But who has not heard of the old adage that nothing new has really been said since the time of the ancient Greeks? The fact remains that Marx was an intellectual entrepreneur *par excellence*. One can speak of the new and the exciting in Marx in the sense that his system represented a unique mixture of existing and sometimes conflicting ideas. It is in that special combination, as a synthesis, that Marx's "message" made its historic impact.

As a final point about the academic side of Marx, how seriously can he be taken as an economist? What, more specifically, can be said about Marx's stature as an economic theorist? Interestingly enough, his contribution here has been understated not only by his enemies but also by his staunchest supporters. Those of the Marxist persuasion have not, at least traditionally, idolized Marx the economic theorist. In part this can be explained in terms of the general attitude on the part of Marxists-Leninists toward pure theorists. In greater part it is that Marx and his system is so much more: an approach to comprehending the total social universe. Marx's critics, of course, have in mind his call to action, his slogans and impassioned phrases, the bitterness with which he lashed out at his foes, and the intensity with which he indicted the existing social order.

A dispassionate look at Marx's economics lends little support to either critics or supporters. Marx was concerned with the same fundamental problems or questions that have preoccupied economists since the time of Adam Smith. He was interested in understanding and exposing to view the process or laws of Capitalist development. That he found these laws to be in contradiction rather than in harmony is not the issue here. Marx relied on and used the same method of induction and deduction as other economists. He was concerned with the predictive value of his economic models. True, Marx also prescribed. But it was his content, at least, that in this case prescription was only the reflection of scientific analysis and description. Like many other economists whose contribution or legitimacy has never been questioned, Marx began his analysis of the Capitalist economy with an investigation of the value-determining process. It is to his credit that Marx did not try to circumvent that which came to pose a thorny theoretical problem for him. Examine *Das Kapital,* better still *Theories of Surplus Value,* and the skill with which Marx utilized both induction and deduction becomes apparent. Such works clearly exhibit the power of his intellect, his gift for the highest level of abstraction, and the order of his logic. Sections of these same works also reflect the breadth and scope of his knowledge of history and the contemporary scene. Modern economic theory has, of course, outmoded or even invalidated significant portions of Marxian economics. It is interesting to speculate about the extent to which the pre-dictive power of Marx's economic models would have been better had Marx had at his command the analytic and empirical tools at the disposal of present-day economists.

Here, in summary, is what one member of the Academy has to say about Marx as an economic theorist. Joseph Schumpeter writes: "As an economic theorist Marx was first of all a very learned man. . . . Geniuses and prophets do not usually excel in professional learning. . . . But nothing in Marx's economics can be accounted for by any want of scholarship or training in the technique of theoretical analysis. He was a voracious reader and an indefatigable worker. He missed very few contributions of significance. And whatever he read he digested, wrestled with every fact or argument with a passion for detail most unusual in one whose glance habitually encompassed entire civilizations and secular developments. Criticizing and rejecting or accepting and coordinating, he always went to the bottom of every matter. . . . This incessant endeavor to school himself and to master whatever there was to master went some way toward freeing him from prejudices and extra-scientific aims, though he certainly worked in order to verify a definite vision. To his powerful intellect, the interest in the problem as a problem was paramount in spite of himself; and however much he may have bent the import of his final *results,* while at work he was primarily concerned with sharpening the tools of analysis proffered by the science of his day, with straightening out logical difficulties and with building on the foundation thus acquired a theory that in nature and intent was truly scientific whatever its shortcomings may have been."[2]

THE REVOLUTIONARY SIDE OF KARL MARX

All the evidence points to the fact that Marx was, indeed, an intellectual giant. Can the same be said about his revolutionary side? Certainly Marx's message has been a potent revolutionary force in the world. It became and remains that, however, in the hands of others than Marx. Why not in the hands of its founder? On the surface it would seem that Marx should have been far more successful as a revolutionary leader than in fact he turned out to be. In some important respects the Europe of the late 1840's appeared quite ready to listen to his call to arms. Marx wished to be and envisaged himself as a revolutionary. The missing ingredients are difficult to isolate with any assurance. But certain facts about the Europe of Marx's day and about the revolutionary facet of his life do shed some light on this question.

Marx's involvement with revolutionary activity began with his entry into a career of journalism. He turned to journalism, however, only after having found all academic doors tightly shut to him. Marx launched his journalistic career by submitting articles to the popular journals. Those published struck with sufficient force to impress the editors of a radical bourgeois paper called the *Rheinische Zeitung,* published in Cologne. In 1842 (Marx was then only twenty-four) he was invited to join the staff of that paper and before long to become one of its editors. His involvement with that first project lasted barely a year. It was a penumbric moment in Marx's life, a stage between youthful philosophical radicalism and the search for a socialist solution. He had been appointed editor of the *Rheinische Zeitung* in order to stabilize the affairs of a paper which already exhibited a philosophical socialist strain; though Marx, himself, was not yet a socialist of any particular description. Early in 1843 the Prussian government modified the divorce laws in a direction that compelled the philosophical radical in Marx to write an atheistically oriented criticism of government policy. The authorities responded by forcing the paper to suspend publication. Thus the hope that Marx would be the one to smooth out that paper's affairs did not materialize. Marx decided instead that he ought to learn more about the existing socialist movement.

In the fall of 1843 Marx resigned from the *Rheinische Zeitung* and moved to Paris, then the center of European socialism. There he joined a Neo-Hegelian named Arnold Ruge in the editorship of a review called the *Deutschfranzosische Jahrbucher* (Franco-German Year Book). The single issue which appeared was true to its intended purpose. The articles, including two by Engels, were sharply critical of the existing social institutions and accepted modes of thought. That issue contained two articles by Marx. One was concerned with the Jewish question. The other constituted a criticism of Hegelian philosophy of law. It is in this latter article that one detects early signs of Marx's departure from the existing current of socialist thought. In it one finds mention of such concepts as class, proletariat, and struggle, as well as an emphasis on political action.

The failure of the *Franco-German Year Book* forced Marx to resume free-lance writing but did not alter his main purpose for having come to Paris. For the record it should be noted that at this time, in the summer of 1842, Marx married Jenny von Westphalen. Jenny, an attractive and well-bred young lady, was the daughter of a German baron (a moderately important Prussian official) and on her maternal side a descendant of English aristocracy. It should be noted, as well, that neither marriage nor the subsequent responsibility of fatherhood deterred Marx from pursuing his mission in life whatever the personal cost to himself and his family. Marx had come to Paris to throw himself into the heart of the socialist movement and he did precisely that.

Among those who interested Marx in Paris, Pierre Joseph Proudhon was then the most important in French socialist circles. Being in Paris enabled Marx to meet and argue with Proudhon at great length and frequency. In 1865 Marx wrote to a friend that it was he who had infected Proudhon with Hegelianism, at least as much of it as the latter appeared capable of understanding. The Parisian intellectual milieu also included the famed poet Heinrich Heine, whom Marx came to know intimately. A close friendship, based on mutual respect, developed between the two despite Marx's earlier and crude attempts at writing poetry. Early in 1844 Marx also met Michael Bakunin, the man who was to become his bitterest enemy. Bakunin's radicalism was already well known to the German and Swiss authorities who had forced him to flee to France. Most important, however, this was the period when Marx reassessed Friedrich Engels.

The co-founders of Scientific Socialism had first met while Marx was still in Cologne. The Engels who initially approached Marx was already a radical of sorts. In fact Marx found him to be too far to the left and unimpressively so. The result was that he dismissed Engels with characteristic rudeness. In 1843 Engels called himself to Marx's attention a second time, on this occasion in a far more favorable light. The circumstance was the appearance of an article by Engels which interested Marx. Thus when they met again Engels found Marx to be much more cordial and willing to talk. There followed some ten days of discussion during which the basis of a lifetime friendship and intellectual partnership was laid.

Marx is known to have been a difficult person to get along with. It is equally well known that Engels was the one associate with whom Marx seldom fought or toward whom he did not ultimately turn bitter. There is universal agreement that of the two Marx was the original thinker, the greater intellect and theorist. There is even some reason to question whether Engels always understood the upper reaches of Marx's abstractions. The strength of this lasting friendship may be accounted for, in part at least, by the various respects in which Engels' personality, ambitions, and talents complemented rather than clashed with those of Marx. Both were Rhinelanders who, in their youth, were subject to a similar intellectual climate. Each, in a special sense, was the product of a *petite bourgeois* environment. True, Karl Marx's father had managed to work up a respectable legal practice. But, as one of Marx's biographers points out, the elder Marx had never really succeeded in learning the art of making money. The Engels family owned two medium-sized, not overly profitable, cotton-spinning factories, one in Westphalia and the other in Manchester. But these enterprises can hardly be regarded as big business even by the norms of that day. On reaching maturity (but with conscious disinterest) Friedrich Engels assumed responsibility for the management of these enterprises. This provided him with both a livelihood and the time in which to pursue his part in a historic partnership. Marx's role in that union is clear. He supplied the high-powered conceptual framework into which Engels could pour the full versatility of his talents. Marx also served as·a pillar of strength and determination; for Engels was by nature a charming, kindly, generous, and easy-going person who, despite his ideology, saw no reason to deny himself all the material fruits of bourgeois civilization.

Engels was an excellent sounding-board and, in turn, was able to influence Marx in several important respects. His association with Marx was certainly important in bringing the latter down from his propensity for purely abstract thinking. The appearance of Engels' *Condition of the Working Class in England in 1844* caused Marx to shift his focus from the less mature Capitalism of Germany to the more advanced Capitalism of England. It also supplied Marx with a richness of empirical evidence on the basis of which to indict the Capitalist system. Engels was also at Marx's side to the full extent of his revolutionary involvement. From 1845 through 1848 both carried on revolutionary agitation in anticipation of the Communist Revolution. Their coauthorship of the *Communist Manifesto* may well be regarded as one of the most significant literary partnerships in history. At a later period Engels participated with and supported Marx in his efforts to organize and direct the First International.

Over and above all of this, Engels assisted Marx financially. His generosity toward Marx paralleled his own financial circumstances. At first the remittances were relatively meager and intermittent. As the Engels enterprises prospered, Marx began to receive a yearly sum. In 1869, on the death of his father, Engels was able to arrange things so that Marx would have a lifetime income of approximately 350 pounds a year. This financial concern extended even beyond Marx's lifetime. When Engels died in 1895 it was found that he had bequeathed most of his property to Marx's children. It must be added that Marx was not unappreciative of either Engels' talents or his financial generosity. On numerous occasions Marx is known to have paid tribute to the quickness of Engels' mind ("Engels is always one step ahead of me") and to have referred to Scientific Socialism as "our theory."

A note about Marx's poverty may be in order at this point. Much, perhaps too much, has been made of the abject poverty in which Marx and his family lived. It is quite true that Marx's financial circumstances were precarious throughout most of his adult life. His only source of *earned* income came from the kind of sporadic ventures into journalism which typically do not yield either an adequate or a stable livelihood. The popular image of Marx's poverty is accurate, however, only in relation to a single period of his life: his early years in London. That was the period when Marx wrote to Engels of his concern over the shortage of wholesome food for the family. Those were the years punctuated by frequent visits to the pawnshop. It was then, too, that his wife Jenny was forced to beg money from neighbors in order to pay for the burial of a child. In this connection one cannot help but wonder why, given her particular background, Jenny Marx withstood such circumstances with so little complaint. It is known that she was deeply in love with the "Moor," as Marx was known to his intimates. It is doubtful, on the other hand, whether Jenny fully comprehended the historic significance of the mission for which Marx had dedicated not only his life but hers and that of the children. Their marriage appears to have been a union which combined the exceptional strength of character and will on the part of Marx and a pronounced submissiveness (politely called devotion) on the part of Jenny. In any case one ought not to confuse cause and effect in regard to Marx's poverty. He was not a radical, as is sometimes implied, because he was poor. He was poor because he was a radical; because he had dedicated himself to a cause which he set above the material well-being of himself and his family.

But let us return to Marx's activities during his two-year (1843-1845) sojourn in Paris and fhat which followed. The French government permitted Marx to reside in Paris for nearly two years before forcing him to leave the country. Marx had become well enough known by this time to bear watching. Understandably, from the point of view of the French authorities, Marx had hardly endeared himself either by his choice of associates or the tone of his articles. The proximate cause of his expulsion was an article he had written for a radical magazine called *Vorwärts*. That article so offended Prussian officialdom that the Prussian government pressured the French to expel Marx.

The three-year period that followed (1845-1848) was the most active revolutionary phase of Marx's life. Engels joined Marx, who went from Paris to Brussels, and together they plunged into propagandistic and agitational activity. Their first step was to establish even closer ties with the European working-class movement in the hope of giving that movement a specific direction. They tried to found a German workers' society and took over a German language weekly called the *Brusseller deutsche Zeitung*. There existed at this time a loosely knit organization known as the League of the Just. It was composed of workingmen (primarily German emigrés) who met secretly in the principal cities such as London, Paris, and Brussels. At first the league had little by way of a formal ideology. Its members searched for the root causes behind their dissatisfaction and advocated corresponding reforms in the structure of the existing economic and political institutions. Marx and Engels began by making it a special point to keep in touch with the various locals of the League of the Just. Before long their connection with and influence over this group became considerable. As a consequence, the organization changed its name to the League of Communists which helped to differentiate it from other socialist or utopian movements of which Marx was so contemptuous. On the eve of the Revolution of 1848 the Communist League decided that it was time to draft a formal program for action. Marx and Engels, who were present at that conference, were asked to draw up such a document and did so under the title *The Communist Manifesto*.

The year of the *Communist Manifesto*, 1848, is central. It was the historic moment when Marx and Engels declared: "A spectre is haunting Europe—the spectre of Communism. . . . Let the ruling classes tremble at a Communist Revolution." This proclamation was based on Marx's already firm conviction that Capitalism had just about run its full course. He saw, or believed he saw, the "objective circumstances" for both the Communist Revolution and the emergence of the next social order all around him. Robert Heilbroner, in *The Worldly Philosophers,* captures the mood of that moment as well and as succinctly as possible: "The specter certainly existed: 1848 was a year of terror for the old order on the Continent. There was a revolutionary fervor in the air and a rumble underfoot. For a moment—for a brief moment—it looked as if the old order might break down. In France . . . the regime of Louis Philippe . . . collapsed . . . and the workingmen of Paris rose in a wild uncoordinated surge and ran the Red Flag over the Hotel de Ville. In Belgium a frightened monarch offered to submit his resignation. In Berlin the barricades went up and the bullets whistled; in Italy mobs rioted; and in Prague and Vienna popular uprisings imitated Paris by seizing control of the cities. . . . The ruling classes did tremble and they saw the threat of communism everywhere. Nor were their fears groundless."[3] Marx and Engels were only too well aware of these circumstances, of the mood of 1848, and of the possibility in the offing. They were not only ready but offered themselves as the leaders of the Communist Revolution.

Given the advantage of hindsight, the following assessment of the Revolution of 1848 by Heilbroner turns out to be more accurate than that of Marx and Engels: "But as it was the uprisings were spontaneous, undisciplined, and aimless; they won initial victories and then, while they were wondering what next to do, the old order rocked invincibly back into place. The revolutionary fervor abated, and where it did not, it was mercilessly crushed. . . . The revolution was over. It had been fierce, bloody, but inconclusive. . . . despite the clarion words of the Manifesto, the demonic note was not a call for a revolution of communism; it was a cry born only of frustration and despair."[4] In the end even Marx was forced to admit that the objective circumstances for the Communist Revolution had not yet fully matured. He estimated that Capitalism had yet another decade, at best two, before finally contradicting itself out of existence. The tiny coterie of politically conscious workers whom Marx and Engels tried to lead during that fateful year had been dispersed. Some were in jail and the remainder scattered themselves throughout Europe in order to escape imprisonment.

The printer's ink barely had time to dry on the copies of the *Communist Manifesto* when the Revolution hit France. That was in February of 1848. Fearful of the radical in its midst, the Belgian government forced Marx to return to Paris. Before long the prevailing unrest spread to Germany and in May of that same year Marx and Engels decided to direct the course of the upheaval from Cologne. Marx was now at the very pinnacle of his revolutionary career. He had openly declared himself prepared to lead the way. As it appeared to Marx, the major obstacle to victory was the erroneous policy being followed by the "middle-class democratic parties." (Marx saw it somewhat differently in retrospect.) He was convinced at the time that reformism, compromise, and indecision were delaying the inevitable. The problem was to convince others. With the aid of friends, Marx and Engels launched a new daily, the *Neue rheinische Zeitung*. As its editor-in-chief Marx used the columns of this paper for two main purposes. He criticized the reactionary policies of the Prussian state. More significantly, he attacked those who advocated or followed a moderate policy of reform and held them responsible for the failure of the revolution to materialize. Marx's most direct call to action occurred in November 1848. The Prussian king had ordered the National Assembly dissolved. The *Neue rheinische Zeitung* responded by urging the people not to pay their taxes and followed this up by an outright call to arms. Cologne fell into a state of siege, the paper was closed down, and its editor-in-chief was arrested and charged with treason. The fact that he was subsequently acquitted of this charge by a *petite bourgeois* jury did not save Marx from being banished from his native land.

Marx was gravely disappointed with the way the Revolution of 1848 had ended. He was concerned over the fate of his revolutionary colleagues who were being hounded or imprisoned. He felt embittered toward the Prussian authorities. In anger Marx renounced his Prussian citizenship, only to regret it some twenty years later when he could not return to Germany in order to direct the affairs of the reorganized workers' movement. His return to Paris in May 1849 was further marred by being presented with a Hobson's choice. The French informed him that he could either settle in a small, isolated town in France or leave the country altogether. Marx decided to move to London and there to await the final phase of the Communist Revolution. He remained in England to the end of his life.

It deserves to be noted that Marx continued his academic writing even during this the most revolutionary episode of his life. The single exception was the year 1848 when he believed that the moment of the Communist Revolution was actually at hand. The Brussels period, for instance, produced some of Marx's most important doctrinal works and essays. It was the interval during which he attacked Proudhon with a book entitled *The Poverty of Philosophy*. Indirectly, at this same time, Marx also attacked Ludwig Feuerbach and so-called "German or True Socialism."

On arrival in England in 1849 Marx's financial straits were such that he was forced to move into the dingiest of quarters on Dean Street in the Soho district of London. The next thirty-four years were spent in continuing study, writing, ideological feuding, and a renewed, but no more fruitful, effort at organizing the European working class. At first he tried to resurrect the shattered pieces of the Communist League but to no avail. Internal strife within the organization, in the face of continued governmental persecution, forced the league to disband. Marx's plan to resume and continue the publication of a revolutionary organ (also called the *Neue rheinische Zeitung*) from London came to no more than six issues. The net result was a series of interesting articles on specific historical events.

Between 1849 and 1864 Marx divided his time, but quite disproportionately, among a variety of activities. He spent a great deal of time in study at the British Museum. He wrote occasional pieces for the *New York Tribune*. He lent his voice and pen in support of various causes and embroiled himself in numerous controversies with political leaders who did not share his views. Usually Marx's polemics would start over some burning issue of the day. In 1859, for instance, the question was the Franco-Austrian War. Almost always, however, controversy would turn into a diatribe for which Marx was more than equally responsible.

In 1864 an event took place in London which enabled Marx to resume a more direct role as revolutionary leader. Workers of different nationalities as well as varying political hues gathered at a London conference in order to further their interests as a class. The fact that Marx had renounced his Prussian citizenship and had been permanently banned from his native land did not prevent him from appearing at this meeting as a representative of the German working class. This turned out to be the organizing meeting of the International Workingmen's Association or, as it is more popularly known, the First International. Within the year Marx became the real though not the titular head of the General Council which set the policies of the First International. It is noteworthy that by this time Marx's approach to revolutionary leadership had gone through a significant transformation from what it was in 1848. He addressed the full membership of the International on numerous occasions' He wrote many of its public statements. Patiently Marx set his views before the General Council. He simplified and elucidated more in the manner of a teacher than a revolutionary. Here one can learn a good deal about Marx's views on child labor, trade unionism, working hours, and education. Marx was not only aware of the diversity of opinion within the International but exhibited an uncharacteristic willingness to compromise on practical political questions. This was also the period, of course, when Marx finally completed and published the first volume of *Das Kapital*.

Again, however, circumstances made even Marx's statesmanlike efforts at revolutionary leadership come to little except as the First International set a pattern for
those that followed. The upsurge of worker unrest in Paris culminated in the Paris
Commune of 1871. Marx's advice to the French workers went largely unheeded. The
emotionalism surrounding the Franco-German War accentuated the difficulties involved in keeping the First International on a single course. The enmity that had developed between Marx and Bakunin came to full growth in the affairs of the International.
Bakunin succeeded in introducing a degree of anarchy into that organization from
which it was not destined to recover. At Marx's instigation the seat of the General
Council of the First International was shifted to New York. But since none of the
fundamental difficulties were thereby resolved the end was near. A mid-summer meeting
held in Philadelphia in 1876 dissolved the First International. Marx is believed to have
been even more deeply disappointed over this than over the failure of the Communist
Revolution to materialize in 1848. In 1850 Marx had been fairly certain that the final
moment of the Communist Revolution would arrive before the close of the decade.
Now, with the end of the First International, he was neither certain nor optimistic.
Marx spent the remaining few years of his life (he died peacefully in bed in 1883) trying
to put certain new ideas in writing as well as reconsidering some of his already published doctrines.

Clearly Marx felt compelled to throw himself into the revolutionary movement.
Struggle and the necessity for participating in the class war represent the very essence
of his doctrine. Nor is there much reason to doubt the genuineness of his desire to see
the working class "saved" from "capitalist oppression." The charge that Marx really
did not care or was even contemptuous of the masses is at best misleading. He was
far more of a realist than the utopian socialists. As Joseph Schumpeter points out: "He
did not weep any sentimental tears about the beauty of the socialist idea. . . . Nor did
he glorify the workmen into heroes of daily toil as bourgeois love to do when trembling
for their dividends. He was perfectly free from any tendency, so conspicuous of some
of his weaker followers, toward licking the workman's boots. He had probably a clear
perception of what the masses are and he looked far above their heads toward social
goals altogether beyond what they thought or wanted."[6] But the fact remains, as
Schumpeter concludes, that "however much of a coffeehouse conspirator he may have
been at some junctures of his life, his true self despised that sort of thing."[6] He had
neither acquired sufficient experience nor did he possess the requisite temperament to
be an effective revolutionary leader. This sheds some light on the disproportionate
time and energy Marx spent on scholarship as against revolutionary activity. It also
suggests at least one factor underlying Marx's weakness as a revolutionary leader. In
the end even Engels admitted Marx's failure in this regard. The focus of Engels' funeral
oration was on Marx the scholar and social philosopher and not on Marx the revolutionary. Marx's truly great achievement, according to Engels, was to have done for the
social sciences what Charles Darwin did for the natural sciences.

Notes

CHAPTER 1

1. R. N. Carew Hunt, *The Theory and Practice of Communism*, new and rev. ed. (New York: Macmillan Co., 1954), pp. 3–4.

2. In order to emphasize that it is the Marxian version of each of these stages of history that is under discussion, each stage or social order will be capitalized from this point on.

3. According to Marxist doctrine, Feudalism is not, even in principle, a bilateral contractual society, i.e., with obligations and rights flowing both ways between the nobility and the serfs.

4. Each succeeding stage of history, according to Marxist doctrine, is characterized by an improvement in the mode of production (i.e., in the capacity to produce) and thus by a corresponding change in the nature of the class struggle and the degree of coerciveness of the state. This aspect of Marxist doctrine will be discussed more fully in Chapter 2.

5. Actually Marxism-Leninism in this case.

6. For some of the complexities involved see Alexander Balinky, "The Proclaimed Emergence of Communism in the USSR," *Social Research*, 28 (Autumn 1961), pp. 261–282.

7. Engels' *Anti-Dühring: Herr Eugen Dühring's Revolution in Science*, 2nd ed. (Moscow: Foreign Languages Publishing House, 1959) comes, perhaps, closest to meeting this requirement.

CHAPTER 2

1. Joseph Schumpeter, *Capitalism, Socialism and Democracy*, 2nd ed. (New York Harper & Brothers, 1947), p. 9.

2. Schumpeter, pp. 9–10.

3. The word "dialectic" comes from the Greek and means to discuss or argue. Plato regarded the existence of contradiction in ideas, for instance, as obstacles to surmount in order to reach the truth. The dialectic is, in that sense, a technique of discussion aimed at eliminating contradiction in order to arrive at the truth. Hegel, on the other hand, insisted that contradiction was at the base of everything and its value was that truth and reality could be reached only through contradiction and the process of its resolution.

4. Karl Marx, *Capital*, Vol. I (New York: New World Paperbacks, International Publishers, 1967), p. 19.

5. In essence, Marx adapted the fundamental character of the Absolute (which, according to some philosophers, includes both mind and body), and applied it to a material world in which mind is only a reflection of matter.

6. This interpretation of Marx's theory of history is defended in Chapter 3.

7. The heaviness with which so much economic theory rests on such essentially un-proven, perhaps unprovable, assumptions about the nature of man is undeniable.

CHAPTER 3
1. Schumpeter, *Capitalism, Socialism and Democracy*, pp. 9–20.
2. Thus, for example, the existing difference in the man-land ratio between main-land China and the United States would be one of the factors differentiating the Chinese from the American productive force, and therefore, the two civilizations.
3. See the following sources: M. M. Bober, *Karl Marx's Interpretation of History* (Cambridge: Harvard University Press, 1927); L. H. Robbins, *An Essay on the Nature and Significance of Economic Sciences* (New York: St. Martin's Press, 1935)! R. N. Carew Hunt, *The Theory and Practice of Communism* (New York: Macmillan Co., 1954); Joseph Schumpeter, *Capitalism, Socialism and Democracy* (New York: Harper and Brothers, 1947); Harry Laidler, *Social-Economic Movements* (New York: Thomas Y. Crowell Company, 1949); G. D. H. Cole, *What Marx Really Meant* (New York: Alfred A. Knopf, 1934).
4. Schumpeter, p. 12.
5. See Schumpeter, pp. 18–19.

CHAPTER 4
1. There is a modest note in the Marxian theory of history worthy of mention. The theory does not claim to account for all of history but only for a given historical period. It is not meant to apply, for instance, to the Presocial segment of historical time. The matter is largely academic, in any case, since Marx was primarily concerned with modern history to which his theory of history is clearly applicable.
2. Karl R. Popper, *The Open Society and Its Enemies* (Princeton: Princeton University Press, 1950), p. 271.
3. Popper, p. 273.
4. Popper, p. 273.
5. M. M. Bober, *Karl Marx's Interpretation of History* (Cambridge: Harvard University Press, 1927), remains one of the best accounts and critiques of the economic interpretation of history. That which follows leans heavily on Bober's assessment.

CHAPTER 5
1. Joan Robinson, *An Essay on Marxian Economics* (London and New York: Macmillan Co., 1964), pp. 1–2.
2. Robinson, p. 22.

CHAPTER 6
1. It has, of course, been argued that the natural agents have a potential exchange value even in their unworked or unimproved state since everyone is aware that labor can or may be applied to such agents.
2. In defense of Marx, it must be added that he is not alone in appealing to the "mystery of the market" for an answer.

CHAPTER 8
1. Note that the rate of profit is calculated not on the expenditure of capital in production but on the advance of capital. When the turnover of capital is unitary, then of course the two are equal.

CHAPTER 11
1. Schumpeter, *Capitalism, Socialism and Democracy*, p. 16.

CHAPTER 15

1. Schumpeter, *Capitalism, Socialism and Democracy,* pp. 38–39.

2. Marx reasoned as follows: The circulating capital component is entirely used up within a given time period of production. It thus reproduces itself within that time period since its full value enters into commodity price. Fixed capital, on the other hand, is only partially used up during any one production period and thus only that element (the extent of its depreciation) currently enters into the valuation process. The actual replacement of physical capital, therefore, does not occur until the end of its lifespan. Those points in time during which there arises a heavy demand for the replacement of such physical capital are associated with periods of prosperity and, of course, vice versa. Implicit in this one of Marx's arguments is that the lifespan of fixed capital, i.e., the time for its reproduction, grows longer as the order of the organic composition of capital becomes higher. Thus the intensity and duration of the cycle varies directly with the lengthening of the lifespan of fixed capital.

CHAPTER 17

1. Schumpeter's translation of the German word *Verelendung.*

2. Schumpeter, *Capitalism, Socialism and Democracy,* pp. 34–35.

3. Schumpeter, p. 35.

APPENDIX

1. R. N. Carew Hunt, *The Theory and Practice of Communism,* p. 9.

2. Joseph Schumpeter, *Capitalism, Socialism and Democracy,* p. 21.

3. Robert Heilbroner, *The Worldly Philosophers,* rev. ed. (New York: Simon and Schuster, 1961), pp. 112–113.

4. Heilbroner, pp. 113–114.

5. See: Isaiah Berlin, *Karl Marx* (New York: Oxford University Press, 1959), Chapter 2.

6. Schumpeter, p. 7.

Selected Bibliography

I. WORKS BY MARX AND ENGELS
A. Karl Marx
Capital (Vol. I), Modern Library Edition, New York: Random House.
Capital (3 volumes), New York: International Publishers, 1969.
The Civil War in France, New York: International Publishers, 1933.
The Class Struggles in France, New York: International Publishers, 1934.
A Contribution to the Critique of Political Economy, New York: International Publishers, 1969.
Critique of the Gotha Programme, Moscow: Foreign Languages Publishing House, 1954.
"The Discourse on Free Trade," *Pocket Library on Socialism, No. 50*, Chicago: Charles Kerr & Co., 1907.
The Eastern Question: A Reprint of Letters Written in 1853–1856 Dealing with the Events of the Crimean War, London: Swan Sonnenchein & Co., 1897.
Economic and Philosophical Manuscripts of 1844, Moscow: Foreign Languages Publishing House, 1959.
The Eighteenth Brumaire of Louis Bonaparte, Moscow: Foreign Languages Publishing House, 1960.
A History of Economic Theories, The Physiocrats to Adam Smith, New York: Langland Press, 1932.
Letters to Dr. Kugelmann, New York: International Publishers, 1934.
The Life of Lord Palmerston and *The Secret Diplomatic History of the 18th Century*, New York: International Publishers, 1969.
Marx on China, 1853–1860; Articles from the New York Daily Tribune, London: Lawrence and Wishart, 1951.
Notes on Indian History, Moscow: Foreign Languages Publishing House, 1947.
The Poverty of Philosophy, Moscow: Foreign Languages Publishing House, 1956.
Revolution and Counterrevolution, or Germany in 1848, London: George Allen and Unwin, 1937.
Theories of Surplus Value, New York: International Publishers, 1952.
Value, Price and Profit, Chicago: Charles H. Kerr and Co., 1913.
Wage-Labor and Capital, Moscow: Foreign Languages Publishing House, 1947.
B. Karl Marx and Friedrich Engels
The Civil War in the United States, New York: International Publishers, 1937.
Communist Manifesto, Socialist Landmark, London: George Allen and Unwin, 1954.
The Communist Manifesto (translated from the German by Stefan T. Passony), Chicago: Henry Regnery Co., 1954.
Correspondence, 1846–95, A Selection with Commentary and Notes, New York: International Publishers, 1936.
The German Ideology, Parts I and III, New York: International Publishers, 1939.

Germany: Revolution and Counter Revolution, New York: International Publishers, 1969.

The Holy Family or Critique of Critical Critique, Moscow: Foreign Languages Publishing House, 1956.

Letters to Americans, New York: International Publishers, 1934.

On Britain, Moscow: Foreign Languages Publishing House, 1953.

On Colonialism, Moscow: Foreign Languages Publishing House, n.d.

Revolution in Spain, New York: International Publishers, 1939.

The Russian Menace to Europe, Glencoe, Illinois: The Free Press, 1952.

Selected Works, New York: International Publishers, 1969.

C. Friedrich Engels

Blood and Iron, New York: International Publishers, 1959.

The Condition of the Working Class in England (new translation), Stanford: Stanford University Press, 1968.

Dialects of Nature, New York: International Publishers, 1940.

Anti-Dühring: Herr Eugen Dühring's Revolution in Science, 2d edition, Moscow: Foreign Languages Publishing House, 1947.

Ludwig Feuerback and the Outcome of Classical German Philosophy, New York: International Publishers, 1934.

II. GENERAL WORKS ON MARXISM

Cole, G. D. H., *What Marx Really Meant*, New York: Alfred A. Knopf, 1934.

Cornforth, M., *The Open Philosophy and the Open Society*, New York: International Publishers, 1969.

Eastman, M., *Marxism: Is it Science?*, New York: Norton, 1940.

Garaudy, R., *Karl Marx: The Evolution of His Thought*, New York: International Publishers, 1968.

Hook, S., *Marx and the Marxists—The Ambiguous Legacy*, Princeton: Van Nostrand, 1955.

Hook, S., *From Hegel to Marx*, Ann Arbor: University of Michigan Press, 1962.

Hook, S., *Toward the Understanding of Karl Marx: A Revolutionary Interpretation*, London: Gollancz, 1933.

Hunt, R. N. Carew, *Marxism: Past and Present*, New York: Macmillan Co., 1954.

Hunt, R. N. C., *The Theory and Practice of Communism: An Introduction* (new and revised edition), New York: Macmillan Co., 1954.

Lichtheim, G., *Marxism: An Historical and Critical Study*, New York: Praeger, 1961.

Meyer, A. G., *Marxism: The Unity of Theory and Practice*, Cambridge: Harvard University Press, 1954.

Parkes, H. B., *Marxism: An Autopsy*, Chicago: University of Chicago Press, 1939.

Popper, K. R., *The Open Society and Its Enemies*, Princeton: Princeton University Press, 1950.

Schumpeter, J., *Capitalism, Socialism and Democracy* (2d edition), New York: Harper and Brothers, 1947.

Scott, A. M., *The Anatomy of Communism*, New York: Philosophical Library, 1951.

Tucker, R., *Philosophy and Myth in Karl Marx*, Cambridge: at the University Press, 1961.

Wolfe, B., *Marxism: 100 Years in the Life of a Doctrine*, New York: Dial Press, 1965.

Zeitlin, I. M., *Marxism: A Reexamination*, Princeton: Van Nostrand, 1967.

III. MARXIAN PHILOSOPHY AND THEORY OF HISTORY

Blakeley, T. J., "The Salient Features of the Marxist-Leninist Theory of Knowledge," in F. J. Adelmann (ed.), *The Quest for the Absolute* (Boston College Studies in Philosophy, volume I), The Hague: Martinus Nijhoff, 1966.

Bober, M. M., *Karl Marx's Interpretation of History*, Cambridge: Harvard University Press, 1927; see also 2d edition revised, New York: W. W. Norton, 1965.

Cohen, M., "Causation and its Application to History," *Journal of the History of Ideas*, III (1942).

Croce, B., *Historical Materialism and the Economics of Karl Marx*, London: George Allen & Unwin, 1914.

Dobb, M., "Marx on Pre-Capitalist Economies," *Science and Society*, Vol. 30, No. 3 (1966).

Dupre, L., *The Philosophical Foundations of Marxism*, New York: Harcourt, Brace and World, 1968.

Federn, K., *The Materialist Conception of History*, London: Macmillan and Co., Ltd., 1939.

Fromm, E., *Marx's Concept of Man*, New York: Frederick Unger, 1961.

Hansen, A. H., "The Technological Interpretation of History," *Quarterly Journal of Economics*, XXXVI (1921–1922).

Jordan, L. A., *The Evolution of Dialectical Materialism*, London: Macmillan Co., and New York: St. Martin's Press, 1967.

Kawakeami, H., "On Marx's 'Forms of Social Consciousness,'" *Kyoto University Economic Review* I, No. 1, July, 1926.

Plekhanov, G., *The Materialistic Conception of History*, New York: International Publishers, 1940.

Regnier, M., "Hegelianism and Marxism," *Social Research*, Vol. 34, No. 1 (1967).

Stace, W. T., *The Philosophy of Hegel: A Systematic Exposition*, New York: Dover, 1955.

Sweezy, P., "The Transition from Feudalism to Capitalism" (a review) and "Reply to M. Dobb," *Science and Society*, Vol. 14, No. 2 (1950).

Tawney, R. H., *Religion and the Rise of Capitalism*, New York: The New American Library (Mentor Book), 1958.

IV. MARXIAN ECONOMICS
  A. General Works

Bober, M. M., "Marx and Economic Calculations," *American Economic Review*, June 1946.

Bohm-Bawerk, E., *Karl Marx and the Close of His System*, New York: Augustus M. Kelley, 1949.

Bronfenbrenner, M., "Das Kapital for the Modern Man," *Science and Society*, Vol. 29, No. 4 (1965).

Domar, E., D. Gordon, and H. S. Gordon, "Discussion on Papers; Das Kapital—A Centennary of Appreciation," Papers and Proceedings of the 79th Annual Meeting of the American Economic Association (December 1966), *American Economic Review*, May 1967.

Dunayevskaya, R., "A New Revision of Marxian Economics," *American Economic Review*, September 1944.

Dunayevskaya, R., "Revision or Reaffirmation of Marxism? A Re-Joinder," *American Economic Review*, June 1944.

Friedman, R., ed., *Marx on Economics* (Harvest Books), New York: Harcourt, Brace & Co. (Harvest Books), 1961.

Gottheil, F. M., *Marx's Economic Predictions*, Evanston: Northwestern University Press, 1966.

Hilferding, R., *Bohm-Bawerk's Criticism of Marx*, New York: Augustus Kelley, 1949.
Horowitz, D., ed., *Marx and Modern Economics*, New York: Monthly Review Press (Modern Reader Paperbacks), 1968.
Robinson, J., *An Essay on Marxian Economics*, London: Macmillan Co., 1964.
Samuelson, P., "Marxian Economic Models," *American Economic Review*, XLVII, No. 6 (1957).
Sweezy, P., *The Theory of Capitalist Development*, New York: Oxford University Press, 1942.
Wolfson, M., *A Reappraisal of Marxian Economics*, Baltimore: Penguin Books, 1966.

B. Significance of Marxian Economics

Bloom, S. F., "Man of His Century, A Reconsideration of the Historical Significance of Karl Marx," *Journal of Political Economy*, Vol. LI (1943).
Bronfenbrenner, M., "Marxian Influences in Bourgeois Economics," Papers and Proceedings of the 79th Annual Meeting of the American Economic Association (December 1966), *American Economic Review*, May 1967.
Bronfenbrenner, M., "Notes on Marxian Economics in the United States," *American Economic Review*, December 1964.
Davis, H. B., "Notes on Marxian Economics in the United States: Comment" and "Reply by M. Bronfenbrenner," *American Economic Review*, September 1965.
Dobb, M., "Marx's Capital and Its Place in Economic Thought," *Science and Society*, Vol 31, No. 4 (1967).
Ise, J., "Significance of Marxian Economics: Discussion," *American Economic Review* (Supplement), March 1938.
Leontief, W., "The Significance of Marxian Economics for Present-Day Economic Theory," Proceedings of the 50th Annual Meeting of the American Economic Association, 1937, *American Economic Review* (Supplement), March 1938.
Patel, S. V., "Marxism and Recent Economic Thought," *Science and Society*, Vol. 11, No. 1 (1945).
Struik, D. J., "Marx's Economic-philosophical Manuscripts," *Science and Society*, Vol. 27, No. 3 (1963).
Varga, E., "Marx's Capital and Contemporary Capitalism," *Problems of Economics 4*, No. 9, January 1962.

C. Methodology

Bronfenbrenner, M., "Academic Methods for Marxian Problems," *Journal of Political Economy*, Vol. LXV (1957).
Dobb, M., "Creative Marxism in Political Economy (Review)," *Science and Society*, Vol. 28, No. 4 (1964).
Dobb, M., "Vulgar Economics and Vulgar Marxism: A Reply," *Journal of Political Economy*, Vol. XLVIII (1940).
Gottlieb, M., "Marx's Mehrwert Concept and the Theory of Pure Capitalism," *Review of Economic Studies*, XVIII, 3, No. 47 (1950–51).
Hodges, D. C., "The Method of Capital," *Science and Society*, Vol. 31, No. 4 (1967).
Hodges, D. C., "The Value Judgment in Capital," *Science and Society*, Vol. 29, No. 3 (1965).
Johansen, L., "Marxism and Mathematical Economics," *Monthly Review*, January 1963.
Lange, O., "Marxian Economics and Modern Economic Theory," *Review of Economic Studies*, June 1935.
Lerner, A. P., "From Vulgar Economics to Vulgar Marxism," *Journal of Political Economy*, Vol. XLVII (1939).
Lerner, A. P., "Marxism and Economics: Sweezy and Robinson" (a review), *Journal of Political Economy*, March 1945.

McConnel, J. W., and others, "The Sociology and Economics of Class Conflict: Discussion," *American Economic Review* (Supplement), May 1949.

Meek, R. L., *Economics and Ideology,* London: Chapman and Hall, 1967.

Meek, R. L., "Karl Marx's Economic Method," in R. L. Meek, *Economics and Ideology,* London: Chapman and Hall, 1967.

Samuelson, P., "Marxian Economics as Economics," Papers and Proceedings of the 79th Annual Meeting of the American Economics Association (December 1966), *American Economic Review,* May 1967.

Schumpeter, J., "Science and Ideology," *American Economic Review,* March 1949.

Schumpeter, J., "The Communist Manifesto in Sociology and Economics," *Journal of Political Economy,* LVII (1949).

Shibata, K., "Marx's Analysis of Capitalism and the General Equilibrium Theory of the Lausanne School," *Kyoto University Economic Review,* July 1933.

Shoul, B., "Karl Marx's Solutions to Some Theoretical Problems of Classical Economics," *Science and Society,* Vol. 31, No. 4 (1967).

Shove, G. F., "Mrs. Robinson on Marxian Economics," *Economic Journal,* April 1944.

Smith, H., "Marx as a Pure Economist," *Economic History* (Supplement to *Economic Journal*), February 1939.

Sweezy, P., "Marxian and Orthodox Economics," *Science and Society,* Vol. 11, No. 3 (1947).

D. Influences on and by Karl Marx

Alexander, S. S., "Mr. Keynes and Mr. Marx," *Review of Economic Studies,* February 1940.

Bladen, V. W., "The Centenary of Marx and Mill," *Journal of Economic History Supplement,* 8 (1948).

Dobb, M., "Classical Political Economy and Marx," in M. Dobb, *Political Economy and Capitalism,* London: Routledge & Kegan Paul, 1937.

Fan-Hung, "Keynes and Marx on the Theory of Capital Accumulation, Money and Interest," *Review of Economic Studies,* October 1939.

Irvine, W., "George Bernard Shaw and Karl Marx," *Journal of Economic History,* May 1946.

Robinson, J., "Open Letter from a Keynesian to a Marxian," in J. Robinson, *On Re-reading Marx,* Cambridge: Students Bookshops, 1953.

Robinson, J., "Marx and Keynes," in J. Robinson, *Collected Economic Papers,* I, Oxford: Blackwell, 1950.

Robinson, J., "Marx, Marshall and Keynes," in J. Robinson, *Collected Economic Papers,* II, Oxford: Blackwell, 1960.

Rosenberg, B., "Veblen and Marx," *Social Research,* March, 1948.

Shoul, B., "Similarities in the Work of John Stuart Mill and Karl Marx," *Science and Society,* Vol. 29, No. 3 (1965).

Tsuru, S., "Keynes Versus Marx: The Methodology of Aggregates," in K. Kurihara (ed.), *Post-Keynesian Economics,* New Brunswick, N. J.: Rutgers University Press, 1954.

Tucker, G. S. L., "Ricardo and Marx," *Economica,* August 1961.

Ward, E F., "Marx and Keynes," *Economic Record,* April 1939.

E. Marxian Economics and Socialism

Holesovsky, J. V., "Karl Marx and Soviet National Income Theory," *American Economic Review,* June 1961.

Landover, C., "From Marx to Menger: The Recent Development of Soviet Economics," *American Economic Review,* June 1944.

Lange, O., "Marxian Economics in the Soviet Union," *American Economic Revi* March 1945.

Nemchinov, V., "Value and Price Under Socialism," *Problems of Economics 4*, No. 3, July 1961.

Rogin, L., "Marx and Engels on Distribution in a Socialist Society," *American Economic Review*, March 1945.

Wright, D. M., "The Economics of a Classless Society," *American Economic Review* (Supplement), May 1949.

F. Value and Price

Chowdhary, M. K., "Development of Labour Theory of Value," *Federal Economic Review*, January 1957.

Debreau, G., *Theory of Value*, New York: John Wiley and Sons, 1959.

Dickinson, H. D., "A Comment on Meek's 'Notes on the Transformation Problem'," *Economic Journal*, December 1956.

Dobb, M., "A Further Comment on the 'Transformation' Problem," *Economic Journal*, September 1957.

Dobb, M., "Requirements of a Theory of Value," in M. Dobb, *Political Economy and Capitalism*, London: Routledge & Kegan Paul, 1937.

Gordon, D. F., "What Was the Labor Theory of Value," *American Economic Association Papers and Proceedings*, 1959.

Johansen, L., "Some Observations on the Labour Theory of Value and Marginal Utilities," *Economics of Planning* (Oslo), No. 2, 1963.

Mandel, E., "The Labour Theory of Value and 'Monopoly Capital'," *International Socialist Review*, July–August 1967.

Mattick, P., "Value and Price," *Science and Society*, Vol. 23, No. 4 (1959).

Meek, R. L., "Some Notes on the 'Transformation' Problem," *Economic Journal*, March 1956.

Meek, R. L., *Studies in the Labour Theory of Value*, London: Lawrence and Wishart, 1956.

Otis, B., "The Communists and the Labor Theory of Value," *American Economic Review*, May 1945.

Robertson, H. M., "Adam Smith's Approach to the Theory of Value," *American Economic Review*, XLVIII, No. 3 (1958).

Robinson, J., "A Reconsideration of the Theory of Value," in J. Robinson, *Collected Economic Papers*, III, Oxford: Blackwell, 1965.

Sowell, T., "Marxian Value Reconsidered," *Economica*, August, 1963.

Stigler, G., "Ricardo and the 93% Labor Theory of Value," *American Economic Review*, XLVIII, No. 3 (1958).

Winternitz, J., "Values and Prices: A Solution of the So-called Transformation Problem," *Economic Journal*, June 1948.

G. Surplus Value

Baran, P., "Economic Progress and Economic Surplus," *Science and Society*, Vol. 17, No. 4 (1953).

Horowitz, D., "Analysing the Surplus," *Monthly Review*, January 1967.

Tajima, K., "New Theory of Surplus Value and the Harmony of the Various Classes of Society," *Kyoto University Economic Review 1*, July, 1926.

Varley, D., "On the Computation of the Rate of Surplus Value," *Science and Society*, Vol. 2, No. 3 (1938).

H. Money, Interest, etc.

Fan-Hung, "Keynes and Marx on the Theory of Capital Accumulation, Money and Interest," *Review of Economic Studies*, October 1939.

Gottheil, F. M., "Wages and Interest: A Modern Dissection of Marxian Economic Models—A Comment," and "Reply by P. A. Samuelson," *American Economic Review*, September 1960.

Morris, J., "Marx as a Monetary Theorist," *Science and Society*, Vol. 31, No. 4 (1967).

Samuelson, P., "Wages and Interest: A Modern Dissection of Marxian Economic Models," *American Economic Review*, December 1957.

Somerville, H., "Marx's Theory of Money," *Economic Journal*, June 1933.

I. Capital Circulation and Accumulation

Bronfenbrenner, M., and Y. Kasov, "On the Marxian Capital Consumption Ratio," *Science and Society*, Vol. 31, No. 4 (1967).

Erlich, A., "Notes on the Marxian Model of Capital Accumulation," Papers and Proceedings of the 79th Annual Meeting of the American Economic Association, December 1966, *American Economic Review*, May 1967.

Evenitsky, A., "Marx's Model of Expanded Reproduction," *Science and Society*, Vol. 27, No. 2 (1963).

Gustafson, B. G., "Rostow, Marx, and the Theory of Economic Growth," *Science and Society*, Vol. 25, No. 3 (1961).

Luxemburg, R., *The Accumulation of Capital*, New Haven: Yale University Press, 1951.

Mattick, P., "Value Theory and Capital Accumulation," *Science and Society*, Vol. 23, No. 1 (1959).

Naqui, K. A., "Schematic Presentation of Accumulation in Marx," *Indian Economic Review*, February 1960.

Schlesinger, R., "The General Law of Capitalist Accumulation: Past and Future," *Science and Society*, Vol. 31, No. 4 (1967).

Steindl, J., "Karl Marx and the Accumulation of Capital," in J. Steindl, *Maturity and Stagnation in the American Economy*, Oxford: Blackwell, 1952.

Sweezy, P., "Rosa Luxemburg's 'The Accumulation of Capital'," *Science and Society*, Vol. 31, No. 4 (1967).

Sweezy, P., "Marx on the Significance of the Corporation," *Science and Society*, Vol. 3, No. 2 (1939).

J. Rate of Profit

Blaug, M., "Technical Change and Marxian Economics," *Kyklos*, III, 1960.

Denis, H., "The Rate of Profit and National Income," *Science and Society*, Vol. 23, No. 4 (1959).

Dickinson, H. D., "The Falling Rate of Profit in Marxian Economics," *Review of Economic Studies*, XXIV, No. 64 (1957).

Dobb, M., "The Falling Rate of Profit," *Science and Society*, Vol. 23, No. 2 (1959).

Gillman, J., *The Falling Rate of Profit, Marx's Law and Its Significance to Twentieth-Century Capitalism*, London: Dennis Dobson, 1957.

Meek, R. L., "The Falling Rate of Profit," in R. L. Meek, *Economics and Ideology*, London: Chapman and Hall, 1967.

Meek, R. L., "The Falling Rate of Profit," *Science and Society*, Vol. 24, No. 1 (1960).

Pasenti, A., "The Falling Rate of Profit," *Science and Society*, Vol. 23, No. 3 (1959).

Robinson, J., "The Falling Rate of Profit: A Comment," *Science and Society*, Vol. 23, No. 2 (1959).

Tsuru, S., "Marx's Theory of the Falling Tendency of the Rate of Profit," *The Economic Review*, July 1951.

K. The Basic Crisis

Bronfenbrenner, M., "The Marxian Macro-Economic Model: Extension from Two Departments," Reprint No. 237, Graduate School of Industrial Administration, Carnegie Institute of Technology, Pittsburgh.

Georgescu-Roegen, N., "Mathematical Proofs of the Breakdown of Capitalism," *Econometrica*, April 1960.

Klein, L. R., "Theories of Effective Demand and Employment," *Journal of Political Economy*, April 1947 (see especially Part 3 on Marx).

Lange, O., "Say's Law, A Restatement and Criticism," in *Studies in Mathematical Economics and Econometrics,* Chicago: University of Chicago Press, 1942.

Shoul, B., "Karl Marx and Say's Law," *Quarterly Journal of Economics,* Vol. LXXI (1957).

Tsuru, S., "Marx's Tableau Economique and 'Underconsumption' Theory," *Indian Economic Review,* February 1953.

L. The Business Cycle

Sherman, H. J., "Marx and the Business Cycle," *Science and Society,* Vol. 31, No. 4 (1967).

Smith, H., "Marx and the Trade Cycle," *Review of Economic Studies,* June 1937.

Tsuru, S., "Business Cycles and Capitalism: Schumpeter vs. Marx," *Tokyo Hitotshu-bashi* Academy Annals, April 1952.

Wilson, J. D., "A Note on Marx and the Trade Cycle," *Review of Economic Studies,* February 1938.

M. Economic Imperialism

Davis, H. B., "Imperialism and Labor: An Analysis of Marxian Views," *Science and Society,* Vol. 26, No. 1 (1962).

Taylor, O. H., "Schumpeter and Marx: Imperialism and Social Classes in the Schumpeterian System," *Quarterly Journal of Economics,* Vol. LXV (1951).

Winslow, E. M., "Marxism, Liberal and Sociological Theories of Imperialism," *Journal of Political Economy,* December 1931.

N. Increasing Misery, The Reserve Army, etc.

Fellner, W., "Marxian Hypothesis and Observable Trends Under Capitalism: A Modern Interpretation," *Economic Journal,* LXVII No. 265 (1957).

Gottheil, F. M., "Increasing Misery of the Proletariat: An Analysis of Marx's Wage and Employment Theory," *Canadian Journal of Economics and Political Science,* February 1962.

Meek, R. L., "Marx's Doctrine of Increasing Misery," *Science and Society,* Vol. 26, No. 4 (1962).

Robinson, J., "Marx on Unemployment," *Economic Journal,* June–September 1941.

Sowell, T., "Marx's 'Increasing Misery' Doctrine," *American Economic Review,* March 1960.

Sweezy, P., "Professor Pigou's Theory of Unemployment," *Journal of Political Economy,* XLII (1934).

O. Marx, the Man and his Time

Beer, M., *The Life and Teachings of Karl Marx,* London: Parsons, 1921.

Berlin, I., *Karl Marx: His Life and Environment,* New York: Oxford University Press, 1963.

Hacker, A., "Capital and Carbuncles," in J. Gould *et al.* (eds.), *Problems in Political Thought: Contemporary Readings,* New York: Holt, Rinehart, and Winston, 1969.

Hammen, O., *The Red '48ers: Karl Marx and Friedrich Engels,* New York: Scribners, 1969.

Korsch, K., *Karl Marx,* London: Chapman and Hall, 1938.

Mehring, Franz, *Karl Marx,* London: Allen & Unwin, 1951.

Micolaievsky, Boris and Otto Maenchen-Helfen, *Karl Marx: Man and Fighter,* Philadelphia: J. B. Lippincott Co., 1936.

Schlesinger, R. J., *Marx: His Time and Ours,* London: Routledge & Kegan Paul, 1950.

Schwarzschild, Leopold, *The Red Prussian,* New York: Charles Schribner's Sons, 1947.

Date Due

APR 5 '72		
MAY 3 '72		
5-26-72		
MAY 9 '73		
NOV 1 8 1981		
AUG 1 8 1982		
DEC 2 2 1998		

Demco 38-297